THE 2010 MELTDOWN

THE 2010 MELTDOWN

Solving the Impending Jobs Crisis

Edward E. Gordon

PRAEGER

Westport, Connecticut
London

OUACHITA TECHNICAL COLLEGE

Library of Congress Cataloging-in-Publication Data

Gordon, Edward E.

The 2010 meltdown : solving the impending jobs crisis / Edward E. Gordon.

p. cm.

Includes bibliographical references and index.

ISBN 0–275–98436–2 (alk. paper)

1. Manpower policy—United States. 2. Labor market—United States. 3. Economic history—21st century. I. Title.

HD5724.G637   2005

331.12'042—dc22   2005018392

British Library Cataloguing in Publication Data is available.

Library of Congress Catalog Card Number: 2005018392

ISBN: 0–275–98436–2

First published in 2005

Praeger Publishers, 88 Post Road West, Westport, CT 06881

An imprint of Greenwood Publishing Group, Inc.

www.praeger.com

Printed in the United States of America

The paper used in this book complies with the Permanent Paper Standard issued by the National Information Standards Organization (Z39.48–1984).

10   9   8   7   6   5   4   3

To Paula, Mark, and Rick, the next generation of my family,
may they always be knowledge workers throughout their lives!

Contents

Illustrations

Acknowledgments

I wish to acknowledge some of the hundreds of people who have given me their valuable information, ideas, and long-term support while I was preparing *The 2010 Meltdown*. They include: Eunice Askov, Distinguished Professor of Education, Co-director, Institute for the Study of Adult Literacy and the Goodling Institute for Research in Family Literacy, The Pennsylvania State University; Lynn Gresham, Editor, *Employee Benefit News;* Roger Herman, CEO, The Herman Group; Kevin Hollenbeck, Director of Publications, W. E. Upjohn Institute for Employment Research; Linda Kaiser, Executive Director, Chicago Workforce Board; Suzanne Knell, Executive Director, Illinois Literacy Resource Development Center; Peggy Luce, Vice President, Education and Training, Chicagoland Chamber of Commerce; Constance Majka, Program Director, Philadelphia Academies, Inc.; Andy McKenna, Jr., President, Swartz Paper Company; Ronald R. Morgan, Professor of Educational Psychology, Loyola University, Chicago; Charles J. O'Malley, Consultant, U.S. Department of Education; James Parker, Coordinator, Midwest States and Work-Based Education, U.S. Department of Education; Judith A. Ponticell, Professor and Associate Vice President, Academic Affairs, University of South Florida–Lakeland Campus.

In particular, I wish to gratefully acknowledge the critical support of John Willig, my publishing agent. His many ideas and suggestions and faith in me as a writer were essential in making this book happen. Thank you, John.

I also wish to thank Nick Philipson, my editor at Greenwood, for his enthusiastic support throughout this project.

Both Sandra Gula and Bonnie Cloer have assisted me with their great computer skills in preparing this book. I heartily express my deepest appreciation to both of them for their invaluable assistance.

My wife, Elaine Gordon, a professional writer and university librarian in her own right, made this book happen. She assisted in gathering information and in editing for clarity of ideas and expression. This book would not be in your hands today without her continuous, expert research and insightful editorial assistance over this five-year period. However, for any factual errors this book may contain, I take sole responsibility.

Edward E. Gordon
Chicago, Illinois

Introduction:
People, Jobs, and Culture

During the past 30 years, the world has undergone accelerated technical and social change. Because of the bewildering combination of these and other cultural forces, many people now worry about their current jobs and the future of America in the world economy

The 2010 Meltdown: Solving the Impending Jobs Crisis addresses the interconnections between technology, globalization, a major worldwide demographic shift, and the increasing global shortfall of skilled and educated people. It spells out solutions to avoid a people catastrophe and a potential economic meltdown for America and the world.

This is a book about culture and change. Most people think about contemporary cultural problems as if the world were a static place; they propose solutions based on how things work today or worked yesterday. That is why the present, static solutions to these jobs and people issues are now being overwhelmed.[1]

Yet the past 30 years have also been a time of marvels and unprecedented prosperity around the world. It is hard for most people to comprehend that only 60 years ago, 40 percent of American families had an annual income of less than $1,000. As historian David McCullough reminds us, "Because you were born into this particular era doesn't mean it has to be the limit of your experience."[2]

The 2010 Meltdown is not just an exercise in nostalgia. Part of my mission is to help the reader roam the past, present, and future to construct new answers for our present dilemmas.

During this current watershed era of change, science has transformed how we live and how long we live. The splitting of the atom and invention of the computer are among the great, earth-shaking developments of our age.

Lest we forget, it was only in 1945, at the end of World War II, that the United States emerged intact as the world's foremost industrial power. During the subsequent Cold War era, through the collapse and transformation of world communism in the 1990s, U.S. history had become world history. Current American culture developed around that success story.[3]

Over the past two decades, technology and world trade created about 40 million more jobs than were destroyed in the United States. These are the past dynamics of successful American capitalism. But the key is to better manage future changes by supporting the transition of U.S. workers to more competitive, higher-paying/higher-skill jobs, not to cling to the low-skill job culture of a past age that is disappearing worldwide.[4]

Part of my motivation in writing *The 2010 Meltdown* is to pilot Starship Earth into a prosperous, peaceful 21st century by emphasizing that people resources are a crucial factor in propelling change. We may often have technology resources, even capital resources, in abundance. But what could be called the smart people resources required to propel us to a better tomorrow simply aren't keeping up with society's demands.

A global economic shift is already under way. The next wave of the Industrial Revolution will make many regions of the United States and communities around the planet regret their current apathy in creating more smart people for the high-tech world economy.

During the past decade, I have been encouraged by the enthusiastic response to my people development ideas from many community leaders around the world who have already heard this message or who have read my prior books on averting this catastrophe. Many have already begun the difficult task of changing the job culture in their local communities. In the following pages, by telling their stories of community activism, I seek to begin the process of winning a real commitment to these changes from a broader range of international readers. If each of us is not willing to invest something in gradual, systemic changes now, we will all pay very dearly 10 to 20 years from now. I agree with the observation of Richard Tomkins in the *Financial Times* that "human achievement is based on sublimating one's own instinct for the greater good and forgoing pleasures today for a better tomorrow."[5]

"America's Meltdown," the first part of the book, is an overview of the broad impact of technology, globalization, baby-boomer retirements, and other interrelated issues. Chapter 1, "The 2010 Crossroad," documents how people are struggling to keep their jobs or find new ones in America's so-called screen saver economy that often seems to be built on greed, illusion, and hype. For the past decade, American business has been in denial about long-term workforce development and, instead, has fixated on short-term profit strategies such as global repositioning, outsourcing, or importing temporary workers. By 2010 an unprecedented number of baby boomers will begin retiring in the United States, Europe, and Japan. We face the sobering reality of a smaller next generation of workers who are less-well-educated and less-prepared with the specialized skills to run a high-tech economy. This smart people shortage will increase the risk that the world's elaborate technological infrastructure will begin falling apart.

In Chapter 2, "The Rise of the Techno-Peasants," we explore how, during the past 30 years, the employee skill bar has been silently rising in workplaces worldwide. Business profits in America and in every advanced, industrialized nation now hinge on using the most advanced technologies operated by more sophisticated workers. Unfortunately, the worker pool of these well-educated, tech-savvy people has not kept pace with workplace demands. Many Americans even lack the fundamental educational skills needed to learn how to use these workplace technologies. The rise of what I call the techno-peasant seriously cripples service and manufacturing productivity worldwide.

Part Two, "Feeding the Sharks," tells us how our culture now traps many people in low-skill or obsolete jobs that are disappearing more each day. Chapter 3, "Where Has the Schoolhouse Gone?", asks if anything has really changed over the past 20 years of so-called school reform. At best, only one-third of all U.S. students are at the twelfth-grade reading level when they graduate from high school, and up to 50 percent of current students drop out of high school. Many people still deny the existence of an education crisis. They maintain that there are plenty of low-skill jobs now available. We only need to raise the minimum wage to make these jobs financially practical for more Americans. Unfortunately, the minority of well-prepared U.S. students in an educational wasteland of mediocrity and ignorance is too small to offset the competition from students of many other nations in the skills race for tomorrow's best job opportunities.

Chapter 4, "Help Wanted in America and the World," explores the broken career machine in the United States and many other nations. The majority of parents, students, and educators suffer from a career culture lag due to outdated information or actual misinformation. Most know too little about the new career opportunities of the 21st century. They know even less about what education and specialized skills it will take to participate in these high-paying careers. The world's labor market seems increasingly out of sync with the growing demands for knowledgeable people to fill careers in many tech-related areas of health care, engineering, the sciences, business, teaching, and even traditional, high-skill craft occupations. The irony is that many individuals who are obsessed with modern technology disdain as "uncool" these high-paying, high-skill, tech-related careers that increasingly make the world go around. This people paradox now grips the globe.

Part Three, "Structuring Renewal," proposes policy solutions to the issues raised in the previous chapters and provides case study solutions. Chapter 5, "Signposts at the Workforce Crossroad," shows how communities from Santa Ana, California to Fargo, North Dakota, as well as across Asia and the European Union, are responding with 21st-century career training and education programs. Small businesses and large corporations are collaborating through local community organizations that include such groups as service clubs, Chambers of Commerce, schools, unions, and parent associations. They sponsor a multitude of different non-governmental organizations (NGOs) that provide guidance to students on a range of new and traditional careers, as well as retraining current workers.

Chapter 6, "The 'Sixth Discipline,'" tells the story of how organizations are better balancing their short-term versus long-term economic needs by investing in growing their people's knowledge. These training and education programs range from those of METRA (Chicago's commuter railroad), Wabash National (a manufacturer of truck trailers), and Will-Burt Company (auto parts) to those of IT companies such as Intel, IBM, and Verizon. They all practice a "Sixth Discipline" by getting a good return on investment (ROI) by developing their human capital and seeking ways of fostering creativity and innovation as part of a business culture change process. They are challenging a Wall Street culture that remains fixated on short-term profit regardless of negative, long-term economic consequences.

The concluding chapter, "Beyond the 2010 Crossroad," explores what we now know about potential practices and policies that can propel us toward an era of reconstruction for a New America and a new world.

The 2010 Meltdown deliberately seeks to challenge many readers' personal prejudices about culture change. In Chicago we have a large Irish community. We also have a local disease known as Irish Alzheimer's—you forget everything but your grudges. I am asking all readers of this book to consider giving up some of their grudges or vested interests to help their communities adjust to the broad, cultural changes demanded by the 21st century. We need to learn from our past mistakes, not dwell on them. Mistakes are seldom irrevocable.

The United States has always been known to the world as a center of energy, change, and optimism. We have become a nation of investors and builders transformed by, and transforming, technology.[6]

Now the nation's critical education mass is falling below a level acceptable for maintaining, let alone expanding, our current standard of living. It has become increasingly clear that "America will not remain highly competitive in global markets unless it builds a world-class workforce."[7]

The entire world is approaching an important economic crossroad that will decide which nations will prosper in the 21st century. If the United States, the European Union, Japan, India, and China fail to redesign their workforce infrastructure from within, it will be redone from without, with a vengeance.

The time has come for more people to band together in their communities and get involved in local civic institutions. America and the world need to move on as we build a more knowledge-based culture for the 2010 crossroad and beyond.[8]

I

AMERICA'S MELTDOWN

1

The 2010 Crossroad

Goods move. People move. Ideas move. And cultures change. The difference now is the speed and scope of these changes. It took television 13 years to acquire 50 million users; the Internet took only five. Not everyone is happy about this.[1]

Two forces today are driving worldwide cultural change—globalization and technology. Which is more important? In terms of creating high-wage jobs, technology will continue to power the globalization express. But the job and career expectations of hundreds of millions of workers will also experience radical changes.

In the United States and many other countries, the demand for highly and specially skilled labor is rising. The need for low-wage, low-skill jobs is in steep decline. One study by William Cline, an economist at the Institute for International Economics, estimated that between 1973 and 1993 technological change was at least five times more powerful than globalization in widening wage and job inequality. If you factor in the current U.S. business outsourcing fad sending jobs to low-wage countries, this trend will continue to accelerate.

Globalization allows more efficient use of the world's resources and usually boosts average incomes. But too many people in low-skill manufacturing and service jobs in richer countries are now finding the demand for their labor is falling. These jobs are being performed more cheaply abroad.

Any effort to hold back technological progress or erect trade barriers to protect jobs is doomed to failure. U.S. and other multinational firms can easily move their operations from one country to another. Protectionism will end up crippling U.S. industry. It will also hamper the creation of new high-tech innovations that have made America the envy of the world.[2]

MEGA-TECH

Like an episode from *Star Wars* or *Star Trek*, 14 giant machines guided by remote computers work throughout the night making gears for lawn sprinklers and computer printers. They drop them into boxes waiting on conveyor belts. It's so-called lights-out manufacturing at a Connecticut ABA-PGT plastics plant. This scene is being repeated at production facilities all over the world.[3]

In the 1940s Thomas Watson, the founder of IBM, predicted a world market of five computers! By 2002 over 600 million computers existed around the world! More than half of all U.S. workers were using a computer at work (72.3 million).[4]

It was only in 1946 that the first programmable computer was built with a memory capacity of 20 words. But it took the spread of mainframe computers, and IBM's later introduction its personal computer (PC), to spark the current technology revolution. Since the 1970s the pace of change has been propelled ever faster, as predicted by Gordon Moore, the co-founder of Intel. In 1965 he forecasted that the processing power of a silicon chip would double every 18 months. He was right. These enormous jumps over the past 30 years in computing power have cut technology costs by 99.999% (or 35% per year) to spread its applications throughout everyday life. A Ford Taurus in 2000 had more computing power than the multimillion-dollar NASA mainframe computers used in the 1970s Apollo space program.[5] But this was only the beginning of mega-tech breakthroughs. Here's what is new and on the horizon:

- Bell Labs has made a transistor from a single molecule—an organic monotransistor one-billionth of a meter long, faster and cheaper than silicon types (2001).
- The NEC Earth Simulator developed by Japan (in 2002 it was the world's fastest computer, equal to the 20 fastest U.S. computers combined).
- IBM's chip with carbon monoxide molecules on a copper surface became the world's smallest operating computer circuit (2002).

- Motorola's Mobile Extreme Convergence Semiconductor cut costs of wireless devices such as personal digital assistants or hand-held DVD players by 40 to 50 percent (2003).
- Intel first invented (2001) the world's fastest silicon transistor, which could switch on/off 1.5 trillion times a second. Then it went on to discover two types of metal to replace silicon in chips and dramatically increase chip speed (2003).[6]

Information technology (IT) speeds up the whole innovation process. Large amounts of data can now be processed more easily and cheaply, thus reducing the time needed to design new products and services. With this increased access to information, IT has made markets work more efficiently.

Information technology is now linked around the world at negligible costs. Technology has helped to globalize production and move business capital anywhere.[7] But these productivity gains were not nearly enough to justify the great 1990s speculative IT bubble.

THE BUBBLE GOES POP

As the world accelerates under the influence of speed-of-light technologies, the "power of now" makes us oblivious to our past. Popular culture is crowding out any remembrance of things past that might save current and future generations repeating a lot of the collective pain from past technology adjustments.[8]

Many previous economic booms were caused by the introduction of a new, general-purpose technology—the telegraph in the 1830s, electricity in the 1920s, IT in the 1990s. Cost savings and spin-off innovations ran wild in the marketplace. But this cascade of new products and productivity was followed by a wave of job obsolescence and a great dislocation of employees. Sound familiar?[9]

Charles Kindleberger, in his classic study of economic bubbles (*Manias, Panics and Crashes*) describes the inherent instability of financial markets and what he calls the "irrational exuberance" of people's belief that share prices will go on rising to the skies forever.[10] In the past, such group mania has assumed many dimensions.

In Holland from 1634 to 1637, tulip mania produced a catastrophic futures trading bubble. Nearly a century later, in an effort to refinance its 1720 war debt, the British government authorized the South Sea Company and other groups to trade their shares for government debt. Investors bought shares in the South Seas Company thinking that the ships were sailing back and forth from the South Seas laden with valuable goods to be sold in London at huge profits for the stockholders. The trouble was that there were no ships and no trade, only human greed. Stock multiplied more than nine times before the South Sea bubble popped. Anyone who remembers the heady days (1990s) of the IT/dot com bubble will be amused to learn that of the 190 trading companies launched in 1720s Britain, only four survived. [11]

The speculative technology of the Roaring Twenties was electric, as was the mass-production economy it spawned. Hot new stocks included General Motors and RCA, the Cisco Systems and Intels of the 1920s. Yale economist Irving Fisher argued that innovation was transforming the economy. The industrials traded at more than 21 times earnings before crashing in 1929.[12]

THE SCREEN SAVER ECONOMY

From the later 1990s until 2000, Wall Street claimed that traditional profit/earning ratios were irrelevant in the new economy. Higher productivity, low inflation, and low interest rates meant that the market had discovered a new paradigm of higher valuations. Short-term profit strategies became the major focus of corporations and investors. Long-term planning became an oxymoron.

Technological change led by IT and the dot coms triggered a bull market that raised the Dow Jones Industrial Index from 5,000 to 11,000 during its five-year run (1995–2002) and the Nasdaq to 5000. The market then collapsed, wiping out close to $7 trillion in investments. The speculative bubble revealed a screen saver economy. "A lot of companies that were funded were not businesses," says Stewart Gross, senior managing director at Warburg Pincus. "They were innovations or products, but were not businesses." Roy C. Smith, Professor of Entrepreneurship and Finance at New York University's Stern School of Business warns that, "In periods of euphoria ... it's faith" in some new idea, rather than hard-edged financial analysis, that often drives investors.[13]

The demise of the IT bubble once again shows that the business cycle has not really been eliminated. If an economy grows too fast, inflation will start to rise. Business share prices still depend on business profits. A more "back to normal" economy hinges on corporate America adopting a sustainable, long-term economic outlook.

An essential component includes the need to develop more skilled people to run a more complex, high-tech U.S. economy. Government still needs to remain on guard against the abuse of monopoly power and human greed.

THE NEW ROBBER BARONS

An Era of Greed

Most financial bubbles begin collapsing with the public revelation of real or imagined corruption. A frenzy of unbridled greed and lavish life-styles recently exemplified by Enron's Kenneth Lay, WorldCom's Bernie Ebbers, or L. Dennis Kozlowski of Tyco Corporation, among many others, captured headlines. Some tried to take the money and run before their alleged swindles were revealed. The crash soon followed.

What really left a bad taste in the mouths of most Americans was the bizarre run-up of the bubble's wealth that created a class of so-called new robber barons. In 1990 the average CEO in America enjoyed a salary equivalent to 85 times that of his or her workers. By 2001 that figure had ballooned to 531 times. No other industrialized country came even close the matching this phenomenon.

This imbalance was made worse when some corporate leaders tried to hide behind barely believable words about how much they value people and their customers. Instead, the fundamental faith of the new robber barons was that the market was God. The market was democratic. It perfectly expressed the popular will. The law of supply and demand, the focus group, the superstore, and the Internet were the grand principles that defined all modern life. Greed was good.

Even Peter Drucker scornfully dismisses any justification for this brand of laissez-faire capitalism. He observed, "A lot of top managers enjoy cruelty. There is no doubt that we are in a period in which you are a hero if you are cruel."[14]

About 100 years ago Theodore Roosevelt surveyed American capitalism's first group of robber barons: J. P. Morgan, John D. Rockefeller, James J. Hill, and Andrew Carnegie, among others. He believed that "the vast individual and corporate fortunes, the vast combinations of capital which have marked the development of our industrial system, create new conditions and necessitate a change from the old attitude of the state and the nation toward property."[15]

Roosevelt vigorously pursued the break-up of business trusts and monopolies that were leaving havoc in their wake. The Sherman Antitrust Act he helped to shape is there for a reason. Monopolies are bad. They give one executive or one business too much power over our lives. But the Sherman Antitrust Act is a relic of Theodore Roosevelt's era. It doesn't work too well anymore. Today, business oligopolies control many markets.

Globalization has permitted mega-business mergers under the guise of deregulation as government has retreated from oversight of the economy.

Oligopolies are the estimated 40,000 global corporations that treat the world as one big market, and can virtually ignore national boundaries and laws. They exist in every economic sector, from defense to college textbooks, and semiconductor chips to pharmaceuticals. They control prices. They can stifle innovations and jobs. The fewer the players, the lower the likelihood that a groundbreaking innovation will be perfected and rolled out into the marketplace. Will the oligopolies go the way of earlier conglomerates and ultimately fail? Over time, their profitability and an international need to prevent abusive monopolistic combinations will tell an interesting tale. (See Table 1.1)

In recent years a compromise between the short-term gains of shareholders and the long-term interests of employees and the wider community has been incorporated in the term *corporate social responsibility*. Its advocates argue that shareholders will benefit if the other stakeholders are dealt with fairly.

The long debate about what companies are for and whose interests they should serve will continue. Businesses will always seek a competitive advantage. Sometimes it will be through new technology, and at other times by cutting costs through mergers, acquisitions, or outsourcing. But woe to any business that fails to develop its people – their innovative ideas, creativity, and skills. In an increasingly competitive world in which technology and a global marketplace call the shots, it is people, not the manipulation of money, that will drive the future of the U.S. economy. Those who fail to grasp this, the so-called champions of cold-blooded capitalism, may soon find their names on the obituary page of *The Wall Street Journal*.[16]

Since 2002 some accounting reforms and governmental oversight activities have been implemented to toughen accounting practices. However, the American public cannot afford to see the combination of lax rules and regulations and unscrupulous individuals continue to undermine the health of the entire economy. America loathes the new robber barons because it treasures the ideal that business should do the country more good than bad.

The Bubble Directors

One of the leading devices motivating executives to pump up their quarterly earnings has been the issuance of stock options. If the stock went up, the option holder made a ton of money. If the stock went down, it was worthless. So the bubble directors and executives "grabbed a cork bat and swung for the fences." They buried themselves in stock options.

Table 1.1
The Oligopoly Watch

Industry	State of Market	Recent Deals	Outlook
Defense Contractors	After a wave of Pentagon-encouraged consolidation, there are five industry titans: Northrop Grumman, Lockheed Martin, Boeing, Raytheon and General Dynamics.	Northrop last week bid $5.9 billion for TRW, soon after buying Newport News Shipbuilding.	Pentagon likely to oppose further consolidation among the biggest players, but giants may snap up smaller firms. Possible targets: L3 Communications, United Defense.
Basic DRAM semiconductor chips	If Micron Technology succeeds in buying the DRAM operations of South Korea's Hynix Semiconductor, the four largest companies would control 83% of the global market, compared with 46% in 1995.	In December Micron agreed to buy U.S. DRAM operations of No. 6 Toshiba. Also, No. 7 Hitachi and No. 5 NEC last year agreed to merge memory-chip operations.	Consolidation fueled by excess capacity and price slump. Reviving demand and mergers help prices rebound. Some small players likely to be squeezed out as four giants dominate.
Cable TV	If Comcast-AT&T broadband deal goes through, three companies will control 65%.	Pending acquisition of AT&T's cable arm by Comcast.	More deals are likely as companies try to compete with Comcast-AT&T. Court decision striking down rules limiting cable companies' scale makes deals easier.
College textbooks	Three companies control 61.5%: Pearson (16.7%), Thomson (21.8%), McGraw-Hill (13%).	Thomson's $2.06 billion acquisition last year of several Harcourt business lines, including its college titles.	Several smaller players could get snatched up by one of the big three, but the biggest remaining player, Houghton Mifflin, has 5.2%.
Job recruitment Web sites	Three players control 66% of industry revenues. Two years ago, at least 10 players were contenders.	Yahoo! This year bought HotJobs.com, and CareerBuilder, who major shareholders are Tribune and Knight Ridder, last year acquired HeadHunter.Net.	No more consolidation likely among three top players. Several major employers, seeking to broaden their options, recently formed a cooperative site.

(continued)

Table 1.1
(continued)

Industry	State of Market	Recent Deals	Outlook
Local TV	Viacom and Fox each reach 41% of homes already. A pending deal would give NBC 30%.	Viacom this year agreed to buy KCAL-TV, last independent station in Los Angeles, for $650 million. General Electric bought Spanish-language Telemundo network and KVEA station in same market last year.	Appeals-court decision last week ordering regulators to rethink ownership cap will spark more deals. Likely targets: Belo and Scripps-Howard.
Pharmaceuticals	Three companies have 26.2% of U.S. sales: Pfizer (10.2%), GlaxoSmithKline (8.8%) and Merck (7.2%).	In 2000 Glaxo Wellcome and SmithKline Beecham agreed to merge and Pfizer acquired Warner-Lambert.	Plenty of room for consolidation remains, but some companies find bigger isn't better as sales growth after deals remains poor.
Wireless phones	Five companies control 71%: Verizon Wireless (23%), AT&T Wireless (14%), Sprint (10%), Cingular, the joint venture of SBC and BellSouth (17%) and Nextel (7%).	Deutsche Telekom bought VoiceStream last year for $26 billion.	Deals likely as major players take advantage of FCC decision last year increasing amount of spectrum any company can own. Major carriers likely to snap up smaller ones, such as Nextel and Northcoast.

Source: The Wall Street Journal (2002).

A leveraged windfall that ran for several years pumped the bubble euphoria in many boardrooms, especially the high-tech ones. Explosive spending and expansion on vast, unprofitable capital investments created serious economic consequences once this bubble burst. Surplus capacity in equipment and workers distorted manufacturing, the telecom-related IT industries, and the labor market.

Enron and the other bubble scandals show the weaknesses of the current system of corporate checks and balances. As David Wessel of *The Wall Street Journal* pointed out, "If companies reward executives for turning up share prices in the near term so they can cash in, at least some of those executives will distort profits to do just that—even at the expense of the long-run interests of the company and its shareholders."[17]

The bubble's flood of stock options began to undermine the fundamental role of management—the long-term welfare of companies makes capitalism work (see Table 1.2). In the so-called new economy, the fox was both inside and outside the hen house. Both managers and investors wanted the highest returns immediately. The financial abuse led to a screen saver economy where managers' wealth depended on artificially propping up their company share price—by any means. The next step was cashing in their stock options even as they led their companies to financial ruin.

Uncontrolled greed can sometimes lead managers to present their financials in the most flattering light. The story comes to mind of a former U.S.S.R. nail factory. The factory's quota was based not on how many nails they made but on the weight of the output. In order to meet its quota, the factory produced one gigantic nail. Warren Buffett and Federal Reserve Chairman Alan Greenspan had long warned that stock options should be treated like any other business expense because they distort shareholder value.

Table 1.2
The New Robber Barons

Issues	Traditional Capitalism	"New Economy" Capitalism
1. Management	Long-term view. 20–30 year careers.	Short-term view. CEO and top people in and out. 4–5 years average tenure.
2. Stock Prices	Based on steady sustainable earnings.	Biggest bang right now. Let someone else worry about the future.
3. Human Capital	Company's revenue and earnings rise – hire more people, fall – layoff people.	Company profitable – layoff through outsourcing, mergers or acquisitions to get stock price up now.

Source: Edward E. Gordon.

By 2002, Standard & Poor's bit the bullet and, over the loud objections of many corporations, changed its stock indexing to take into account the true cost of stock options. By the fall of 2003, over 120 U.S. companies, including Coca-Cola, General Electric and Amazon.com began treating stock options as expenses. Microsoft has abandoned the use of options.[18]

Millions of Americans had invested in a screen saver economy that simply went away. Millions of employees despaired over their shrunken 401(k) retirement plans. Many also lost jobs and saw careers end. Yet these economic effects may be mild in comparison to the labor-market changes coming soon to your local economy.

DEMOGRAPHIC MELTDOWN

United States

It is a mistake to think that U.S. economic gains for the past few decades will continue based solely on technology breakthroughs and historical financial data. There has never been anything like today's aging population or, on several fronts, the potential economic meltdown it might bring.

The so-called baby boomer generation of 79 million people was born between 1946 and 1965. They have long distorted the U.S. population balance. The baby boomer generation has about 27 million more people than the generation that preceded it, and about 10 million more than the one that follows.

From 1980–2002, the U.S. workforce exploded by 50 percent due to the addition of 38 million baby boomers. Women also flooded into the workforce. Now the baby boomers are aging. By 2008 the labor force median age be will be 40.7 years and going ever-upward. (It was only 38.7 years in 1998). Today the labor force is growing more slowly—dropping to a 0.8 percent annual rate over this decade, then sliding to a tiny 0.2 percent per year indefinitely into the future (2020 and beyond).

By 2020 the ranks of working men age 55 to 64 will swell by 33 percent to about 20 million. As baby boomer retirements accelerate, the U.S. will have 27 "Floridas" by 2025. The portion of the population over 65 compared to the working age population (15 to 64) will rise by mid-century from 22 percent (2000) to 38 percent (2050).[19] See Table 1.3.

The U.S. Census Bureau, Department of Labor, and the Immigration and Naturalization Service all agree that the population younger than 45 is in a steep decline. In 2003 the U.S. experienced its lowest recorded birth rate. By 2010 the native-born labor force will begin to dwindle, even

Table 1.3
Percent of Population over 65 Compared to Population 15–64,
2000 and 2050 Projection

Nation	2000 (%)	2050 (%)
USA	22	38
Australia	20	47
Austria	25	55
Canada	20	46
Czech Republic	22	58
France	27	51
Germany	26	53
Ireland	19	44
Italy	29	67
Japan	28	65
Norway	26	41
Spain	27	66
Sweden	30	46
United Kingdom	26	46

Source: Standard & Poor's (2004).

though in the 1990s America admitted the largest number of immigrants it had ever recorded in one decade. Thirty-three million people now living in the United States were born elsewhere. However, this latest flood of immigrants will only partially offset the overall population decline in the workforce.

In the decade following 2010, the principal talent pool for managers and workers under age 45 will shrink by 6 percent. The structural demographic forces are now in place for a real skill war for talent during at least the next 20 years.[20]

In 2010 the meltdown will become even more apparent, warns Social Security Trustee Thomas Saving, because that is when the oldest baby boomers turn 65 and will start to retire. In 1950, 16 people were working for every person drawing Social Security benefits. By 2030, only about two people will be working for every beneficiary.

In 2000, 27 percent of the U.S. population was 18 or under, and 21 percent were 55 or older. Fast-forward to 2020, when 25 percent will be 18 or under, and 30 percent will be 55 or older. This raises many red flags, including the solvency of pension programs and business competition for the human resources to do all the work.

Eighty percent of all boomers say they plan to work part-time after retirement. Another 20 percent also want to start a business. Even so, by 2010 surpluses in the Social Security trust funds will begin to decline. Thomas Saving believes that the money needed to finance the federal retiree programs will start to have an effect on other government spending.[21]

Motivating more men and women to put off their retirement might help. Already, 68 percent of men aged 55 to 64 are working. However, just to add another million men would require that figure to jump to 74 percent by 2010. (Seventy-seven percent of all women are now in the workforce.) But companies are reluctant to hire older workers on a part-time or full-time basis because many executives believe that you cannot "teach old dogs new tricks." Also, there is the perception that older workers are a liability and that even if they are highly skilled, they can't be worked as hard or adapt to change as rapidly as their younger counterparts. As we will see later, most of this business culture is based on faulty executive "street smarts." These arguments just don't hold up to the convincing data on older workers' performance on the job.[22]

An Aging World

Germany is the world's third-largest economy. By 2050 over half of its people will be over age 65, compared with one-fourth today. Unless the birth rate recovers, the total German population of 82 million today will shrink to somewhere between 70 million and 73 million. The number of Germans under 35 will shrink about twice as fast as the older population will grow. The total workforce will decline by 25 percent, from 40 million today to 30 million.

Germany's demographics are far from the exception. Today in most European countries, there are three employees for each older person. But after 2010, the trend changes sharply. The Organization for Economic Cooperation and Development (OECD) predicts that by 2030 there will be only two workers left for every retiree.

Due to low birth rates, the populations of 33 countries are projected to shrink by mid-century. In 2004, nearly 20 percent of Japan's population was over age 65, and in 2050, U.N. projections place this figure at over 35 percent. The percentages are far higher when the population over 65 is compared to the working age population. In 2000, those over 65 constituted 28 percent of those aged 15 to 64; by 2050, the percentage is projected to be 65 percent.

Russia has one of the fastest-shrinking populations on earth. From a population of 145 million (2001), it is projected to fall to 137 million

(2025) and then to 128 million in 2050. This meltdown is being fueled by both declining life expectancy and a big drop in the birthrate.

Even China is beginning to experience dramatic population aging in response to the government's one-child policy. The United Nations predicts that China will have about 630 million people aged 50 and above in 2050. This compares to only about 78 million children below the age of five, and only 324 million children and teenagers below the age of 20. China will have almost twice as many people above 50 as below age 20![23]

For France, Germany, Italy, and Spain, the demographic mix is even more explosive. In 2050 there will be severe labor shortages of not just skilled workers, but also the unskilled. By then more than half of the European Union (EU) population will be over 65. A November 2004 *New York Times* article reported that Frank Schirrmacher, author of *The Methuselah Conspiracy*, stated: "Spain, Italy, and Germany will be the first societies in human history with more older people than children. What will it mean for popular culture? How will they vote?"[24]

The Race against Time

The global, bottom-line demographic problem is that too many skilled people are dropping out of the world economy at one time. There simply aren't enough skilled Generation X or Y workers to keep economies humming. Beverly Goldberg, vice president of the Century Foundation, thinks that the business downturn after the IT bubble took pressure off companies that had not yet come to grips with impending labor shortages. "Labor force participation by those over 55 has to increase by 25 percent starting in 2011 to have enough workers to maintain productivity, never mind business growth," she said.

Politicians have no interest in facing up to this demographic meltdown and the skilled worker shortages it will produce. James Vaupel, a professor of demography at the Max Planck Institute for Demographic Research in Germany, says, "The official government forecasts distort people's decisions about how much to save and business investing in current and future workers' skills. They have given politicians a license to postpone painful adjustments."

In a wide-ranging demographic report, the U.S. Center for Strategic and International Studies indicated that, "[C]ountries will have to race against time to ensure their economic and social fabric against the 'shock' of global aging." Of all the shocks, the greatest is the "staggering fiscal cost." A big part of that bill is a labor market out of sync with the world marketplace.[25]

DO YOU KNOW WHERE TO FIND A GOOD ——?

A New Kind of "Crash"

Although Manhattan is usually snarled in traffic jams, the billions of daily transactions of the New York Stock Exchange (NYSE) flow flawlessly around the world. At least until one June morning (June 9, 2001), when a botched computer software installation halted trading for an hour and a half. This set off computer ripples to the Chicago Board of Trade and the Chicago Mercantile Exchange, which abruptly stopped trading options and futures products tied to the NYSE-traded stocks. Earlier, in October 1998, a similar human technical glitch had brought down the Big Board. A rare instance, you say?

Three weeks later, a technician sitting at a single computer in Connecticut disabled two of Nasdaq's main trading platforms for about two hours. To compensate, Nasdaq kept its stock exchange open for an extra hour. The glitches reverberated across the nation's exchanges and trading desks.

In September, 1999, 2,000 of Citibank's automated teller machines shut down intermittently for two days. In 2004, human error caused American Airlines and U.S. Airways to be temporarily unable to access critical takeoff information in their computers systems, forcing three-hour flight delays affecting thousands of passengers nationwide. Also in 2004, a flawed software installation shut down *Chicago Tribune* computers; that day, 40 percent of subscribers didn't get a newspaper. "You're going to see more failures because there are more systems," says Avivah Litan, an analyst at Gartner Research. Bank mergers are combining old and new computer systems. Today the programmers who can read these languages are declining in number. John Billota, a vice president at Charles Schwab, observed, "It is very difficult to find new people who are willing to work with this stuff."

Then there are the crashes that didn't happen. After addressing the Virginia Military Institute, President George W. Bush boarded his Marine One helicopter. Five minutes later he scrambled across a grassy field, boarded the backup helicopter and took off. What happened? Marine One broke down. "It was a mechanical problem," explained White House spokesman Ari Fleischer. "These things do happen from time to time."[26]

Finding "Smart" People

Sometimes Jeff Taylor, chairman of Monster.com, sounds like a nut case when he talks about the critical shortages of skilled workers now and into the future. "The knowledge worker is going to be at the center of company desperation." He says there will be a so-called smart-people gap as wide as the Mississippi. Taylor urges all American to look at the numbers. About

70 million baby boomers, some highly skilled, will exit the workforce over the next 18 years, with only 40 million workers coming in.

As the baby boomers begin to retire, skill shortages throughout the entire economy will reach crisis levels. Companies need to take steps to retain and retrain current workers, as well as better prepare and recruit the next workforce generation. Most executives and most Americans haven't yet faced up to the powerful combination of how the technology and demographic slide is propelling us all to a 2010 meltdown.

An issue accelerating labor shortages, says John A. Challenger, CEO of Challenger, Gray & Christmas, Inc., is that "[M]any of today's workers, as well as future generations of workers, lack both basic and specialized skills needed in the present and future workplace." Challenger warns, "The lack of skilled workers in technology and other sectors that face labor shortages could have devastating effects on companies' ability to compete in the increasingly global marketplace."[27]

Despite the tight, post-bubble U.S. job market, the labor market suffers from a shortage of people educated and trained to industry-specific jobs. Many of these jobs require specific training and, for some people, changing careers may mean going back to school. In some fields such as nursing and health-related technical careers, the shortage exists today. In many other areas, experts predict that the economy will experience a severe job shortage over the next 20 years—similar to the low unemployment rate of the late 1990s before the bust of the dot com boom.[28]

Simply stated, today in America there are just too many people trained for the wrong jobs. Many jobs have become unnecessary, technically obsolete, or will become so with increasing rapidity. Worse yet, the job/career aspirations of too many current and future workers are at serious odds with the changing needs of the U.S. labor market. Our current training and education systems were never designed to respond rapidly to these rapidly changing conditions. Unless resolved quickly, this labor market imbalance will have serious economic consequences, possibly including a devaluation of the U.S. dollar due to the huge U.S. trade imbalance.

By 2010 many aspects of daily life in America will become more difficult. Throughout the entire economy, the United States lacks adequate numbers of appropriately skilled workers to support high standards in personal or professional services, or properly maintain the physical and technological infrastructure upon which everyone relies and takes for granted. By 2010 the United States will reach a crossroad in what has become an incredibly challenging environment.

The U.S. Bureau of Labor Statistics (BLS) predicts that in 2010 that the economy will support about 167 million jobs, but the population will be able to fill only 157 million of them. Then we must factor in the education gap. Perhaps add another 10 million vacant positions? As futurist Roger Herman notes, "[T]he fastest growing occupations are those requiring postsecondary education, either for a vocational certificate or an academic degree ... [E]conomic growth continues to create these high-skilled jobs at an accelerating pace".... [29]

Though a shortage of 20 million people looks terrible, the BLS assures us that over the long term, labor supply and demand will balance. They don't see a shortage. Unfortunately for most Americans, that long-term adjustment could be quite painful and of a long duration. Many experts predict by the time this labor meltdown becomes obvious to most people, we will be well into a skilled worker shortage. As we approach the 2010 crossroad, accelerating baby-boomer retirements could extend the effects of this meltdown for several decades. Larger numbers of skilled people cannot be produced overnight because of our outdated training and educational systems.

Economist Mark Henricks sees an evaporating pool of properly skilled people. "The size of the pool gets smaller and smaller, and the demand for those skills gets bigger and bigger. So you have more companies competing for a smaller and smaller group of talented people."[30]

The slump in the job market at the beginning of this decade seems to belie these statistical prognostications. In the first 22 months of the recession that began in March 2001, employers eliminated 1.75 million jobs—eventually 2 to 8 million jobs were lost. A large part of this was produced by technology-driven productivity gains, or the off-shoring of low-skill jobs to lower-wage countries. The U.S. jobs that remain are more complex, requiring higher personal skills. Though technology continues to automate, more skilled humans still beat out robots. People have flexibility and the right education that increases their adaptability at performing new services or making new products.[31]

Jobs for the Future

What are some of these areas of potential job shortages? Professional specialty occupations are projected to grow by 5.3 million new jobs by 2008: teachers, nurses, radiologists, computer technicians, skilled machinists, and other areas. However, jobs in occupations that require a technical certificate, degree, or apprenticeship will increase at a faster rate than all other categories as the technology revolution spreads to even more jobs: computer technicians, lab technicians, airplane mechanics, auto mechanics, electricians, carpenters, electronic machine repairers, and many others.[32]

Here's a brief survey of selected job opportunities and their related dilemmas.

Nursing

A critical shortage of nurses is already apparent, but the future projections are even more frightening. Of the 570 nursing schools operating across the United States in 2002, 38 percent reported faculty shortages to the American Association of Colleges of Nursing. By 2010 the Bureau of Labor Statistics projects that 1 million new and replacement nurses will be needed.

A wide variety of data attest to the extent of the nursing shortage:

1. Actual and Projected Nursing Shortages

Year	Number	Source
2000	110,707	U.S. Department of Labor
2003	126,000	Joint Commission (UCAHO)
2008	450,000	U.S. Department of Health and Human Services
2020	808,000	U.S. Department of Labor and Department of Health and Human Services

2. Supply

2.7M Licensed nurses
2.2M Working (1:10 not working as a nurse) (American Association of Colleges of Nursing)

3. Age (in California)

Younger than 30	Less than 10%
31–50 (average age 45)	45%
Older than 50	33%
Over 60	15%
By 2010 over 50	40% (Health Care Association of Southern California)

4. Nursing School Enrollment

Year	Student Enrollment
1995	128,000
1999	61,646
2000	60,435
2001	62,671
2002	67,684[33]

In 2002 the U.S. Department of Health and Human Services reported that overall health care spending ($1.55 trillion) accounted for nearly 15 percent of the nation's economy. That represented an average of $5,440 for every American. Yet low pay remains one of the main reasons for the nursing shortage ($45,000 per year, 2002, U.S. Labor Department). Women today have more career opportunities than did their mothers. Nurses feel overworked, undervalued, belittled by doctors despite their many years of professional schooling and more direct contact with patients. Many nurses are frustrated and angry. Barbara Blakeney, president of the American Nursing Association (ANA) told a recent healthcare meeting, "You need to know that when nurses are overworked, when there aren't enough nurses on the floor, things happen to patients."[34]

In 2002 California moved to become the first state to improve nurse-to-patient ratios. The current ratios of one nurse to six or more patients shrank to only five patients in 2003. Because California already faced the most serious nursing shortage in the nation, this mandate helped to accelerate the closure of 60 hospitals over the last decade (26 were opened) since not enough nurses were available to staff patient beds.

By 2004, in desperation, a hospital in Palm Springs, California began offering free trips for two to Hawaii (including airfare, hotel, and car rental) to lure new nurses. Other equally pressed hospitals in Missouri and New Mexico put up billboards along highways advertising a nursing signing bonus of up to $10,000.[35]

U.S. hospitals have met with some notable success with more aggressive nursing recruitment. More than 100,000 registered nurses were hired in 2002, the highest level since 1994. Married registered nurses over age 50 and foreign-born nurses accounted for almost all the new hires. Nursing schools and hospitals have stepped up their efforts to recruit both nurses and nursing professors from Mexico, Puerto Rico, Venezuela, Spain, and the Philippines. Some hospitals pay recruiters up to $18,000 for every foreign nurse they enlist.

The health issues involved recruiting from overseas has, in turn, raised education and language skills for these students. But even if English 101 and 102 are not the issue, advanced education can also be a problem for native-born American students. College-level nursing work is difficult; it requires science, math, and excellent reading skills. Many young adults lack the appropriate high school preparation. They can become easily discouraged when they find out that they will need extra college math, science or even reading courses, before they can even begin a nursing-career education program. Another significant issue has been that nursing school enrollments have not increased fast enough, even though there are waiting lists of qualified students. A shortage of Ph.D. nursing faculty is preventing the expansion of many school programs.[36]

Health Technologists

The number of mammography centers is slipping. The American College of Radiology reported a decline from 9,873 to 9,534 in 2001 alone. The chief reason is a shortage of radiologists and technologists specializing in mammography. The American Society of Clinical Pathologists is certifying about 2,400 medical technology students a year, while the demand is closer to 5,000. This is happening just as an increasing number of women are swelling the age group for which annual mammography screening is recommended,

Other health occupation areas that will experience sharp growth range from medical assistants to lab technicians to home health aides (see Table 1.4). In few, if any, of these other career areas will the anticipated supply meet the expected demand. Educational and training requirements, low pay, and lack of awareness about these jobs tops the reasons for public indifference in pursuing health-care-related careers.

Even the once-prestigious health occupations of doctor and dentist are attracting too few new entrants. Nationwide, there are about 152,000 active dentists, more than 33 percent of whom are over age 55. About 4,000 new dentists graduate each year. This falls below the replacement number level leaving the workforce for retirement. Even though breakthroughs in dental hygiene have reduced the need for larger numbers of dentists, there are now severe shortages in large parts of the Great Plains, southern Texas, Nevada, Maine, as well as poorer and rural areas in many other states. Thirty-one million people are already affected. The American Dental Association estimated a shortage of 4,650 dentists (2003) that will continue to grow.[37]

Table 1.4
Health Care Jobs
2000 versus 2010

Demand for health care expertise to surge.
The government projects the growth for jobs in the health care field will be strong in the next several years.
FASTEST-GROWING OCCUPATIONS
Total number of jobs in 2000 and projected for 2010

Occupations	2000	2010	Percentage Change
Personal & Home Care Aides	414,000	672,000	62
Medical Assistants	329,000	516,000	57
Social & Human Services Assistants	271,000	418,000	54
Physician Assistants	58,000	89,000	53
Medical Records & Health Information Technicians	136,000	202,000	49
Home Health Aides	615,000	907,000	47

Source: U.S. Department of Labor.

Air Traffic Controllers

In 2004, 53 percent of the 1.8 million federal workers became eligible for retirement. People at the U.S. Social Security Administration and the Internal Revenue Service are all affected. This also included 15,000 air traffic controllers.

The majority of the controller workforce (7,000 people) will leave the Federal Aviation Administration by 2010 due to a mandatory retirement age of 56. It takes three to five years to properly train new controllers. Washouts are high. By 2010 the United States could easily have "[A] situation where in very short order, we simply will not have enough people to keep the system operating at its present level," says Ruth Marlin, executive vice president of the National Air Traffic Controllers Association. The U.S. Department of Transportation projects that there will be one billion passengers per year by 2010 and two billion per year by 2020.

In 2004, a narrowly averted mid-air collision near Chicago's O'Hare Airport prompted charges that the FAA had already fallen behind. Due to a shortage of staff at O'Hare, the FAA then brokered a deal with United and American Airlines to reduce flights during peak hours. Too few controllers can lead to many errors. "We are in a dire situation today," said Raymond Gibbons, president of the controllers' union.[38]

Airplane Mechanics

Back on the ground, you many never leave the gate. As the airplane mechanic workforce ages, there is today an outright shortage of airplane mechanics among small carriers and the maintenance and repair contractors who work on private aircraft. Even the large commercial airlines are hiring applicants straight out of vocational training programs rather than requiring five years of previous experience. The job has lost prestige and requires advanced training. Not enough younger workers are entering the field. The frequency of airplane maintenance errors is rising. John Goglia, a member of the National Transportation Safety Board and a former mechanic, says he is "very concerned" about the shortage and the industry's creeping "loss of skills."[39]

Technicians

Many plants have introduced new technology, reducing the need to hire new people. With mergers and restructuring, more of the younger generations faced layoffs. Cummins Engine Co. operates a big engine plant in Columbus, Ohio. Over 65 percent of its 1,100 older workers can retire in 2004. Unfortunately, Cummins has curtailed its hiring of younger workers. It is worried about filling high-skill jobs with younger, technically certified workers who lack the experience and training of the older workforce.

Across the United States between 2005 and 2015, many other companies like Cummins will all have to replace large numbers of retirees.

The nation's auto industry faces the same critical shortage of skilled technicians. According to a 2002 Wirthlin Worldwide survey, only about 2 percent of young adults aspire to careers in the auto industry. Parents, in particular, are likely to believe that employment as a mechanic (entry-level salary of $40,000 annually) is not enough of an intellectual challenge.

"The day of the 'grease monkey' is dead," says Jim Willingham, chairman of *Automotive Retailing Today*. "But these high-paying jobs ($70,000–$100,000 a year for a master mechanic) go wanting because most people don't understand that the industry has changed drastically." More than half of the auto dealers surveyed in 2004 say they face this labor shortage. The Bureau of Labor Statistics estimates that dealers face an annual shortage of 35,000 auto mechanics through 2010.

Have you recently tried to get your lawn mower repaired? Or any other small household appliance? Join the waiting line. A shortage of small-engine technicians has created lengthy backlogs in lawn mower and small engine repair shops nationwide. In the Chicago area, three- to four-week waits are not unusual. Virgil Russell, executive director of the Equipment and Engine Training Council, estimated (2000) a shortage of over 30,000 qualified service technicians in the country. More parents and children are steering toward white-collar careers. Fewer younger people are opting to be trained to fix outdoor power equipment such as lawn mowers and snow blowers. The same can also be seen in office technology service and repair. Have you ever tried to fix your computer yourself while talking to a service center in India? Technicians to keep technology humming are increasingly in short supply.[40]

Skilled Trades

Avondale Shipyard, upriver from New Orleans, is owned by Northrop Grumman Ship Systems, a prime contractor for the Navy. It has a backlog of work upgrading Coast Guard ships and aircraft. Wood Oge, director of business affairs, mourns the "notable void in blue-collar trades." He talks about the shortfall of plumbers, electricians, and welders. Each year he has 500 vacancies left by retirements and other causes. "We did the wrong thing in telling kids that to make something of themselves they had to go to college," he says.

The same dismal picture is being repeated across the nation. In California, this author addressed 150 skilled trade apprenticeship supervisors in 1996 on how to attract more young people into careers as carpenters, brick layers, electricians, or plumbers. "My own son just doesn't want any part of the business," one plumbing trade representative told me. "He just wants to go to college and work in some office."

Even in Chicago, a bastion of union labor, some local councils have begun to advertise the availability of apprenticeships. These spots had traditionally for generations been passed from father to son, or a close relative. They were coveted, high-paying, lifetime careers. But they all require long-term, specialized training through apprenticeship and journeyman programs. They are increasingly high-tech occupations as materials, tools, and computer-assisted designs now are often used to complete a project.[41]

Teachers

Every spring, recruiters from Alaska, California, Texas, and Europe caravan through Illinois colleges looking for new teachers. Some run newspaper ads like this:

Chicago Area Teachers Bring Your Teaching Degree to CALIFORNIA. You'll get better pay. A better lifestyle. And more opportunities in school districts statewide.

It's true. The opportunities in California for K-12 teachers are as golden as our sunsets!

Cal Teach (Source: *Chicago Tribune*, 2001)

The retirement wave of teachers is worsened by an abnormally high concentration of baby boomers who entered the field in the 1960s and 1970s. As a result, America's teaching corps has grayed all at once. Now baby boomers' children and grandchildren again are raising school enrollments. In 1992 the United States needed 156,000 new teachers; now that number is up to 220,000 per year for the next decade.[42]

A report by the National Commission on Teaching and America's Future described an even more serious issue than retirement—the continuing problem of high teacher attrition rates. In 1999–2000 the number of teachers who left the profession exceeded new entrants by over 20 percent. 232,000 new teachers were hired, but 287,000 left (out of a nearly 3.5-million-teacher workforce).

A major study by Richard M. Ingersoll at the University of Pennsylvania confirmed the inability of U.S. schools to adequately staff classrooms with qualified teachers. Teachers left because of job dissatisfaction and to pursue other better-paying, more culturally respected jobs. Segun Eubanks, at the National Education Association, confirmed these trends: "We lose 20 percent of new teachers within their first three years in the classroom. In urban communities we lose up to 50 percent within the first three years." Within the first five years, 30–50 percent of new teachers quit.[43]

Teachers' wages were often cited as the reason for leaving. These range from a state average high of $53,000 in New Jersey to a low of $30,000 in North and South Dakota (1992).

Some states used their starting salaries as an incentive to lure teachers away from their poorer neighbors. The Dallas schools ran an advertisement in *The Oklahoman* newspaper offering a salary of $34,000 for new teachers. This is about $7,000 more than Oklahoma pays. Dallas offered up to $4,500 as a signing bonus, a $250 stipend for classroom supplies, extensive health insurance, and even threw in a free laptop computer. Such wage price-war tactics will probably become more common as the decade advances.[44]

By 2003 many jobless persons were turning to teaching. Accelerated certification programs were often putting enough bodies to fill classrooms, but not always. And of what quality? Shortages persist in math, science, special education, and bilingual education. By 2010, as the pool of workers again tightens, teacher shortages will again appear across the nation.[45]

Technologists

According to the American Society for Training and Development (ASTD), "[T]here is no evidence to suggest that the entire U.S. IT workforce will be replaced by lower-wage professionals in other countries. Higher-skill-level jobs such as strategy development and business process improvement will remain in the United States, lower skill area jobs including call centers, programming, system maintenance or application development may go elsewhere" (see Table 1.5).

In 2003 alone, the Information Technology Association of America (ITAA) reported a demand for 1.1 million IT jobs:

199,000	Network Systems
530,000	Service and Support
161,000	Software and Programming Development
195,000	Interactive Media

Between 2000 and 2010, demographic experts predict 2.2 million new IT jobs, including computer engineers (+108%) and computer support services (+102%). This prediction was at least partially confirmed in a study by Catherine L. Mann, senior fellow at the Institute for International Economics in Washington, D.C. She found that the number of computer- and math-related jobs in the United States. grew to 2.8 million in October, 2003 from 2.6 million at the end of 1999. This was at a time of an economic downturn and major business layoffs.[46]

But will the people be there? Engineering Bachelors' degrees peaked at 77,572 in 1985 and had plunged to 60,914 in 1998. By the mid-1990s more U.S. students were getting degrees in "parks and recreation" than in electrical engineering, and the majority of those degrees were being given to foreign transfer students. "There is a critical shortage," says Daniel Sullivan at Qualcomm, "in entry level experts in computer-assisted design, integrated-circuit design and even radio-frequency design for digital wireless R&D." Nicholas Donofrio, a senior vice president at IBM agrees, "The long-term trend suggests there's going to be a problem."

Even the National Aeronautics and Space Administration (NASA) feels the pressure to find IT people with certain specialties such as propulsion systems and robotics. NASA's woes reflect a lack of skilled workers throughout the entire aerospace industry. "The generation who went into aerospace engineering to go to the moon, Mars, and beyond is retiring. You cannot have large numbers of people retire and not have others to back them up," says William F. Ballhaus, president of Aerospace Corp.[47]

Table 1.5
Technology Jobs
2000 versus 2010

Demand for technology expertise to surge.
The government projects the growth for jobs in the technology field will be strong in the next several years.
FASTEST-GROWING OCCUPATIONS
Total number of jobs in 2000 and projected for 2010

Occupations	2000	2010	Percentage Change
Computer software engineers, applications	380,000	760,000	100
Computer Support Specialists	506,000	996,000	97
Computer Software Engineers, Systems Software	317,000	601,000	90
Network and Computer System Administrators	229,000	416,000	82
Network Systems and Data Communications Analysts	119,000	211,000	77
Desktop Publishers	38,000	63,000	67
Database Administrators	106,000	176,000	66
Computer Systems Analysts	431,000	689,000	60
Computer and Information Systems Managers	313,000	463,000	48

Source: U.S. Department of Labor.

Boeing should know. The company has been laying off lower-skilled workers by the thousands as their current aircraft production has shrunk. On the other hand, in 2004 Boeing ran half-page ads in the *Los Angeles Times* and the *Wall Street Journal* promoting the "Boeing Interview Event." Boeing's ad listed "some of the key skills we are seeking for open positions in California, Virginia, Oklahoma, Kansas, Washington (state), and Washington, D.C." The positions included over 10 engineering categories and other IT professional areas.

In a 2001 speech at the National Tech Prep Conference in Dallas, Rick Stephens, vice president and general manager of space and communications at Boeing, lamented the lack of sufficient numbers of young American workers entering engineering and technical careers. Boeing and other tech manufacturers have filled many vacancies with foreign workers hired under the federal temporary H-1B visa program for six-year temporary employment. These workers, once they have returned to their own countries, often share U.S. industrial and defense secrets. Stephens warned "the shrinkage of a U.S. technically able workforce is the greatest threat to our national security."[48]

The Commission on the Future of the United States Aerospace Industry, composed of leading industry representatives, was even more blunt:

Our policy makers need to acknowledge that the nation's apathy toward developing a scientifically and technologically trained workforce is the equivalent of intellectual and industrial disarmament and is a direct threat to our nation's capability to continue as a world leader.

The lack of sufficient numbers of new, entry-level workers across the entire industry led the commission to recommend in its final report that "[T]he nation [should] immediately reverse the decline in, and promote the growth of, a scientifically and technologically trained U.S. aerospace workforce."[49]

OUTSOURCING GONE MAD

Creative Destruction

The global movement of jobs is a potential creator of world economic growth. Yet cutting costs has become a major U.S. business priority. Low-cost outsourcing is the latest management strategy to move so-called non-core business activities to lower-wage foreign locations. In three and a half years since June, 2000, U.S. manufacturing lost 2.8 million jobs to outsourcing.[50]

Economists use a term to describe the shrinking job market—"creative destruction." Coined by Joseph Schumpeter, the scenario goes like this: Weak U.S. industries and businesses have to be destroyed so that thriving ones become more competitive.[51]

Ask Lewis Burkett, a plant worker in Douglas, Georgia, if he likes being "destroyed." Tecumseh Product Company closed its plant, lured just seven years earlier from a higher-wage northern city. Douglas had pitched a cheap and willing workforce, a job-training program, tax breaks, and ready-built factory buildings. These were low-skill jobs and nearly half of the Tecumseh workers lacked a high-school diploma. So where have these jobs gone?

Lewis Burkett saw first-hand when he arrived to help smooth the transition of the former Douglas wire shelving factory into the northern Mexican city of Cuauhtemoc. He was surprised to see a new, spotless building housing most of the same machines from Georgia, only rebuilt and repainted. "The Mexican workers were doing the same things we did," says Burkett. The only difference was they worked for $8 a day instead of $11 an hour in Georgia. [52]

Low-skill U.S. factory jobs will disappear overseas. But as the world's consumers continue to demand higher-quality products, these low-tech jobs will also, in turn, shrink around the world.

Forrester Research (2003) reported that American employers will lose about 3.3 million white-collar jobs and $136 billion in wages abroad in the next 15 years. This would include 1 in every 20 tech jobs as well as professionals in the computer, banking, health care, and insurance sectors. A Deloitte Consulting survey (2003) found 2 million financial service jobs at risk in the U.S. and Europe. At the top of the offshoring list are the 51,000 low-end, white-collar call center jobs. Three million people earning an average of $20,000—$28,000 a year (2004) are ripe pickings for outsourcing, according to Datamonitor, a business intelligence firm. A 2003 Gartner, Inc. survey, *U.S. Outsourcing Structural Changes "Big Impact,"* correctly predicted that 1 of every 10 jobs in the U.S. computer services and software industries would disappear to low-cost Russia or India by 2004.[53]

Foreign Direct Investment

Many labor-market experts still believe that innovation will ensure U.S. high-skill/high-wage jobs, just as it has in the past. Future products and services will be increasingly customized. Positions in computer and mathematical occupations are expected to increase by 29 percent in the coming decade (U.S. Department of Labor). The little-reported fact is that many U.S. executives are very worried about serious projected shortages of highly skilled technologists, machinists, and other specialists.

Despite the widely held notion that U.S. business is outsourcing mainly to snare the cheap labor of Mexico, China, and India, in reality U.S. business is heavily invested in other high-wage countries! A study by Deloitte Consulting (2003) found that U.S. manufacturers sent 94 percent ($23 billion) of their foreign direct investment (FDI) to overseas plants they own in high-wage/high-skill countries. Europe ranked as the top FDI destination, with Germany the largest single recipient of investment.

Why do they go? Because, says Peter Cappelli, professor and director of the Center for Human Resources at the Wharton School of the University of Pennsylvania, major U.S. companies cannot bring in enough workers to meet their needs, despite flat-out hiring of entry-level, high-skill people! More than a third of Intel employees are now offshore, admits Craig Barrett, the computer chip giant's chairman. "We are going to go after the last international resources wherever they are," he said. And the next 10 years, he says, will bring "major, major dislocation."

A knowledge-based workforce is qualitatively different from a less-skilled one. What does that portend for the future of the tech industry in the United States? Gordon Moore, Intel's founder, has this answer:

Well, it certainly weakens it. Many American companies operate pretty much globally, and we find ourselves putting technical jobs in places where technical people are available. And things that we would ordinarily do in the U.S., we're likely to be doing in Europe or Russia or China, and India ... and we're actually exporting some of those very good jobs.

Adds Barrett, "The established economies ought to worry like hell about their education, infrastructure, and R&D."[54]

This human capital issue motivated Advanced Micro Devices (AMD), the U.S. semiconductor giant, to set up its first non-U.S. microprocessor factory in Dresden, Germany. AMD transferred key chip-making technology from America to Germany, built a cutting-edge facility, and trained the local workforce with the relevant skills. Over a five-year period, AMD had looked at other sites in California and Texas. But it decided that it would be difficult to find the necessary pool of qualified entry-level people in these communities.

Jim Doran, senior AMD executive, who set up the Dresden plant, explains that Germany has traditionally been associated with good standards of technical education and a positive attitude toward work. "The workforce has been quick to learn and highly focused," he says.[55]

Feeding the Sharks

Foreign plants, however, are not always a key to profit. Before a business outsources or builds an overseas facility, the CEO should talk to Joe Charles, chief executive of Charles Industries, Ltd., a telecom equipment business in suburban Chicago. "What happens when you go offshore," says Charles, "is your inventory increases, productivity tanks, and you have little control over quality. I don't think you save money. I've tried it, and it just didn't work." Charles plans to keep his plants in Illinois, Nebraska, and Missouri. Charles Industries lost money by using workers in Mexico, the Philippines, and Haiti.

This experience isn't at all unusual for many American businesses. In a recent (2003) outsourcing business survey by P.A. Consulting, 60 percent of respondents said they were disappointed with financial returns, 17 percent saw no benefit, and only 23 percent said outsourcing met their financial goals. "Outsourcing has become just another fad," says Michael Porter, a Harvard Business School professor. What looks like a good deal initially turns out to be a lot more expensive later.[56]

Economist Stephen Golub, at Swarthmore College, explains that low-wage countries usually go hand-in-hand with low productivity. Poorer countries often have low levels of general education, and poor public infrastructure and transportation services.

In China's current, pre-modern condition, political influence and corruption are endemic. The legal system is primitive. Technology is vulnerable to theft, and competition takes place in a jungle. Authorities in Beijing recently (2002) exposed 10,000 phony police officers who had plagued business. This has aided industrial piracy. The Chery, China's fastest-selling car, is a virtual replica of a Volkswagen model, the Jetta. China can be a quagmire for U.S. business. Unfortunately, according to Michael Porter, in the long term the companies that have outsourced their production or services "have often lost the ability to do the job themselves." Think of all the industries that the United States dominated in the past: television, shoes, clothing, home entertainment electronics, steel, automotive, aerospace. In every case, we either no longer make these products or our market share has seriously diminished. Now even U.S. high-tech industries are massively outsourcing somewhere else. Companies have been giving away something too important to be left to outsiders—the creativity of their own employees.

India has its eye on professional services for its 1.5 million English-speaking college graduates. Foreign call centers, software developers, and multinational operations now employ 650,000 of them. (2003) This business-process outsourcing is driven by very low professional wages. But most Indians still live in rural villages that have very poor basic education for boys and virtually none for girls. Nevertheless, India's small middle class is growing, as is the overall economy. As India's economy expands, it is expected to absorb more of its own high-skill workers, and wages will begin to rise.

This has all happened before. Back in 1970, unit labor costs in Korea, Taiwan, and Singapore were less than half of U.S. levels. Over the next 20 years, overseas workers' wages increased, closing this gap. From 1977 to 1996, real wages in South Korea have risen eightfold. Now it's China's and India's turn.[57]

The outsourcing dogs of U.S. business will always be chasing their low-wage tails in a race they cannot win. As soon as low-wage outsourcers see a country to invest in, they begin to push wages higher and kill the golden goose.

"We have watched with accelerated horror as the dual ills of transplanting technology to other regions of the world were combined with the educational indifference of our own population," says Douglas Swanson, president of Erie, Pennsylvania-based Swanson Systems, a designer and manufacturer of mechanized manufacturing processes. According to Swanson, U.S. manufacturers have not been slow in noticing these trends. They've either become indifferent to what is happening, thereby causing their own operations to decay, or they've profited by these shifts to get their shoes, cars, TVs, and everything else hand-assembled with low-cost, non-unionized, overseas labor.

"This cannot be reversed without a great effort—by instilling some pragmatism in the manufacturing management who will someday learn that the uncontrolled distribution of proprietary manufacturing know-how to more ambitious, more motivated, lower-cost areas of the world is but feeding the sharks," Swanson says.

Kosuke Shiramizu, a senior executive in charge of global production for Toyota, Tokyo, apparently agrees with Swanson's strong beliefs about the negative side of outsourcing IT secrets. In a recent *Financial Times* interview about the reasons behind Japan's (and Toyota's) high productivity, he said that "[S]ome of the company's most developed machinery was not exported to its factories abroad to prevent it falling into the hands of rivals." Many other foreign manufacturers are responding to competition by keeping key technologies at home while moving only low-valued-added production and assembly operations overseas.[58]

THE 2010 CROSSROAD

So is a high-skill worker shortage coming? The answer is already apparent, and it will be worldwide. A study (2003) by the All India Management Association estimated a net workforce shortfall of 32–39 million knowledge workers by 2020 in the developed countries. Here's the country breakdown:

United States	17 million
Japan	9 million
Russia	+6 million

France	+3 million
Germany	3 million
Britain	+2 million

Both India and China have now begun reporting shortages of high-skill technical workers. In China even low-skilled farmers are becoming less interested in repetitive factory work as agriculture becomes more profitable.[59]

In the past 20 years, multinationals shopped the world for knowledge workers and then relocated operations in high-skill/high-wage countries worldwide to fill their worker void. Or they have used the H-1B visa to import millions of tech-savvy workers into the United States. Now that the world pool of these smart knowledge workers is drying up, businesses will have to think again as they arrive at the 2010 crossroad. "There's a frenzied competition for this same group of people worldwide," states Sandra Boyd, who chairs Compete America, a coalition of U.S. companies lobbying for more H-1B visas. "Without question it's going to be a phenomenon," says Neil Lebovits, president of Ajilon, a global consulting/staffing firm. "A lot of people think the worker shortage of the late '90s was a one-time aberration and we're telling them, think again."[60]

The unique combination of socioeconomic events—the rise of advanced technologies, globalization, the 1990s bubble and its collapse, and a massive worldwide demographic shift—have now all combined to produce a 2010 meltdown.

A great people paradox is the result. On one hand, we have too many untrained people or people trained for the wrong jobs. On the other hand, we will increasingly lack enough people to fill the jobs that support the world's leading high-tech economies.

The 2010 crossroad through which we must all pass will cause a high degree of pain for some workers. In an address to a London financial conference, Federal Reserve Chairman Alan Greenspan said:

Competition from abroad has risen to a point at which developed countries' lowest skilled workers are being priced out of the global labor market. The diminishing of opportunities for such workers is why retraining for new job skills that meet the evolving opportunities created by our economies has become so urgent a priority.[61]

The longer choices are postponed, the harder they become. They've already been delayed so long that they will no longer be easy. The basic problem is not just numbers, but in motivating people to prepare for jobs and careers in high-tech applied fields. According to the Statistical Abstract of the United States (2000), here is a basic breakdown of how the American workforce was distributed in 2000:

133M	People at work
40M	Executives, managers, professionals
38.9M	Sales/technical
17.9M	Low-end service jobs
14.5M	Technical support, crafts[62]

Millions of American workers have lost their jobs since 2000. Some were low-skilled workers, others were well-educated technicians and managers who suddenly became redundant when the high-tech bubble popped and devastated many companies.

People who are unemployed and poorly educated will probably remain unemployed, unless they accept menial jobs or are personally motivated to accept training and education that enables them move up the job skills ladder. Other better-educated workers can either change business sectors or accept re-education for new careers, or probably face retirement. Alan Greenspan, in his 2004 testimony before Congress, acknowledged that the outsourcing of U.S. jobs has created hardships for many Americans. He again reiterated that the answer "was better education and job training, not higher trade barriers."

"If you're a Web programmer," says Atul Vashistha, a leading offshoring consultant, "you have no right to think you can keep your job in the U.S. if you're using the same technology that existed four years ago. You've got to keep moving up. You've got to keep going back to school.... If you're not going to do that, you're going to lose your job."[63]

As the skilled people who are running the economy retire, and the number of younger, entry-level workers continues to fall, the underlying great mismatch of lower-skilled people to high-skill jobs will rise to stellar heights. Unemployment rates will drop as high-skill jobs go unfilled, or businesses will leave the United States entirely in search of more high-skill, job-ready workers elsewhere. Potentially, millions of the lower-skilled workers or people educated for careers that aren't growing will sit on the economic sidelines, either unemployed or condemned to a low-wage future.

At issue here is not just to do more job training. As Gordon Lafer, at the University of Oregon's Labor Education and Research Center, points out in *The Job Training Charade* (Cornell University Press, 2002), generic, one-size-fits-all, government-run job training programs have been an almost universal failure. He found that after 40 years of federal and state programs, on average most of the participants failed to move up to high-skill/high-wage jobs. However, job training does work where business provides the job training, or closely collaborates with local educational institutions to prepare individuals for specific jobs.[64]

In order to avoid a gradual meltdown of the U.S. high-tech economy, the message is clear. For the United States to thrive, economic flexibility built on the higher educational abilities of more smart people has become essential. Henry Chesbrough, a professor at Harvard Business School, agrees. In *Open Innovation* (Harvard Business School Press, 2003), he points out that knowledge expertise and new ideas are more widely distributed today than ever before. Skilled people are as likely to be found in Bangalore or Beijing as in Silicon Valley, Seattle, or Boston. While low-wage countries may grow for a time by competing on price, high-wage countries like the United States must modify their business and societal culture to develop more of their own well-educated labor force of knowledge workers, so that they can provide the right talent at the right time and place—in both the short and long term. Otherwise, they may lose the worldwide skills wars.[65]

There will be high rewards for those American companies that have the strategic vision and leadership to meet this challenge. In the short-term (2005–2010), U.S. business will probably just move more jobs offshore; perhaps consider keeping some older workers for a few extra years; and just continue trying to replace people with more technology.

But as America approaches the 2010 crossroad, none of these strategies will provide long-term solutions. For 2010–2020, business must drastically increase its investment in training the current workforce. By 2015 America have little choice but to support massive career preparation efforts that dramatically address cultural attitudes that lag behind the employment opportunities demanding a smarter workforce in every American community. For America to prosper, "[I]n the global economy it is education, not location, that determines the standard of living," says Albert Hoser, president of the Munich, Germany-based electronics and electrical engineering company, Siemens.

American business has long been a consumer of smart people. Can America change its cultural attitudes to increase the supply? After considering these future trends, do we have any choice?[66]

2

The Rise of the Techno-Peasants

Workers can't find jobs and companies can't find workers.
—*The Wall Street Journal*
November 22, 2004

Clyde and Robert Lane are brothers who built their adult lives around working for the Western Electric Company, a former AT&T subsidiary near Chicago. Western Electric was the Bell system's major supplier of telephone equipment, and 48,000 people worked at its sprawling 141-acre campus. The Lane brothers did very well, garnering pay raises as their skills advanced. By the mid-1980s they had mastered the company's most sophisticated machinery.

Then technology began to change. Heavy copper wire was replaced with new fiber optic cables that can carry more calls. In an instant the Lane brothers found out they had spent years learning skills that were now obsolete. A state-of-the-art fiber optic plant opened in Atlanta, and the Cicero plant closed. "I've kind of wised up to the fact that most manufacturing companies don't stay in business that long," says Clyde Lane.[1]

WATERSHED ERA'S NEW WISDOM

What really happened to Robert and Clyde, and millions of others, was that they got caught in a watershed era of change. On one side was the time of the wrench, with large numbers of semiliterate, unskilled workers who could earn good pay in the mass-production-oriented 20th century.

On the other side is a new era of advanced technology demanding a highly skilled, highly paid, versatile workforce. Many workers are now caught in between these two very different eras.

Over the past 20 years the United States, the world's largest economy, created around 40 million more jobs than were destroyed. Yet, according to the U.S. Department of Education, up to 50 percent of America's adult population today lacks the advanced skills that are the foundation for most future high-paying jobs in today's complex knowledge economy. Should we be concerned?

Back in the 20th century, the answer might have been "No." In the past, a more industrial-based economy had high-paying, low-skill jobs in sectors such as services and manufacturing. There were also plenty of other job opportunities for the less-well-educated.

Today it's a high-skills world. More advanced literacy skills are the foundation needed just to qualify for most higher-wage jobs and to keep up with the constant changes in every employment area. Some people believe the cruel fiction that plenty of good, low-skill jobs still exist. Just raise the minimum wage for these low-skill jobs to enable middle-class people to exist. This flies in the face of reality. According to the U.S. Departments of Labor and Education, 80 percent of all the new jobs now being created have specific, high-skill requirements.

Today, America's workforce is divided into three parts: about 25 percent are the "smart people" who are well educated and also have special career skills; another 25 percent are the "walking dead," victims of mergers or technical change and need to acquire new skills in order to change jobs or even careers (like the Lane brothers); and up to 50 percent are the "techno-peasants," poorly educated adults with few if any special career skills.

Even *The Wall Street Journal* has acknowledged, "One conundrum that continues to vex the U.S. job market is this: Workers can't find jobs and companies can't find workers." In November, 2004, the State of Pennsylvania reported nearly 350,000 unemployed workers. Yet 24 percent of businesses tell that state they can't find enough qualified workers.[2]

A major study by the Organization for Economic Cooperation and Development (OECD) observed that "[W]orkers not only must have higher levels of education, but the ability to adapt, learn and master new skills quickly and efficiently." Today's U.S. and world economies are knowledge-based. As we emerge from the current transitional period into a new era, individuals must possess more complex skills to compete for high-paying jobs. What does this mean?

Simply stated, for most Americans very strong reading and math skills are key. This includes being able to clearly understand text in newspapers, books, maps, schedules, charts, graphs, and digital formats. Many also need skills in mathematical computation, simple geometry, and algebra, and good communication skills—both verbal and written. Many experts across the United States and abroad have identified these skills as being the so-called new wisdom necessary for every person to survive and prosper in advanced industrial countries. The new wisdom's common denominator is a very good liberal arts education plus special career education components (with constant skill updates throughout one's lifetime). This is not an either/or proposition. Every American will need both of these educational components to become the so-called knowledge worker that Peter Drucker first identified nearly half a century ago. Now every company will want these smart people, who are increasingly in short supply.[3]

A CULTURE CRISIS

What will it take to overcome the cultural barriers to reach this very ambitious goal? Craig Samuel, Hewlett-Packard's chief knowledge officer, has said that "[Complex technology] is only 10 percent of the problem, we've all got [sic] so seduced. Work processes are another 20 percent, and 70 percent is cultural."

Every person has a stake in acquiring this new wisdom of useful skills and knowledge. Today, more than ever, companies must strive to find smarter workers in order to compete, survive, and grow. By their very nature, the people of the United States have shown themselves to be very resourceful and competitive, as well as leaders in innovation. These are all national characteristics that have served our people well in past times of change and crisis.

Nevertheless, American popular culture seems stuck in denial regarding the new world of work and international competition. "Indeed, the supply of highly skilled, educated and creative workers is increasing internationally as other countries invest in their own workforces," reports the Computer Systems Policy Project, a consortium of major American information technology (IT) companies. In 2004, they issued a severe storm warning that states, "The United States needs to focus on educating and constantly training its current and future workforce, especially in science, mathematics and engineering, to maintain and create more opportunities for American workers."

In *Choose to Compete* (2004), the consortium provided a long list of what they consider their powerful, well-established, multinational competition: Awia, Fujitsu, Hitachi, Infosys, Legend, Minolta, NEC, Nokia, Philips, Samsung, Seiko, Siemens, and Sony. The American IT leaders ominously noted that in 2001 almost half (47 percent) of U.S. technology patent applications were filed by foreign competitors (U.S. Patent and Trademark Office).

Many of these nations and companies have growing numbers of workers who are highly educated, skilled, and creative. "Americans who think that foreign workers are not a match for U.S. workers in knowledge skills and creativity are mistaken," warns the report.

Just to drive their point home, the report fires a warning shot above the heads of the American workforce: "Because U.S. companies are operating globally, they must hire qualified workers around the world to meet customer demands and expand their capabilities—a business model that makes sense, given that increasing corporate revenues come from abroad."

In other words, if leading-edge American technology companies cannot find sufficient numbers of knowledge workers inside the United States, they will shop the world and relocate operations to take advantage of local talent anywhere, any time. This is why General Electric already has built a gleaming, new steel and glass research center north of Munich, Germany. This is also why IBM maintains five of its eight laboratories outside America. These leading U.S. technology companies have found elsewhere the knowledge technologists who are not available in their home country. How many more of these jobs will be exported because America lacks enough of these smart people?[4]

NO LONGER #1 OR #2

Technology companies have some legitimate reasons for concern. In 2005, Samsung displaced Intel from its position as the largest buyer of chip production equipment. Samsung ranked second to Intel in chip production. It is the world's biggest maker of memory chips and has overtaken Intel in the production of flash memory used in cell phones, digital cameras, and computers.

On another technology battlefront, Japanese giant Toyota Motor Corp. sped past Ford Motor Company in 2004 to become the world's second-largest car company, behind General Motors. Starting as a welding factory in 1918, Toyota was selling over 20,000 cars and trucks per year by 1966, and the company's worldwide retail sales climbed to 6.78 million vehicles in 2003. By 2005 quality and efficiency in Japanese car manufacturing is such that it takes about 27.9 worker-hours to build each vehicle, resulting in a lower cost advantage of $350 to $500 per vehicle.

Much of the credit for Toyota's growth can go to W. Edwards Deming, the American management consultant whom the Japanese revere as the

Father of Quality. Deming's "profound knowledge" approach asked management to think about manufacturing as a dynamic system of what he called enlightened humanism that could function only if it evolved toward greater efficiencies. A vital component was a rigorous system of continuous employee education and skill-building.

So Toyota opened a Global Production Center in Toyota City. On any given day you can see how Chinese, Filipinos, Americans, and workers from around the world are being taught to assemble Toyota vehicles. To break through language barriers, trainers use video recordings and interactive DVDs that help ensure workers thoroughly comprehend Toyota's way of doing things.

Despite years of similar efforts, the American Big Three automakers (GM, Ford, and DaimlerChrysler) continue to lose market share. From a high of 80 percent of the world's automotive market in the 1950s, U.S. auto manufacturers now control about one-third. Though Ford began giving their employees home computers and Internet access in 2000, many still lack the advanced skills to compete as knowledge workers.

Part of the problem is the education level of the Big Three's entry-level workers. Recently at DaimlerChrysler's Detroit, Michigan car plants, only one out of four applicants could pass a test requiring tenth-grade skills. This critical shortage of younger knowledge workers is hurting the U.S. automotive industry's ability to compete. This problem is not unique to Detroit or the auto industry. The American Diploma Project's recent (2004) study found that the high school diploma, once considered a springboard to success, now has little meaning in determining whether students are ready for college or work. These findings were from a two-year review by an alliance of top education officials from the former Clinton and Reagan administrations. This study warned that, "Only a comprehensive change, including more rigorous English and math requirements for all students, will restore the significance of high school graduation."[5]

To get the whole picture, expand this problem to every business across every region of America.

THE TECHNOLOGY PARADOX

Since 1970 America's manufacturing output has more than doubled. Even after the recession, output rose by almost 50 percent between 1992 and 2003. Yet at the same time the U.S. manufacturing sector lost 2.7 million jobs from June, 2000 to September, 2003, an 11 percent drop.

Contrary to the wisdom on the street, American manufacturing workers weren't the biggest job losers. Brazil had a 20 percent decline in that time period, Japan shed 16 percent of its factory workers, and even China lost 15 percent of the manufacturing workforce! What is going on?

Economists at Alliance Capital Management Holding, LP found that from 1995 to 2002 in 20 of the world's largest economies, more than 22 million low-skill manufacturing jobs disappeared—a decline of over 11 percent. Joseph Carson at Alliance said that productivity gains from newer technologies and competitive pressures have forced factories to become more efficient—allowing them to do more with fewer workers. Even as worldwide manufacturing employment declined, global industrial output rose more than 30 percent. Bill Belchere, chief economist for Asia at J. P. Morgan Chase in Hong Kong, predicts, "There's going to be a further shakeout as we move forward."

That big sucking sound you hear drawing low-skill/low-wage jobs to Mexico and China is not an illusion. It's just the sound from flushing these low-skill jobs first overseas and then into the sinkhole of oblivion.[6]

But the catch-22 of the technology paradox remains for U.S. manufacturers who have laid off millions of these low-skill workers. At the same time, they cannot find enough high-skill people to fill jobs that require using advanced technology and special, cutting-edge skills. Stan Donnelly, owner of Donnelly Custom Manufacturing Co. in Minnesota, notes that a brilliant new idea or product is worthless unless you have the know-how to make it into something tangible. "That is what drives the economic wealth of a society," he said.

He's right in thinking there are big links between the economy and people's wisdom. Any country with higher average skill levels will also have a larger proportion of knowledge workers. These are the people who are best prepared to contribute to U.S. technological development in any field, as well as to adjust more effectively to continuous technological change. Unfortunately, a recent study by the Hudson Institute (2002) found that 60 percent of all the jobs we are creating will require skills that only 20 percent of the current U.S. workforce actually possesses. Clearly, the United States has work to do if we are to overcome this technology paradox and raise the overall educational level of our population.[7]

Knowledge Technologists

Innovations of new products and services are hard to come up with year after year. Yet that is exactly what businesses (large or small) must do to survive. The main focus must be on a community or company culture that values creativity and change.

The United States needs a new breed of workers—knowledge technologists—in every field. Indeed, it is these workers' knowledgeable use of technology that can enhance the value of any organization's products or services. Knowledge technologists also have discrimination, analysis, and interpretation skills. They can solve problems and coordinate projects. Knowledge technologists have three main development needs: formal education that gives them a firm general educational foundation; specialized career education; and continuing education and training throughout their working lives to keep themselves up-to-date.

Today only a few countries provide the knowledge technologists with systematic and organized skills preparation. This will change. Over the next few decades, individuals, businesses, and government will begin to demand that all educational institutions (elementary, secondary, and post-secondary) prepare more people to become knowledge technologists. This has all happened before. American popular culture in the recent past demanded the establishment of general education institutions for the 20th-century's mass-production era.

But this time around, Americans need to accept that both the majority of people must be skilled at far higher levels than ever before and that these skills must be continually updated through lifelong education. Unlike traditional skills learned in school, which change very slowly, 21st-century knowledge rapidly becomes obsolete.[8]

A mighty skills chasm stretches between where America's culture is today and where our culture needs to move for tomorrow. Let's now examine why America has, unfortunately, become the land of the techno-peasants.

Revenge of the Techno-Peasants

Surprise! Surprise! America's well-educated are suddenly scarce on the ground! Our tech-based lives may suffer a meltdown! American competitiveness may tank in the world marketplace!

Of all the danger signals on the path to the 2010 crossroad, the under-skilled workforce flashes brightest on the horizon. The issue has been studied to death. Nevertheless, the rise and implications of America's techno-peasant underclass remain a blatantly ignored cultural issue. Payback time may be coming soon.

The scope of this problem has become so large that most people just don't want to deal with it. Let's take a look at the numbers:

- *$60 billion per year* cost in lost business productivity (National Institute for Literacy, 2001).

- *45 million U.S. adults* read below eighth-grade level. This means that about 50 percent of the adult population cannot fill out a job application; read a driver's license manual, newspapers, or *Reader's Digest*; or compute change when making a purchase [National Literacy Survey (NALS), U.S. Department of Education (1993, 1998); International Adult Literacy Survey, (OECD, 2000, 2004)].
- *The United States ranks 49th out of 158 nations in literacy.* Sixty percent of adults never read books; only 6 percent read one book per year (United Nations, 1998).
- *47 percent of job applicants* lacked the reading, writing, and math skills for the jobs they sought (American Management Association, Workplace Testing, 2000).
- *73 percent of U.S. employers* cited "very" or "somewhat" difficult conditions hiring qualified workers. Forty percent said applicants have "poor or no employment skills." (Center for Workforce Preparation, U.S. Chamber of Commerce, Washington, D.C., 2002).
- *50 percent of U.S. manufacturers* found that their current workers had serious reading, writing, and math skill problems (Grant Thorton Survey, National Association of Manufacturing, 1997).
- *8 million U.S. workers* (5 percent of all American adults) speak English so poorly that they cannot hold high-paying jobs (Center for Law and Social Policy, 2003).
- *6 in 10 U.S. mayors* report a serious, widespread, and increasing shortage of highly skilled workers in technology, health care, manufacturing, and construction (U.S. Conference of Mayors, 1999).
- *53 percent of adults in Los Angeles* have literacy skills so low that their ability to work and be productive is threatened (Literacy Network of Greater Los Angeles, 2004).
- *90 million Americans* (nearly half of all adults) face higher health risks because their low literacy leads to trouble understanding medical terms and following directions (National Institute of Medicine, 2004).[9]

These studies represent only the tip of a giant iceberg. Over the past 20 years, literally thousands of business, government, and academic studies, surveys, and blue-ribbon commissions have all reached the same basic conclusions: More Americans need more skills for the new jobs being created by technology in virtually every economic sector.

As mentioned earlier, there remain many naysayers who will tell you that this is not true. There are plenty of low-skills jobs still available across America. For several reasons, they are correct. New retail clerk and cashier positions represent the highest numbers of new jobs now created across the U.S. economy (2000–2010). Warehousing, restaurant, hotel, resort/entertainment, and practical nursing jobs are also increasing. However, the vast majority of these positions are not only low-skill jobs but are also low-wage, dead-end jobs. They are concentrated in the service sector. Because these jobs cannot be outsourced, they often attract new immigrants to the United States. The concept of raising the minimum wage, so that many of these jobs will pay more, will never turn them into desirable, high-wage, middle-class jobs. Where have those jobs gone?

Three Waves of Technological Change

Until the 1970s only about 25,000 computers existed worldwide; today there are about 200 million. They are leading all of us into a so-called third wave of technological change.

The first wave was the early Industrial Revolution (1820–1910), powered by steam. Railroads were the big players in the U.S. economy. In the second wave (1910–1970), mass production took over. The automobile industry is representative of that era. Many industries created low-skill/high-wage jobs for a large, blue-collar middle-class. In 1950 this represented 60 percent of U.S. jobs being created.

In the 1970s all the rules began to change. The creation and spread of the personal computer (PC) saw memory power skyrocket and prices fall dramatically. The third wave of technological change flooded the world with the products we now take for granted: cell phone, VCRs, DVDs, CDs, soft contact lenses, microwave ovens, Stealth fighters, new building materials, food products, medical breakthroughs—an endless list that grows longer every day. However, a knowledge undertow began dragging down the demand for unskilled labor. In 1991 these jobs represented only 35 percent of new job creation and, by 2000, only 20 percent.

New technology continues to raise the education bar in every workplace worldwide. Eighty percent of all new jobs created in the United States will be high-skill by 2010, predict the U.S. Departments of Labor and Education. Government figures indicate that 50 percent of these jobs will be technology-centered; Bill Gates places that figure at 70 percent. "The fundamental problem is that long-term, we are not providing enough high-skill, labor-force entrants to meet the demand," says Jerry Jasinowski, president of the National Association of Manufacturers.

The severe shortage of knowledge technologists won't go away any time soon. A major U.S. cultural disconnect feeds this problem, sustained by people's education and career expectations from a bygone era.[10]

CULTURE AND SKILLS—THE NEW TECHNO-PEASANTS

At the start of the 21st century, American culture is almost in the same position in regard to education and skills for work as it was at the beginning of the 20th century. Around 1900 the technological changes of that era, including the development of automobiles, electricity, telephones, radio, and motion pictures, began to touch the lives of ordinary people across the nation and world. More and more people began to see that to get ahead, some education and skills were essential.

Between 1890 and 1920 the United States embarked on a long and bitter, state-by-state, cultural battle to enact laws requiring public schooling for everyone up to age 16. The average parent realized that basic, functional, educational skills would lead to a better life for their children—both boys and girls. Business leaders supported this first American education revolution because they understood that a basically skilled workforce was a requirement for a mass-production economy. Union leaders supported this revolution because it removed children from the workplace and brought higher wages. Community leaders and politicians supported it to help assimilate millions of new European immigrants. Education for both social and economic democracy became the American cultural way of life.

For most of the 20th century, through two world wars, the rise of the middle class, and the end of the Cold War, this skilling and schooling formula worked very well. It was organized on the premise that we needed to educate about 20–25 percent of the population to the highest skills and knowledge levels for professional or managerial careers. However, although almost everyone went to school, many received a minimal education.

Here is how the culture worked in that era: Twenty-five percent of the population graduated from college; another 40 percent graduated from high school, but some got additional technical or post-secondary education; the remaining 35 percent had a difficult time in school and some dropped out—more with each passing decade.

American culture adjusted to support this skill/education game plan, since it worked very well for so long and for so many people. Popular culture came to believe that only the brightest in the population could really benefit from a higher-level skills education. Then the world began to change.

The latest technology revolution, beginning in the 1970s, started to rewrite the rules of the skills game. What it meant to be a skilled, literate person in America took a quantum leap by 2001. Now most people need reading, math, and writing skills beyond the high school level to survive and thrive.[11]

About 20 percent of adult Americans today have the advanced skills needed in the high-tech workplace (International Adult Literacy Survey).

Another 30 percent are reading at about the tenth-grade level. But half of the U.S. adult population is still at risk. Many read below the sixth-grade level and, as such, are the new techno-peasants—virtually certain to be unemployed or trapped in low-pay, low-skill jobs for life.

In 1993 the U.S. Department of Education issued the first National Assessment of Adult Literacy Survey (NALS). It painted a bleak picture of too many adults lacking the foundational education needed to prosper in a 21st-century world. In 2005 the second National Assessment of Adult Literacy (NAAL) will be released. Most literacy experts, including Robert Wedgeworth, president of ProLiteracy Worldwide, predict an upswing in the number of poorly educated Americans and a grimmer picture of this nation's overall adult literacy equation. "Balancing the equation requires cross-cutting strategies from our policy-makers, our health, education, labor, and welfare system, our prison system, and last be not least, business and industry," Wedgeworth stated.[12]

In 1998 about 4 million adult students across the United States participated in basic education, adult secondary education, or English as a second language (ESL) programs. But those numbers had declined to 2.67 million in 2000–2001. We seem to be headed in the wrong direction![13]

Some might argue that these dramatic skill-level differences in the U.S. adult population are only natural and will fade over time. School reform has been addressing these problems for years. Others may believe that the way the statistics were compiled in the 1993 NALS was faulty and that adult literacy really isn't that bad. Yet other studies, such as that conducted by the Educational Testing Service, support the opposite conclusion. It analyzed U.S. elementary and secondary school student reading and math test scores on the National Assessment of Educational Progress (NAEP), and the Third International Math and Science Study (TIMSS, 1999). These studies found that inequalities in skill levels are either rising or, at best, stable. In the 2003 Program for International Student Assessment (PISA) study of 15-year-olds conducted by the Organization for Economic Co-operation and Development (OECD), U.S. students ranked 15th out of 29 OECD nations in reading, and 24th out of 29 nations in mathematics. These poor rankings are due in great part to the wide gap that exists between America's best and worst students, which is greater than in most other high-income countries.[14]

The United States must maintain what I call a certain education critical mass in its population's skills if it wishes to remain a world economic leader and a stable democracy. How can America remain the technological giant of the world if its manufacturing base disappears and a growing digital divide prevents 44 million under-skilled adults from accessing

21st-century technology? "Folks, if you can't read, you can't use the Internet," states Jim Barksdale, former CEO of Netscape. "The Internet is a reading medium. The most boring application in the world, if you can't read, is e-mail."[15] Even the competitiveness of the vaunted U.S. service economy will be threatened.

By 2010 the number of techno-peasants across the United States may begin to undermine America's education critical mass. By then there will be just too many ill-educated, poorly skilled people. The techno-peasants are a cultural anachronism embedded in the 1970s and earlier, which we can no longer afford to ignore. Many Americans have become complacent about educational standards in general. They see the techno-peasants as living an alternative lifestyle that has little to do with them. But by 2010 this poorly skilled underclass will have become so large that it may threaten the cultural and economic foundation of our entire society. Even the competitiveness of the vaunted new service economy will be threatened.

The United States must prepare itself to meet its demographic and educational date with destiny. Part of the solution will be in reshaping what is taught inside U.S. elementary and secondary schools. Where has the schoolhouse gone as we approach the 2010 crossroad?

II

FEEDING THE SHARKS

3

Where Has the
Schoolhouse Gone?

We are in gridlock. We are just denying the existence of a problem.

—Craig R. Barrett
Chairman, Intel

WHO HAS TIME TO READ?

Thirty years ago the United States was the undisputed leader in educating its population. Now other countries seem to be quickly catching up or even surpassing American education. Is this the truth? If so, why?

It is also 30 years since the baby boomers entered school in record numbers. Now their children's offspring comprise over 50 million students. Between 2010 and 2020 the U.S. teen population will swell to 44 million. These are Generation Y, also called the "millennials" (born in 1981 and later).

They have a different culture, different vocabulary, and different media preferences. They have no patience with passive learning—they crave fast-action screen images. They insist that school and work must be more like play, and don't expect them to play without an immediate payoff.

Millennials are exposed to a constant media barrage of popular culture that makes Elvis and the Beatles look like Sunday school preachers. For many children these cultural icons define their attitudes toward life. Millions of young Americans, covered with tattoos and body piercings, are unable to speak proper English and are unwilling to read a book or a newspaper.

Clutching their cell phones, iPods™, and Palm Pilots™, they are experts at more and more complex video games.

How will many in this generation compete for good jobs in our information-driven world? The answer, if nothing changes, is that millions of millennials will become the latest recruits to the ranks of the techno-peasants doomed to a low-wage, low-skill existence.[1]

With lives defined by gee-whiz, techno-entertainment gadgets, their lives revolve around a steady diet of mind-numbing clicking and tapping. Back in 1922 Thomas Edison predicted, "[T]he motion picture is destined to ... supplant the use of textbooks." Now schools are packed with computers. "I can't tell you how excited I am," said a 32-year veteran teacher in Newport Beach, California schools, "It will be infinitely better."

This compelling cultural fascination with technology as an end unto itself is fueling an alarming trend toward aliteracy. According to a Gallup/ *Washington Post* survey, over the past 20 years a growing number of young and old Americans who can read, don't bother to. As many people tell this author, "Who has time to read?" Instant technology is replacing books, newspapers, and magazines as information sources. Increasingly, the reading skills that Americans are taught focus on skimming to get information. As Ronald Smith, a history professor in the Massachusetts State College system, states, "Students no longer are into the culture activity of reading the way they used to be."[2]

For some people, reading a book has been an irritating experience. Until now they thought the United States had moved beyond an era of a semiliterate, unskilled workforce. They thought there were more important issues than reading books, such as using technology to educate more people. In fact, the term "aliteracy" was coined in the 1980s to describe this.

The demise of the book has been predicted almost since the day Gutenberg invented moveable type. People are reading fewer and fewer printed books, magazines, and newspapers. In 1991 slightly more than half of Americans read 30 minutes or more each day; by 1999 this had dropped to 45 percent. A 1999 Gallup poll reported that only 7 percent of Americans finished more than one book a week and about 60 percent read fewer than 10 books a year. Many people didn't read at all.

Yet what about the staggering number of books—2.5 billion—sold annually in the United States? In 2003 alone, 170,000 new titles were published. Then there is the book club boom and numerous Internet sites that now propel a $30-billion book market. But that same survey reported that only half of the books purchased are actually read. Many end up in our bookshelves and bed stands, never opened.[3]

Equally dismal news was issued in the 2004 National Endowment for the Arts (NEA) report, *Reading at Risk*, analyzing the results of a survey on reading conducted by the U.S. Census Bureau. This survey found that only 47 percent of adults read fiction and only 57 percent read any book at all. This was a decline of 10 percent (an astonishing loss of 20 million readers) over the past two decades. For young adults aged 18 to 24, the drop was 55 percent, greater than that of all the other adult groups.

It's the invasion of the Internet and other electronic space invaders into the home that seems to have killed off reading. This lines up with other academic studies that show a change in children's cultural attitudes toward reading. Fewer children, whether or not they are skilled readers, engage in reading as a leisure activity (National Reading Panel, 2000).

Reading at Risk gives concrete testimony that a bedrock cultural legacy is now disappearing among younger Americans. Just as *A Nation at Risk* (1982) warned that "[A] rising tide of mediocrity" had overtaken the nation's schools, *Reading at Risk* reveals a more insidious situation—a culture at risk.

Almost 90 million Americans today don't read books. "As more Americans lose this capability," states NEA Chairman Dan Gioia, "our nation becomes less informed, active, and independent minded. These are not qualities that a free, innovative, or productive society can afford to lose."[4]

We must also factor in another reason why people don't read. Up to 50 million Americans with poor reading skills find much of the Web just too complicated to navigate. "Just because somebody has a computer doesn't mean that they're going to be downloading Shakespeare," says Mark Warschauer, professor of education and information and computer science at the University of California, Irvine, "It's another tool that adds to the repertoire of what people can do in school, but it's not a magic bullet."

Yet a mountain of studies shows how technology has made learning faster, cheaper, and more individualized. Except that it doesn't. Very few studies actively compare students taught with computers versus teacher-led instruction. However, research published in the *Economic Journal* (2002) did just that. A joint study by the Massachusetts Institute of Technology and the Hebrew University of Jerusalem showed that the use of computers in teaching is no better (and is perhaps worse) than traditional instructional methods.

An analysis by the Organization of Economic Co-operation and Development (OECD) of 2000 survey data from the Program for International Student Assessment (PISA) showed the availability of home computers actually had a significant negative relationship to achievement. Also, the relationship between computers at school and student achievement, while not negative was statistically insignificant.

As many parents know, the average child knows more about the Internet and computers than does Bill Gates. However, the study pointed out that the idea that computers allow students to learn at their own pace turns out to be wrong. Most educational software is very much one-size-fits-all. Moreover, the study picked up signs that computers might actually make things worse. Fourth-graders who were taught math without computers did better than fourth-graders taught with them.

Take, for instance, using the Computer Algebra System calculator (CAS) to spit out the answers to even the most difficult equations. "This is just another excuse for letting people go forward without a conceptual understanding," says Wayne Bishop, a math education professor at California State University. "The kids become absolutely helpless, and yet they are given credit for algebra." Many U.S. teachers lack the training to clearly explain the underlying mathematical principles and logic that would help students understand the basis of these calculations (National Science Foundation).

Instead, billions of dollars have placed computers in the classroom rather than improve teacher training. Yet what politicians want an old-fashioned, cultural answer like that? The bottom line for computer education, says Dr. Angrist of Hebrew University, is "[T]he costs are clear-cut and the benefits are murky."[5]

Other aspects of this culture war are equally troubling. A survey of students from four top college-prep schools in suburban Chicago revealed most spent less than an hour a day preparing for school. Seventy percent read less than three hours in a week. "Students think reading is boring because there are many more interesting things to do with their time," said 17-year-old Derek Falk, former student body president at Glenbard North. Though he said he spent more time in high school on schoolwork than most, the distractions were many, including video games, the telephone, the computer, and friends. Reading has plummeted even for the best students at the best schools.

Numerous other studies by the Brookings Institution, Public Agenda, and UCLA all confirm that students at all levels are studying less, not more. Also, students describe much of their homework as "busywork" (Met Life Inc. Survey).

At the same time, the public's perception is that students are overwhelmed with homework reading assignments, "Homework Hours Triple Since 1980" (Associated Press); "Too Much Homework" (*Time*); "Four Hours of Homework for a Third Grader?" (*People*). Yet Tom Loveless, director of the Brown Center at the Brookings Institution, found that even the PTA's guideline of 10 minutes per grade per night is not being followed. By twelfth grade, students should expect 120 minutes of reading/ homework, but most do only 50 minutes.

"One reason for this is when we actually assign homework that takes a little bit of time, many parents complain," admits Anthony B. Harduar, president of the National Association of Elementary School Principals. Yet even some so-called progressive educators rail against homework. A recent issue of *Teacher* magazine described homework as a form of "academic violence."

However, decades of contrary evidence shows that there is not enough time in the school day for students to practice their reading, math, and other skills. Learning through practice at home is both a necessary and essential part of the basic, twelve-year schooling process that helps a student become a literate person. Sadly, what the Brookings study actually found is that U.S. students, on average, spends six times as many hours every week watching television or playing video games as they do on homework reading.

Even more interesting, the same homework researchers also discovered a significant difference among students in France, Italy, Russia, and South Africa. In their final year of high school they spend twice as much time on homework than do their American counterparts. It's a culture thing.[6]

"I'm not anti-libraries," says Carlos Wells, a Carter County, Kentucky magistrate. "After several weeks of study, I didn't find facts indicating that we needed a public library." Carter County, an eastern Kentucky farming area wherein half of the residents have very low level reading skills, is one of the few counties in America without a public library. Kentucky ranks last in the United States in the number of people over 25 who have graduated from high school (33 percent).

Carter County residents pay plenty of taxes already, Wells believes. They have done as well educationally without a library as neighboring counties have done with one, he says. Ask resident Roy Seagraves, who dropped out of school in the eighth grade. He now earns $800 a week working in a factory making plastic bumper guards for cars. He doesn't read much. Now that his three children are grown, all the reading material he needs is the Bible, a set of encyclopedias, and some magazines. It's a culture thing.

Cultural attitudes stubbornly resist change, and then modify very slowly. Cultural change often produces much reactionary nostalgia for the "good old days"—unless pushed by a contemporary catastrophe or widespread disaster felt across a society.

Some recent signs of America's current education culture are very troubling:

- In western Kentucky, a rural school district moved to a four-day school week to save money. Zach Cato, a high school senior there, spends his extra day off mowing lawns and watching football games. Rural schools in Arizona, Colorado, Kansas, Louisiana, Arkansas, New Mexico, Oregon, South Dakota, Wisconsin, and Wyoming have all made similar moves.
- In 2003 Colorado began considering entirely eliminating the twelfth grade and establishing a year of preschool instead. Lawmakers said, "It would better prepare students for college by giving them an early start, and also could save money."
- Public Agenda recently released a decade of research on cultural attitudes toward education indicating that teachers today are troubled by a lack of parental support and poor student behavior.
- A dramatic culture gap exists between ratings by employers and college professors of the skills of high school graduates, and how parents and teachers rate them.
- K–12 textbooks and library budgets are being slashed to buy more computers and software.
- Will reading and reporting on a book come to be considered a boring and inefficient use of time because a synopsis can be quickly found on the Internet and downloaded? (Digital Cliffs Notes)
- Does "doing research" come down to just using a "search engine"?
- "I'm seeing my students' attention spans wane and their ability to reason for themselves decline. I wish the university's computer system would crash for a day," says David Rothenberg, associate professor of philosophy, New Jersey Institute of Technology.
- Mel Riddile, a high school principal in Falls Church, Virginia, says that, "Computers are important, but not as important as literacy. The kids have to be able to read or they can't even use computers. Here we spell hope 'r-e-a-d.' We make them 'haves' by teaching them to read. It's no guarantee, but it's essential."
- Children aged six months to six years spend about two hours a day watching television, playing computer games, or using a computer, versus just 39 minutes a day reading or being read to. (Kaiser Family Foundation Study, 2003).
- Sixty-one percent of U.S. parents rate themselves as "fair" or "poor" at raising their children. The study, *A Lot Easier Said Than*

Done, conducted by Public Agenda, shows parents are struggling at instilling positive cultural values in their offspring.[7]

Popular culture is something that flows from the daily living patterns of a people. It is sometimes influenced by what experts tell us is good for us. Prominent educational groups, including the International Reading Association, the U.S. National Association for the Education of Young Children, the National Center for Family Literacy, and the American Academy of Pediatrics offer clear advice to parents:

- "Reading is the fundamental skill upon which all formal education depends."
- "Family is the root of a child's early literacy."
- For every hour per day that children aged 1 to 3 watch television, they face a 10 percent risk of developing attention-deficit problems by age 7.
- "Learning to read and write is critical to a child's success in school and later in life."
- "A vast store of research . . .has confirmed that what young children learn . . .is deeply affected by their relationships with parents, the behavior of parents, and the environment of the homes in which they live."

Yet U.S. popular culture has stubbornly ignored the so-called experts in its mainstream internal attitudes regarding a personal commitment toward education. Education reform has been on the American front burner for more than 20 years. Yet as the OECD's survey of international education shows, external efforts such as reduced class size or spending more on education does not necessarily bring better results. Internal family attitudes and behavior are more important and more difficult to alter.

By contrast, South Korea has experienced remarkable improvement at all levels of its educational system. South Korea has both large academic class sizes and relatively low public spending. However, South Korea has shown spectacular progress in reforming its educational system within the timeframe of just one generation. Why? After the Korean War (1949–1954), Korea was literally destroyed and most South Koreans placed a strong internal cultural value on education to help build a modern nation over the ensuing decades. As a result of parental demand, standards have been driven upward and improved education has become one of the pillars of the Korean economic miracle. It's a culture thing.[8]

REINVENTING REFORM

What is the state of education in America? More than 20 years ago (1983), the commission appointed by the Secretary of Education, and which produced *A Nation at Risk,* stated that the nation's schools produced "a rising tide of mediocrity." Has anything really changed? Or is the alternative spin offered by some people true—that it is all a big lie—and there is no education crisis? What is the reality regarding how many students really learn, and at what levels, throughout the nation's schools?

In this author's search for answers, several years ago I was struck by two news stories that appeared on the same day in the *Chicago Tribune.* On page 18, reporter Judith Graham's article on the world's biggest supercomputer conference in Denver, "Try Swallowing a Byte of This," gave a peek into the future from what she called "the minds of the leading data mavens on the planet." Think TeraGrid, "the ultrafast network linking supercomputers... it will conduct more than 13 trillion operations per second, running 16 times faster than the fastest computer networks today." "TeraGrid" is the brainchild of the University of Illinois, Argonne National Laboratory, the University of California, and the California Institute of Technology. It represents why the United States has become the world's technology leader.

Then I turned to page 20 in the same section of the *Chicago Tribune,* "12th Graders Score Low on Science Test." According to that article, new national test scores (National Assessment of Educational Progress) showed that only one in five high school seniors had a solid grasp of science, and only half of them could explain simple scientific principles. Only 18 percent correctly answered the most difficult questions, down from 21 percent four years earlier. Former astronaut George Nelson commented, "The vast majority of our students today are learning very little science."

U.S. Education Secretary Rod Paige called the situation "morally significant." "If our graduates know less about science than their predecessors four years ago, then our hopes for a strong 21st-century workforce are dimming just when we need them most," he said.[9]

The educational system is central to the long-term development of a nation's intellect—call it the formation of America's critical education mass. During the last 100 years, the United States led the world in the creation and expansion of a general education system for everyone. It became a leading contributor to America's dominant position in the current world economy. If any reader doubts this, I suggest he/she throw away this book now.

So what are the origins of today's problem? According to Tony Wagner, co-director of Harvard University's Change Leadership Group, "The problem is that fundamental changes during the last quarter century in the nature of work, in expectations for citizenship, in our understanding of what must be taught and how, and in student's motivation for learning—taken all together—have rendered our system of education totally obsolete." Today's policy needs to concern itself much more with quality of education issues rather than only maintaining the quantity of free access for all. Though completion rates for high school and college have remained about the same for the last 25 years, in most U.S. high schools "at least 50 percent of the student population is leaving school completely unprepared for either skilled-based work or responsible citizenship." Wagner believes that America faces the problem of "how to educate all—not just some—students to higher standards and how to prepare them for continuous learning."[10] Too many schools amount to no more than free day care, or places of religious indoctrination. Neither alternative stretches the minds of youth by rigorously preparing them for a lifetime of career challenges and as thinking citizens of this republic.

Where Has the Schoolhouse Gone?

The National Assessment of Educational Progress (NAEP) has been the only accurate national survey of U.S. student achievement. Since 1990, its so-called Nation's Report Card has tested fourth-, eighth-, and twelfth-grade students in core academic subjects at 13,600 schools in all 50 states. On a 0–500 scale, all students are rated at three levels of learning: Basic, Proficient, and Advanced. The Center for Education Statistics in the U.S. Department of Education gathers and reports this data from the states.

A comparison of math and reading scores from 1990 to 2003 shows that overall student achievement has been basically flat or rising very slowly. For example, the fourth-grade average math score of 213 in 1990 had risen to 234 by 2003, an increase of about 1.6 points per year over 13 years. This means that most U.S. fourth-graders were deficient in math (63 percent). Most of these children have only partially mastered basic math skills. Fewer than one-third were considered proficient.

Eighth-grade students scores rose to 276 in 2003 from 263 in 1990, or one point per year. Unfortunately, that means that 75 percent of eighth-grade students are at a basic math skills level, and only about one-third are math-proficient (See Figure 3.1). Even worse, a 2004 report from the Brown Center on Education Policy at the Brookings Institution challenged the difficulty of the NAEP math test questions. They found that the test often only required math skills that are several years below the students' grade level.

Reading scores were far worse, showing little, if any, real improvements over the past 13 years. Most fourth- and eighth-graders read at a basic level. High school seniors showed an actual drop in their scores. In 2002, 74 percent were rated basic and 36 percent proficient in reading (See Figure 3.2).[11]

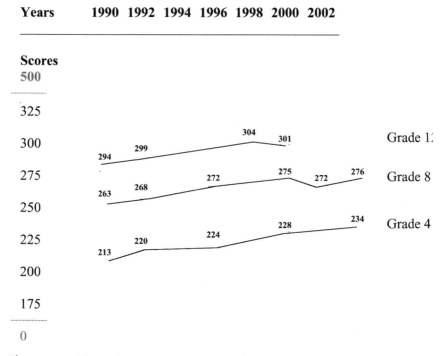

Figure 3.1—National Average NAEP Mathematics Scores of U.S. Students, Grades 4, 8, and 12: 1990–2003
Source: National Center for Education Statistics, NAEP 1990, 1992, 1996, 2000, and 2003 Mathematics Assessments.

"We need a more comprehensive approach to teaching reading," states Lesley Mandel Morrow, president of the International Reading Association (IRA), "that engages all students in all grade levels." Observes Stanford math professor R. James Milgram, "We are still in a position of having a long way to go." That is something of an understatement considering that as recently as 2000, only 2 percent of high school seniors were at the advanced level on the NAEP math exam.

In other areas such as science, high school senior test scores have fallen slightly or remained flat. "Despite the urgent need for science literacy, the ... results provide alarming evidence that most of our students are not being prepared for the challenges ahead," says George D. Nelson, the director of science education for the American Association for the Advancement of Science.[12]

What the NAEP scores make abundantly clear is that America has reached an important educational crossroad. After more than two decades

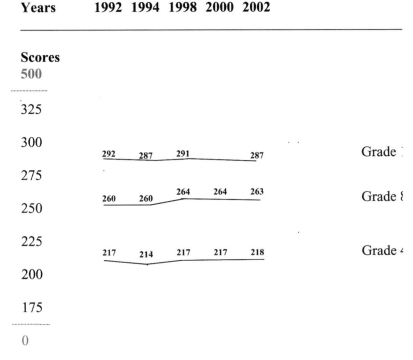

Years   1992 1994 1998 2000 2002

Figure 3.2—National Average NAEP Reading Scores of U.S. Students, Grades 4, 8, and 12: 1992–2002
Source: U.S. Department of Education, Office of Education Research and Improvement.

of pursuing education reform and increasing school expenditures, U.S. student achievement appears stagnant. The majority of U.S. students are deficient in areas of the basic knowledge they need to live successfully in a democratic, technologically complex nation.

LOSING OUR FUTURE

How do you learn if you are not in school? MPR Associates, a Berkeley, California research organization, found that on an average school day, 93 percent of U.S. high school students actually attended school (1997). This means that in a typical 180-day school year, the average student missed 13 days or 2.5 weeks of class time.

But there are many urban schools that don't come close to the national attendance average: Baltimore, 77.3 percent (1999); Los Angeles, 85 percent in seven schools, less then 90 percent in 29 schools (1999–2000); and

Oakland, California, Chicago, New York, and San Francisco (to name just a few) show several high schools with attendance of less than 88 percent.[13]

Chicago public high school teachers, in interviews with the author, discussed a related issue. Many high school students were not absent from their school, but they were tardy from attending class. Students were somewhere else inside the school building, or perhaps outside it, but not in the classroom. This calls into question the validity of at least some schools' attendance records and obviously frustrates teachers who daily deal with students who often disappear.

Problematic school attendance can obviously lead to a student dropping out. The U.S. Department of Education reported an 86.5 percent high school completion rate for the class of 2000. Unfortunately, several recent studies now show other disturbing trends masked by this number.

The Manhattan Institute (2003) found that when only recipients of regular high school diplomas were counted, the national graduation rate plunged to 69 percent. This means that more than 3 of every 10 U.S. students drop out of high school, with overall national graduation rates of 55 percent for African Americans, 53 percent for Hispanics, 57 percent for Native Americans, 79 percent for Asian Americans, and 76 percent for Anglo-Americans. But this still does not give us a complete picture regarding U.S. high school completion.

Between 8 and 9 percent of 18- to 24-year-olds hold a General Educational Development (GED) high school equivalency certificate. Each year during the past decade, about 800,000 people have taken the GED exam in the United States, and 500,000 per year have passed it. Educational and labor market research studies have reported both the negative and positive impact of the GED on a student's future wages, employment, annual earnings, and continued post-secondary education. "Although there is value to getting a GED," states Jay Smink, executive director of the National Dropout Prevention Center," I don't want to downplay that, but it is not a high school diploma and it sends a different message to employers."[14]

A related study on high school dropouts was conducted by the Pew Hispanic Center (2003). The researchers found that one in three of America's more than half-million high school age Hispanics are dropouts, and typically they are recent immigrants who have little or no contact with U.S. schools.[15]

The Civil Rights Project at Harvard University and the Urban Institute issued by far the most damning report, *Losing Our Future*, on the rising tide of America's high school dropouts. The researchers discovered that school districts nationwide "seriously inflate" their graduation rates. They discovered that in reality only about half of all African American, Latino, and Native American students are graduating with regular diplomas in four years. For instance, the analysis found that the Chicago public schools' graduation rate was only 49 percent, compared with 70 percent the system reported to the state. Other Illinois school districts showed comparable, overstated numbers (See Table 3.1). Overall, Illinois's graduate rate of 75 percent ranked the fifteenth-highest in the nation. However, the differences in graduation rates of racial groups were among the largest of all the states.

Across America, the method used to calculate graduation rates measures the difference between how many twelfth-graders graduate in one year versus the number of ninth-graders enrolled four years earlier, minus the transfer students. Too many schools assume that a student who leaves school has just transferred, even if the school never receives any written notice indicating where the student went!

"It's just devastating," said State Senator Miguel del Valle, Illinois Senate Education Committee chairman. "We've been complaining about this issue for a long time.[16]

These abysmal high school completion numbers have serious consequences for the entire nation. For instance, several national studies have found that from one-half to two-thirds of the nation's state and federal prison inmates lack a regular high school diploma.[17]

What these studies also show is a disturbing international trend that has been growing in recent years. For generations, the United States has had a higher percentage of its people graduate from high school than any other industrialized country. America is now starting to lag behind. More than 75 percent of Americans aged 55 to 64 have a high school diploma; this is far higher than any other developed nation. But this dominance is beginning to disappear among adults 25 to 34. In South Korea, Norway, Poland, and the Czech Republic, 87 percent of adults have diplomas.

Table 3.1
Illinois High School Graduation Rates

School District	Graduation Rates Percent Reported to the State	Percent Found in Harvard Study
Chicago	70	49
Elgin District V-46	Overall–95	77
	African-American–90	53
Waukegan District 60	61	49
Rockford District 205	81	50

Source: "Losing Our Future," Harvard University & the Urban Institute, 2004.

In a 1998 OECD comparison of our 17- to 19-year-olds, the United States ranked dead last behind all other 26 industrialized countries (OECD, 1998). Unfortunately, America's current high school graduation dilemma is probably even worse. The OECD international ranking was done six years before the recent studies on the inflated official U.S. graduation rates![18]

In *The Hidden Crisis*, researchers at Boston's Center for Labor Market Studies at Northeastern University warn that, "The high concentrations of school dropouts, especially male dropouts, in many of these large central cities should be viewed as the new 'social dynamite' of the 21st century." Today, 34 million adult Americans lack a high school diploma.

The growth of these severe dropout rates is about to send culture shock waves across America. As the Boston researchers point out, "They will only intensify problems of labor shortages, structural unemployment, working poverty, crime, family breakdown, child poverty, and economic dependency in the years ahead."[19]

What is being taught in the nation's schools is a significant part of the America's high school dropout phenomenon. Many students aren't being mentally challenged, or they fail to see some application of what they learn to their future life. Too many rapidly lose interest in attending school. Others who do remain run the risk of acquiring little useful knowledge for the new America taking shape.

The Crayola Curriculum

Education writer Mike Schmoker toured hundreds of early-grade classrooms. He often saw unsupervised groups of students involved in so-called learning activities. "Students were not reading, they weren't writing about what they had read, they weren't learning the alphabet or its corresponding sounds; they weren't learning words or sentences or how to read short texts," he wrote in *Education Week*. "They were coloring. Coloring on a scale unimaginable to us before these classroom tours."

Kati Haycock, director of the Education Trust, echoed Schmoker's observations. She, too, was stunned to see kids in thousands of disadvantaged schools being given "more coloring assignments than mathematics and writing assignments."

Dubbed the "Crayola Curriculum" by Schmoker, this trend is appearing in high schools, as well. College English professor Donna Harrington-Lueker points to a teacher workshop on writing skills that advised using early-grade-school picture books with high school students. Even more troubling was Lueker's survey of teachers, professional journals, and on-line postings of so-called high school writing assignments. For example, she found an honors class for freshman in writing that offered 13 options to write a short story. But "[O]nly a handful involved actual writing," she said. Students could create a map to illustrate the story's setting. They might make a game on the story's theme, or put together a collage of magazine photographs. While these projects teach organizational skills, is it any wonder that, as she said, "[K]ids are often showing up at college unable to write?"[20]

How much of a surprise was the *Public Agenda Survey* (2002) that reported that three out of four employers and college professors rate high school graduates' grammar, spelling, and writing skills only "fair" or "poor"? Another recent study shows that more than four in ten of today's college freshmen must take a remedial course in writing.

The Neglected 'R': The Need for a Writing Revolution (2003) contends that, "Of the three Rs, writing is the most neglected." Issued by the National Commission on Writing in America's Schools and Colleges, the report states that only about 25 percent of fourth-, eighth-, and twelfth-graders can write a thoughtful essay free of grammar, spelling, and punctuation errors.

The situation is so serious that the commission called for all Americans to join in what is called a writing revolution to demand improvements. Writing, the report contends, allows students to connect the dots of learning in preparation for educational and career success. One reason for this problem, say writing experts, is that students don't read enough. Also, 75 percent of high school seniors never receive a research writing assignment in history or social studies.[21]

High school junior Dominique Houston was a straight-A honors student in Covina, California. She hoped to take a double-major in marine biology and political science at UCLA. But the problem was that she had written only one research paper while in high school. When interviewed in 2003, Houston fretted over being able to do college research.

"Bibliographies?" she scoffed. "We didn't really even know how to do those. I didn't even know how I would write a 15-page paper. I didn't know how I would begin." Remarkably, Dominique eventually became a candidate for class valedictorian! A survey on high school research papers found that most teachers now only require essays or summaries of assigned readings. The result is the awful quality of most college term papers.

"I read every paper line by line," says J. Martin Rochester, a political science professor at the University of Missouri–St Louis. "It's one of the most painful ordeals you can ever go through. Students today cannot write a complete sentence."[22]

Spamming the World

Survey after survey reveals the U.S. high school students' unbelievable lack of subject content knowledge. Take, for example, American history. When asked on a multiple-choice test which U.S. president opened up diplomatic relations between America and Communist China, only 37 percent of high school seniors correctly picked Richard Nixon [National Assessment of Educational Progress (NAEP), 2002]. Nearly half of the fourth-graders tested didn't know that slavery was a major cause of the American Civil War. Based on the NAEP, American students know less about history than any other academic subject.

"Clearly our high schools are failing to teach U.S. history well," says historian Diane Ravitch. "Seniors are very close to voting age, one can only feel alarm that they know so little about their nation's history.[23] Knowledge of history per se isn't really the issue, as E. D. Hirsch, a proponent of cultural literacy, pointed out. "Without a framework (history) for understanding—the ability to identify key figures, major events, and chronological sequences—the world becomes unintelligible and reading a newspaper well might be impossible," he said.[24] This is probably one good reason why daily newspaper readership has fallen so abysmally among younger readers.

Another thing young American adults don't know is their geography. When they were given a map of the United States to locate 10 states, a large majority identified only Texas and California. Many couldn't locate New York (49 percent) or New Jersey (70 percent).

All the recent news coming from the Middle East doesn't seem to have helped much, either. A *National Geographic* survey (2003) that polled more than 3,000 18- to 24-year-olds in the United States and other industrialized countries showed that only 13 percent of Americans could locate Iraq or Iran, just 17 percent could find Afghanistan, and 24 percent could find Saudi Arabia. "If our young people can't find places on a map and lack awareness of current events, how can they understand the world's cultural, economic, and natural resource issues that confront us?" asked John Fahey, National Geographic Society president.

Asked the size of the U.S. population, one in three Americans selected 1 billion to 2 billion as the answer (actually it was 289 million in 2002). Only China and India have populations of the size guessed. Young Americans scored worse than their peers in seven of the eight other countries surveyed. Fahey explains, "This is not the fault of young people, but the responsibility of the culture that has reared them. Their lives are spammed with information and entertainment alternatives. As a result they are highly skilled at tuning out that which they do not need to know. Unfortunately, that seems to include knowledge of the world they live in."[25]

At a time of expanding U.S. globalization and international involvement, school districts faced with funding shortages are taking the axe to their foreign language programs. Elementary schools are often eliminating entire programs. High schools are curtailing German, French, or Spanish offerings.

Some might argue that English has become the dominant language for business deals and international relations of all kinds. But the fact remains that 75 percent of the world doesn't speak any English. Also, students who complete at least four years of foreign language study seem to score higher on college entrance tests such as the SAT.

Another issue is the languages being studied. One million U.S. students study French, a language spoken by only 80 million people worldwide. Yet fewer than 40,000 study Chinese, the language of about 1.3 billion people. Only a handful of U.S. states (including New Jersey and Wyoming) have the insight to require foreign language instruction in their elementary schools.[26]

Luckily, there are some bright spots on the high school horizon. The average SAT college-entrance exam math score has risen to 516, the highest in 32 years (2002). This is, in part, because more college-bound high school students are now taking pre-calculus (45 percent) and calculus (25 percent). At the same time, SAT verbal scores have remained flat or experienced a slight decline. The number of U.S. high schools offering students English composition courses shrunk to 67 percent in 2002, from 81 percent in 1992. What U.S. students achieve or lack will clearly have an impact on American higher education.[27]

Raising the Bar

A high school diploma in what could be called the Old America of the 20th century was once considered the admission ticket for the road to success. No longer. It now has become a hollow symbol that guarantees little or nothing—neither college success nor the opportunity for a good job.

This is the verdict of the American Diploma Project, an organization that includes top education officials in the former Reagan and Clinton administrations. What this group calls the New America of technology and globalization demands comprehensive change—more rigorous English and math mandated for all students. Raising the bar, this group thinks, might restore the significance of a high school diploma and restore some sanity to American higher education, as well.[28]

With the arrival of large numbers of high school graduates who have not been prepared for college work, too many of America's colleges and universities have seen their graduation rates plummet, financial resources diverted into remediation rather than higher education, and faculty increasingly frustrated with grade inflation and watered-down course content. A 2004 study by the testing service that is responsible for the American College Testing Program (ACT) college-admission test found that 78 percent of the students who took the test were not prepared for college-level English composition, algebra, or biology.

This has not prevented politicians from preaching that everyone must get a four-year college degree to participate in the American dream. Banks and other businesses bombard the airwaves daily with their advertising for student loans, college savings plans, and so forth, further popularizing this cultural icon. Signs that popular education culture has responded are everywhere. For instance, a 2004 study found that only 58 percent of 1972 high school seniors attended a post-secondary institution. By 1992 that proportion had risen to 77 percent, a figure Clifford Adelman at the U.S. Department of Education called "stunningly high." A recent Metropolitan Life Survey found that 71 percent of students expected to go to a four-year college. Yet their teachers thought that only 32 percent were academically ready for higher education. This is confirmed by the fact that, despite the influx of students, college graduation rates have held steady for the 30 years (at about 27 percent).[29]

Remediation is gradually taking over too much of American higher education. Nationally, in 1995 nearly 3 out of 10 (28 percent) first-time freshmen enrolled in at least one remedial course. This trend is still going upward. By the fall of 2000, 42 percent of freshmen at public two-year colleges and 20 percent at four-year public institutions took a remedial class.[30]

Take, for instance, the California State University report that 59 percent of new freshmen needed remedial math or English. Nevertheless, to be admitted these students had to rank in the top third of their high school classes and have at least a B average. At the same time, the percentage of all college-bound students carrying an A average has risen from 28 percent 15 years ago to 42 percent now, according to the College Board. Is this the harvest of grade inflation?[31]

The *New York Times* tells another tale of remediation at the City University of New York. The Board of Trustees finally dropped their open admission policy. A flood of remedial students, clearly not prepared for college work, nearly destroyed the institution. Graduation rates plummeted. Remediation rather than higher education became the faculty's teaching focus. Those who fail a not-very-demanding entrance test in reading, writing, and math are now sent to the local community colleges.[32]

But this approach offers little help for another basic college enrollment issue. Between the mid-1980s and mid-1990s, the number of degrees awarded in engineering, math, and computer sciences in America went down. Graduate engineering enrollment dropped from 435,000 in 1993 to 407,000 in 1997. The National Science Board labeled this trend "alarming." U.S. colleges awarded 37 percent fewer degrees in computer science; 24 percent fewer in math; 16 percent fewer in engineering; and 2 percent fewer in the physical sciences. "We're fishing the pond. We're not restocking it," says NASA administrator Daniel Goldin.[33]

The United States is today clearly lagging behind other nations in these areas of higher education. A study by the Computer Systems Policy Project, a consortium of high-tech U.S. companies, found that in 1999 American colleges and universities granted only about 61,000 Bachelor engineering degrees, compared to over 103,000 in Japan, over 134,000 in the European Union, and more than 195,000 in China. By 2002 the U.S. accounted for only 7 percent of the 868,000 Bachelor engineering degrees granted worldwide (National Science Board's Science and Engineering Indicators).[34] More young Americans must study math and science or the United States risks losing its competitive edge. These are real challenges that are not going away.

The equally distressing fact is that about 27 percent of all graduate students in science and engineering are foreigners (2001). Until recently, the number of Americans enrolling has been falling while the number of foreign students has been climbing. In 2001, nearly 40 percent of the graduate students at the Massachusetts Institute of Technology (MIT) were from abroad. Michigan State University reported 153 applicants in 2001 for its graduate program in statistics—7 from the United States and 123 from China. As *The Wall Street Journal* pointed out, "Counting on a continued flow of foreigners because the professions can't attract Americans is a risky strategy."

Just how risky became apparent in 2004. The need for increased national security has resulted in extensive foreign student background checks. At that time, this took an average of 67 days to process, even longer for students from India, Pakistan, China, or Russia. Sixty percent of research universities reported a decline in international graduate student applications. A study by the American Council on Education and the Council of Graduate Schools found that international students perceived the United States as "an unwelcoming climate."[35]

This dearth of American graduates in high-end math and science seems destined to produce a human resources train wreck for technology-related jobs. The U.S. Bureau of Labor Statistics predicts that new jobs involving science, engineering, and technical skills will balloon by 51 percent by

2008. Some 1 million new jobs will be created for engineers, physical sci-entists, and technicians. Disappearing foreign graduate students may leave crucial jobs unfilled or delay projects that require special talents that can't be found in the United States. Not to worry—we can always outsource them. And that is exactly what is now beginning to happen.

This knowledge gap is of particular concern to Rockwell Scientific, which depends on U.S. defense contracts for 70 percent of its business. With minor exceptions, you must be an American citizen to work on these projects. "In military defense, we have a clear superiority," says Rockwell's chief executive, Derek Cheung. "But can we maintain it with the number of graduates we are turning out?"[36]

None other than America's greatest living symbol of high technology—Bill Gates—showed just how serious the situation has become. In early 2004 Gates went on a campaign tour described by the *New York Times* as "trying to reinvigorate his base, as they say in politics." He addressed students at elite universities (University of Illinois in Urbana, Carnegie Mellon, Cornell, MIT, and Harvard), trying to reverse the decline in the number of students majoring in computer science. Gates told students at Harvard, "We need your excitement."

But students like Matthew Notowidigido, 22, intend to go into bank-ing or other jobs that are less prone to outsourcing. This at a time when companies like Microsoft, Intel, and Boeing simply cannot find enough capable, entry-level, 25- to 35-year-old workers to fill the ranks for the next generation of tech careers.[37]

As technology and globalization continue to push life in the 21st century forward, personal reading, math, and science attainments have never been more important. People with strong skills in these areas will have tremen-dous opportunities to succeed.

The solution to this tech labor market meltdown must begin in the K–12 grades. All states must mandate for every student the math and science foundation skills that are essential to every academic discipline and the future of a New America. If we lack the political will to face up to these vital educational issues, there are other nations who will pass us by on the road to the future. In fact, this has already begun.

"Islands of Knowledge" versus "The Big Lie"

How do U.S. students stack up against their overseas counterparts? Between 1995 and 2003, many international test comparisons included American students. Here are some highlights of results.

I. Third International Math and Science Survey (TIMSS) (38 nations):

1995

4th-graders—Math above average; science average close to top

8th-graders—Math and science below average

12th-graders—Math and science below average

1999

4th-, 8th-, 12th-graders—Overall scores improved

Affluent U.S. suburban school districts tested above average, while large, urban school districts were at the bottom in science and math. For example, only Chile, the Philippines, Morocco, and South Africa scored lower then the 352,000 students from Miami, Florida's Dade County School District.

In response to these scores, U.S. Secretary of Education Rod Paige stated, "We have islands of excellence, but islands of excellence is not what we seek." The Brookings Institution estimated that even if U.S. student gains in math continued at the present rate, it would take 125 years for most American students to match their counterparts in top-scoring Singapore and 83 years to reach their peers in Japan. This also assumes that those countries don't improve.[38]

II. Program for International Student Assessment (PISA) conducted by the OECD (2000 data included 32 of the most industrialized countries; 2003 data compared 29 industrialized countries) In both years, 15-year-olds were tested.

2000

12% of U.S. students had scores at the highest reading level.

18% of U.S. students were at or below the lowest level. The gap between America's best and worst readers was wider than any other country's.

2003

2% of U.S. students had scores at the highest level in the overall test of reading, math, and science (the international average was 4 percent).

25% of U.S. students were at or below the lowest level in math. For reading, math, and science OECD country rankings based on mean scores, see Table 3.2.

Table 3.2
2003 PISA Rankings of OECD Countries

Country	Math	Reading	Science
Finland	1	1	1
South Korea	2	2	3
Netherlands	3	8	5
Japan	4	12	2
Canada	5	3	8
Belgium	6	9	11
Switzerland	7	11	9
Australia	8	4	4
New Zealand	9	5	7
Czech Republic	10	20	6
Iceland	11	17	18
Denmark	12	16	26
France	13	14	10
Sweden	14	7	12
Austria	15	19	20
Germany	16	18	15
Ireland	17	6	13
Slovak Republic	18	27	17
Norway	19	10	23
Luxembourg	20	23	24
Poland	21	13	16
Hungary	22	21	14
Spain	23	22	21
United States	24	15	19
Portugal	25	24	27
Italy	26	25	22
Greece	27	26	25
Turkey	28	28	28
Mexico	29	29	29

Source: OECD.

Craig R. Barrett, Chairman of Intel Corporation, feels threatened by the results of these international tests, since he sees U.S. twelfth-graders' science and math scores in the lower 10 percent of the industrialized world. "The educational system basically hasn't changed in the past century," he says, "It hasn't fully recognized that the standard of living is going to be dependent on the quality of the workforce."

Yet many educators believe that these international test comparisons are unfair to American students. William Murdick, an English professor in Tallahassee, Florida, argues that foreign countries only educate their elite through high school and weed out the rest earlier. This counter-argument misses the major point in any comparison of U.S. students to their overseas peers. The United States does have the challenge of educating a more ethnically diverse student population than a country like Finland. Yet Fernando M. Reimers, an associate professor of education at Harvard University, believes that such a challenge is not an excuse for some of America's poor educational results. "The reason the U.S. is average, on average, is that many do badly," says Barry McGaw, OECD deputy director for education. "What the U.S. needs to do is pull up the bottom. You don't have to sacrifice quality to get equality."

"The variance in American schools is higher than in most countries such as Japan," believes Uri Treisman, director of the Charles A. Dana Center and a math professor at the University of Texas. She thinks that PISA shows the great inequities among American schools. "We have the technology and knowledge to educate some children at high levels. But it's really a question of will."[39]

"I visit about 30 countries a year," states Intel's Barrett. "In every country I go to, there's a recognition that the future of the economy depends on educating young children.... I get a totally different reception in just about every country from that I get in the United States on this topic.... We are in gridlock. We are just denying the existence of a problem."[40]

IT'S A CULTURE THING. WHEN WILL AMERICAN CULTURE CHANGE? A QUESTION OF WILL—THE CULTURE FACTOR

In Old America for most of the 20th century, the United States took comfort that our best and brightest students were on a par with their counterparts in other nations. True, there was a wide gap between our best and worst schools, but the United States had the brainpower to remain on top. But this is no longer the case.

In the New America of the 21st century, U.S. twelfth-graders taking advanced placement courses in calculus and physics are, for example, average or even below-average compared to their foreign counterparts. Let's put aside all the excuses and empty rhetoric. What is happening in our culture, and the value we put on learning?

Culture is a tough idea to pin down. It exemplifies how ordinary people live, their daily habits, and what they think their lives will be like tomorrow.

Many subtle forces—both direct and indirect—shape and drive cultural attitudes. Changes usually come slowly. Old habits and personal attitudes are fiercely defended but change does come, for better or worse.

Recent examples of cultural change appeared in a Sunday edition of the *Chicago Tribune*. On the front page was "Reading, Writing, Retailing: Field Trips Flock to Stores," and on page 3 of the same newspaper was "New Train of Thought in Mexico." The field trip story related that many schools across America are now sending students to shopping malls rather than museums because it is cheaper. Ten thousand to twelve thousand such excursions are happening nationally each year, paid for by retailers. "We'll go anywhere where there's an opportunity to learn. We make it easy for the teachers and it's free," said Susan Singer, president of Field Trip Factory, Inc. Is locking in brand loyalty an appropriate cultural value for schools to convey?

The other *Chicago Tribune* article describes a program aimed at the 4.7 million daily subway riders in Mexico City. Mexico's largest city has begun handing out 250,000 books to subway riders as they board a train. These free anthologies of Mexican literature are being distributed in the hope of promoting more reading and lowering the subway crime rate. Readers are asked to return the paperbacks, with 60–70 percent doing so, thus far. Earlier, Tokyo initiated a similar program whereby dozens of small paperback libraries were set up in Japanese train stations.

Mexico City Mayor Andres Manuel Lopez Obrador's book campaign seeks to combat the lack of regular reading among average Mexicans. Going to a mall and reading a book are both cultural activities. Which one contributes more to America's future? You cannot force people to form the habit of reading if they don't have it at home. "What we hope is that we can help people discover that reading can be a pleasure. We need to create the necessity to read, "said Paloma Saiz of Mexico City's Cultural Department. Added Claudia Calderon, 26 and a student of orthodontics, "I do hope this opens the door to spreading a culture of reading."[41]

In Old America in 1985, the President's Commission on Industrial Competitiveness sounded the cultural alarm bells. At that time a group of leaders from business, labor, education, and government saw the erosion of America's ability to compete in either the emerging high-tech or the low-wage global marketplaces. This commission urged massive cultural change across the board to keep America strong—massive R&D in new technology, quality education for more students, and retraining workers for new jobs within every economic sector.

In today's New America, if that formula for cultural change sounds familiar, it should. Old America was the most innovative country on earth; New America won't stay that way if we run away from the new cultural realities of the global economy. "We must do what Americans have always done," says Carly Fiorina, former chairman of Hewlett-Packard, "Work to keep our country in the lead, by making it the most competitive and creative of all nations. We don't have a second to waste. The rest of the world isn't waiting."[42]

Thus far, New America isn't doing too well. The so-called agents of no-change have watered down education. Paul A. Gigot wrote in *The Wall Street Journal*, "Washington's education lobby is the equivalent of 'North Korea'" in negotiating change, and the business community as a whole might be said to resemble Genghis Khan on its side of the bargaining table.[43]

Playing the blame game won't get us very far in closing a widening education gap in the New America. Thus far, we have seen general agreement on creating higher academic standards in our schools. But what are the key components in enabling schools to implement this transformation in standards?

1. *Good Local Leadership.* A school's principal needs to be both a good administrator and a superb people manager of both teachers and parents. The principal must energize the change process and get all of the teachers as well as parents to buy into the improvement plan that is adopted.

2. *Great Teachers.* The Roman orator Cicero once said that teachers need to know their subject, their audience, and themselves. Great teachers love their subject and know it inside and out. Especially at the high school level, teachers should have completed a college major in the subject that they teach. Great teachers love children and adolescents, and they want to spend their entire adult lives with them. Teachers must be viewed as respected members of their community so that they are motivated to become to very best teachers they can ever possibly be.

3. *Supportive Parents.* It is essential that parents make it clear to their children that learning in school comes first. Parents should demonstrate interest in their children's classroom learning, and respect and support for classroom teachers. This includes making sure homework is done well. Parents need to realize that achievement and aptitude develops very slowly throughout childhood and adolescence. How parents share culture and knowledge day-to-day will vary, based on their child's personal interests, ethnic background, ability, and accessibility to books, computers, museums, music, sports, and so forth. However, parents have the major role

of setting the educational priorities that the classroom teacher can then build upon. If parents do not make clear in word and action that they value learning and support the long-term schooling process, it is very difficult for any teacher to motivate children or adolescents to put their best efforts into classroom learning.

Much of successful education is up to parents. But what are the cultural expectations of parents regarding the impact that education has on their own life and the future of their children? To a large extent, the future of the United States hangs on the answer to this cultural question. This culture area or, as I call it, the "C" (Culture) factor, is the base that drives the future of the United States. Do we as a people have the will to improve U.S. culture, this C factor, to better prepare more youth for a New America?

All states need to toughen their elementary and high school curricula to reflect the reading, math, English, and science requirements that students actually need to succeed in life (American Diploma Project, 2004). In 2005 the National Governors Association met in Washington D.C. for a weekend education summit on the nation's high schools. Thirteen states announced their participation in a national high school project to raise graduation standards. Six philanthropic organizations pledged $23 million to help launch these reform efforts. This is a move in the right direction. Schools also need to relate a liberal arts education to the real world. Parents need accurate information from a school on how their child's personal aptitudes and interests align with potential career opportunities in the 21st century (National Research Council, 2003).[44]

Non-governmental organizations can be a means of mobilizing key sectors in local communities for making these educational changes. We

Table 3.3
The "C" (Culture) Factor

Culture	X	Literacy	=	Education	X	Marketplace	=	GDP
A nation's attitudes and motivation regarding the importance of personal learning & applying it throughout life.		Personal reading practices and formal schooling.		The "critical mass" of a nation's knowledge		The socio-economic forces driving business, government and non-profit activities		Gross Domestic Product: The Wealth of a Nation

will later examine (in Chapters 5 and 7) how some U.S. communities are already taking action, and how to get started where you live and work.

The consequences of technological change, globalization, and outsourcing need not be a new, permanent American underclass. If U.S. culture changes over time, students can receive the educational preparation needed for the high-skill/high-wage occupations being created across America.

We have time to address this cultural change between now and 2020, before the demographic shift makes this transformation much more difficult. But first the U.S. must address the C factor that keeps too many people from participating in a high-skills-based modern society (See Table 3.3).

4

Help Wanted in America
and the World

I can't see how we can move forward in this economy without
having the right people. The purpose of education is to allow
people to move up to jobs requiring high skills as quickly as
possible. . . . There's no alternative to teaching people.

—Alan Greenspan
Chairman, Federal Reserve Board

THE UNITED STATES "OPTING OUT"

Allan Greenspan's 2004 testimony to the U.S. House Education and
Workforce Committee had a blunt message: The United States cannot
prosper in a global economy without a larger population of highly skilled
people who can handle demanding jobs and generate new ideas.[1]

Yet twenty years of reform has failed to produce major changes in the
quality of typical high school graduates or the U.S. workforce. "This coming September (2003) about 3.5 million young people in America will
begin the eighth grade," said Tom Vander Ark, executive director of education for the Bill and Melinda Gates Foundation. "Over the succeeding four
years, more than one million of them will drop out. . . . Another 1.5 million
will muddle through with a collection of credits that fail to prepare them
for college, work or citizenship."[2]

Even more sobering is the fact that at the height of America's tech-
bubble job boom (2000), about 14 percent of youths aged 16 to 19 were
unemployed. This was four times the overall jobless rate of 3.4 percent.

African American young adults fared even worse, with a national unemployment rate of 27.9 percent. Too many young people will never be ready for high-wage, entry-level jobs.[3]

This has prompted major American technology leaders to wave the white surrender flag. As long ago as 1999, Renee Lerche, director of workforce development at Ford Motor Company told Congress, "I am afraid that the slow pace of change will tempt any businesses and other partnering organizations to 'opt-out' of the public education reform effort."[4] Why should today's outsourcing debate be a surprise, if Ford already saw the handwriting on the employment wall in the 1990s?

Business is becoming impatient. Those that are able will shop the world for high-skill entry-level people. The local American communities they will leave will probably have lost these jobs forever. If Americans don't choose the careers of tomorrow, companies will travel where they can find people who are interested in these careers.

On the Road to Nowhere

More U.S. students enter post-secondary education (52%) than any other major industrial country (1996). This reflects the strong contemporary cultural belief, as expressed by W. J. Reeves, professor of English at Brooklyn College of the City of New York, "There exists a goal that the majority of the nation's youth should go to college and that access should be the byword for higher education. On the surface, this sounds like a great idea, in reality it is not."

What happens—or doesn't happen—once a student gets to college? For too many, the answer is "not much." As we have seen, large numbers of students are placed in remedial courses after they are admitted to college. The survival rate is very low: 37 percent drop out, while about 27 percent will ultimately get a four-year degree. Those who quit may experience disappointment, disorientation, and difficulty in finding desirable employment.

The important news for parents and students, according to the U.S. Bureau of Labor Statistics, is that 42 percent of new, entry-level job growth will require a two-year associate degree or a technical training certificate, not a four-year degree. This is good news for many students, as total four-year college costs will continue to soar to over $100,000. Also, high-paying technology careers are good alternatives for those students with the motivation and aptitudes to pursue them.

Some good questions for mom and dad are: In what areas does your child show talent and interest? Do they translate into a traditional four-year degree in business, liberal arts, or a technical career area? When your child does graduate from a post-secondary institution, wouldn't it be nice if a good-paying career awaits him or her rather than just a high mountain of debt and a low-paying job?

One of the key questions for U.S. communities to consider at the high school level is how to combine more rigorous academic studies with career-related applications or career-based learning, or both. This will help more high school graduates succeed in higher education and start desirable careers.[5]

One Best Solution?

The U.S. career mess did not happen overnight. High school education has evolved slowly over the past 125 years.

In 1874 the Michigan Supreme Court confirmed that all boys and girls had a basic right to a comprehensive and advanced education. This helped establish the precedent that the United States would not have two high school systems, one for vocational education and another teaching liberal arts, as was the case in much of 19th-century Europe. Instead, America would have one system offering a comprehensive high school education program for all.

In 1906 one of the first vocational education programs began at the University of Cincinnati. By 1914 in Dayton, Ohio, businesses helped launch the first vocational high school. Students spent half of their time in the schoolroom and the other half at the workplace in employer-supervised education.

By the 1920s larger, urban high schools were offering students a comprehensive curriculum of general, college preparatory, and specific career-education courses. Then most students used their high school diploma as the entry-level ticket to the workplace.

It was not until after the Second World War that vocational education began its steady decline. The G. I. Bill paid for veterans' technical or college education. A college degree began to be seen as the best guarantee for an individual to achieve the American dream.[6]

During the Cold War, the Soviet Union's successful launch of Sputnik I (1957), the first human-made earth satellite, created a new demand for U.S. technical education. The resulting National Defense Education Act of 1958 was America's answer to the space race challenge by reforming education to stress science, math, foreign languages, and related vocational education for students and adults. This program was designed to prepare them for employment as technicians or skilled workers in scientific or technical fields. However, the United States won the race to the moon in 1969 with the Apollo landing. Our victory once again reduced interest in technical education programs.

Vocational education enrollments started a steady decline in the 1970s. However, the passage and reauthorization of the federal Carl D. Perkins Vocational Education Act (1984, 1990, 1998), as well as the School-to-Work Opportunities Act (1994), encouraged about 150,000 high school students in the 1990s to graduate annually with some vocational/technical credits. About 8 percent of all high school students are now enrolled in these programs. Around 50 percent of U.S. high schools provide such opportunities.[7] Yet this remains inadequate to fill many new, high-skill tech jobs now being created across the U.S. economy.

Lack of interest by students, not employers, seriously hurt the federal school-to-work program (STW). Columbia University researchers discovered that not enough students wanted to participate in tech career education programs. Only 2 to 3 percent of high school students took part in learning that combined academic classes with work-based education. In part, this was because only 23 percent of school-to-work schools integrated academic and career teaching. Another reason was that few high schools clearly linked career studies to post-secondary college courses. In only a handful of states did STW high school courses count toward college-entry academic credit. No wonder students stayed away from STW in droves!

The negative impact of this tech education failure is now all too apparent. Over the past 20 years in America's leading high-tech state, California, 75 percent of technology-related courses have gone by the wayside, according to a study by the *Los Angeles Times*. One reason cited was California's sagging school budgets, making tech classrooms very pricey to equip with modern technology. But this excuse is a smoke screen for society's indifference. In most of the past 20 years, California (and especially the Silicon Valley) profited hugely from high-tech industries built on a skilled workforce. Yet these skills are now in increasingly short supply throughout California's K–12 school system.[8] So if most students spurn occupations that are related to technology, how are today's students making their future career choices?

Career Confusion

A number of recent studies concerning which careers young Americans think about suggest that many teenagers have wildly high expectations about their futures. Beginning in 1992, researchers at the University of Chicago and the National Opinion Research Center have asked a national sample of some 1,000 students in grades 6–12 what they want to be when they grow up. The answers are amazingly unrealistic.

The researchers found that most young Americans expect to have high-status and high-paying jobs. Almost one in three expects to have a professional career. Ten percent expect to work in the sports or entertainment industry. Another 10 percent think they will be doctors. Few imagine themselves working in service, craft, or technical industries. Yet government labor and economic indicators predict that most new, high-wage jobs will be created by these business sectors over the next 10 to 15 years.

"Our kids' aspirations, overall, represent a considerably more potent, better-rewarded economically high-status set of occupations than probably these kid are going to enter," says Charles Bidwell, one of the principal investigators for this career study.

The study also found that the vast majority of young people expect to graduate from a four-year college, and a large number expect to go as far as a Ph.D. degree. Yet they have scant knowledge about what specific careers actually entail. When asked for precise information about the fields they hoped to enter, such as the average income, the educational requirements, or the prospects for job openings, few students could provide it.[9]

A Metropolitan Life Survey (2000) confirmed that many students have an unrealistic view of most careers. About 33 percent listed entertainment as an area of interest. Education and high-tech tied for second place with 26 percent, while health care and law were next at 25 percent. Yet these same students had taken little in the way of math, science, history, or English literature courses in high school to prepare for these potential careers.

Students also listed having "a meaningful job" in fourth place among the elements of a successful adult life, following "earning lots of money," "having time for personal activities," and "having fun at work."

This interest in money as the ultimate driving force for one's education for life was also confirmed in the American Freshman Survey released by UCLA in 2004. In this study of over 267,000 students, 73.8 percent listed being "very well-off financially" as very important or essential. As USC freshman Dustin Grant said, "The reason you go to college is to get the degree so you can make a lot of money." Period. Forget altruism, forget that 86 percent of college freshmen once said (1967) "it was important to find a meaningful life philosophy." This is today's American culture. The "greed is good" message has really penetrated all the way down to the next generation.[10]

In view of these current student values, the swelling enrollment in four-year colleges is hardly surprising. Government study after study indicates

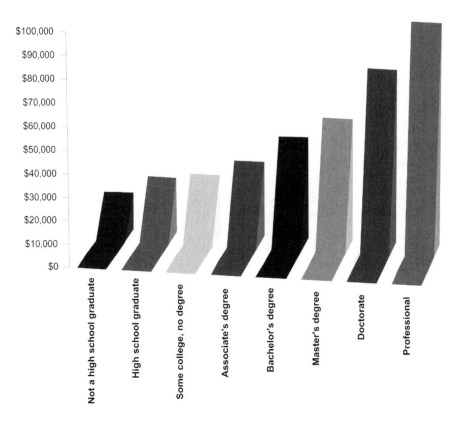

Figure 4.1—Average Annual Earnings in the United States by Level of Education
Source: Statistical Abstract of the United States, 2001.

that a college degree leads to higher annual earnings (see Figure 4.1). Yet the career world is changing. Over the next decade, many holders of technical professional jobs will become high wage earners, surpassing many who received B.A. degrees.

The University of Chicago study also argues that schools need to provide better career information to both students and parents about the knowledge and skills required for a broad range of occupations, and to integrate that information throughout elementary and high school curricula. Today's high school counseling is focused primarily on college, not careers. The social status and economic prosperity of individual communities seem to be the main influences on whether students are channeled into four- or two-year colleges or enter the job market right after high school.

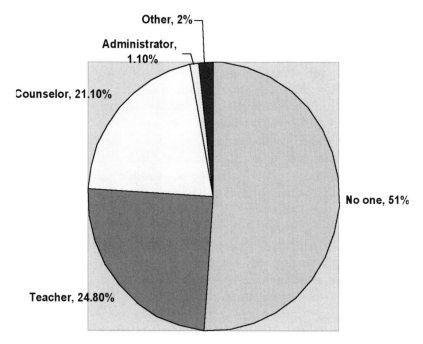

Figure 4.2—Students See Little Career Guidance
When asked who in high school has been helpful in advising on career or future education options, more than half of 800 high school junior and seniors nationwide said "No one."
Source: Ferris State University, 2002.

Phyllis Eisen, vice president of the Manufacturing Institute and executive director of the Center for Workforce Success, agrees that students are getting little or no career advice from high-school guidance counselors (see Figure 4.2). After reading *Decisions without Direction* (2002), a six-month study by Ferris State University in Michigan, she agreed with the report's call to action on career preparation. "It is criminal what we are finding in our high schools. The K–12 education system is cracking from the lack of career counseling," she said.[11]

In the past, high school counselors were attacked for sorting students into two major tracks: the labor market or college. Today, counselors in the mainstream have embraced the popular culture notion that all students should go to college. This is what Barbara Schneider, a professor of sociology at the University of Chicago found in her review of how the current career system works and fails so many students. More and more students are expected by parents, peers, and society to obtain Bachelor's or post-graduate degrees. Popular culture demands this even if they are academically unprepared, lack the motivation to sustain the long-term effort, or have aptitudes and intelligence that do not center on the detailed, written research and study required by a traditional four-year college program. Students become caught in what Schneider terms an "ambition paradox"—students with high ambitions choosing an education route with low odds of success.[12]

Another alternative has been suggested by George L. Wimberly and Richard J. Noeth. In "College Readiness Begins in Middle School," an ACT study (2005) of nearly 3,000 students, they found that most students in middle school had given little realistic thought to how their aptitudes and interests might someday translate into worthwhile careers. As a result, many high school students who haven't begun thinking about their post-high-school plans early enough, and even those who have, may not take the right classes to prepare to meet their goals.

"Schools can help students by helping their parents," said Noeth. "Information is vital. If parents understand what their children need to meet their goals, then they can properly advise and encourage them to make the right decisions on course planning."

To do this, career aptitude and personal interest assessments need to be provided in middle schools. These types of formal assessments and follow-up student/parent counseling is now seldom found in U.S. middle schools.

Unfortunately, most current career education is based on a commonly held myth that a Bachelor's degree is the best route to a good job and secure lifetime career. The reality is that for a few students, the 15 to 25 percent who will earn any degree, a B.A. or B.S. degree does provide access to the upper tier of American society. The vast majority of future entry-level jobs with career-growth potential will require only a year or two of post-secondary education and continuing lifelong educational updates.

The new definition of "career" focuses less on a progression up a career ladder in a profession or corporation, and more on recognizing opportunities and adapting. Rather than focusing on a one-career preparation path, current and future workers need a higher quality of education that integrates general knowledge in both the arts and sciences with emerging technology. The well-educated technician, such as depicted in the cast of the television series *ER*, provides a more realistic, 21st-century career model than the attorneys and politicians of *The West Wing*, or the media stars of television, news, movies, or the recording industry.[13]

America's Broken Career Machine

Both Alison Wolf of the University of London and Professor Kenneth C. Gray agree on one vital point: It's important to "have the right qualifications, in the right subjects, from the right institutions." In *Does Education Matter? Myths about Education and Economic Growth* (Penguin Books, 2002), Wolf questions whether ramming more people through college while letting the quality of K–12 schools stagnate is good public policy. This has placed increasing financial burdens on families, while dumbing down the average quality of a university or college degree.

Without expanded career-education options, four-year college degrees alone will not automatically fill the nation's job requirements or our economic needs. Professor Gray notes that many high schoolers, even those who dislike formal studies, opt for college because they don't know what else to do with their lives. Ironically, he concludes, "A number of good-paying, prestigious jobs are still available that do not require a four-year college degree but which continue to go begging."[14]

America's career machine is badly broken. The future U.S. economy is in great peril if we don't fix it. Americans simply can no longer afford to cling to the by-gone career culture attitudes of 20th-century Old America. Unless this dramatically changes, high-skill/high-wage technology jobs being created by 21st-century New America could disappear overseas. Or will they?

Ironically, the same technology and globalization forces have also raised the career-education stakes around the entire world. How big a threat outsourcing or foreign direct investment becomes to the average American worker will be largely dependent on which nations win the skill war that will upgrade their population's overall education.

ASIA'S PAINFUL TRANSITION

China's "Secret" Market

In the 1980s, Japan, Inc. was on the road to taking over the world's economy. Faltering American businesses enviously studied Japanese companies. Rockefeller Center in New York, Pebble Beach in California, and large chunks of Hawaii were purchased by titanic Japan. Land values in Japan soared, at one point reaching such a height that the acreage of Tokyo's Imperial Palace was more valuable than the entire GDP of Canada. Then, in the early 1990s, the bubble of Japan's invincibility burst, returning them to earth with a dismal economy for the next decade. Now it is suddenly China's turn to eat America's lunch. Pundits predict that China's ability to manufacture almost anything cheaply will permanently devastate American production and jobs.

The rapid change in China can be seen across its landscape: the ultra-modern face of Shanghai, and a McDonald's restaurant in Beijing. Designer sunglasses on Chinese youth are now as ubiquitous as Mao's *Little Red Book* was a generation ago. In time for the 2008 Olympic Games, Beijing alone aims to teach about 400,000 Chinese people to speak English.

At the forefront of this revolutionary change are China's university graduates. Since 1999 the government has been rapidly increasing enrollments. About 2.8 million students graduated in 2004 from institutions of higher learning in China. This is double the number of 2002 graduates. The number may be as high as 3.2 million in 2005.

Though this sounds impressive, 900 million people still live in the impoverished rural areas of that nation. China's industries are crying out for skilled labor that is currently in short supply. "It's very difficult to find good or suitable engineers who can come and work for our company," says Hiroshi Matsuo, general manager of China operations at Sharp, the Japanese electronics company. With a limited supply, and demand building, salaries for skilled employees are rising at a "crazy" rate, stated Angel Leung, senior consultant at Tak Consulting, a Hong Kong recruitment firm. Though salaries for Chinese engineers are still at least 25 percent below the U.S. equivalent figures (2004), the gap is narrowing rapidly. This shows the difference between the huge supply of Chinese techno-peasants employed as cheap factory labor and the tightening supply of available knowledge technologists.

Also at issue is the quality of Chinese higher education. Too many graduates cannot find jobs. Critics say China's schools place too much emphasis on rote learning and test scores. Students are not prepared for the real world. Professors have little hands-on experience of what they teach. Universities have a long way to go in overhauling business curricula and allow more creativity (see Table 4.1).

China's overall educational system is woefully inadequate for supporting long-term economic development. In 2003 the United Nations reported that, overall, Uganda was doing better than China in guaranteeing every child a basic education. China spends only 2 percent of its GDP on education. The government provides only 53 percent of school funding, lower than most other countries with compulsory education systems.

This shows up materially in the inadequacy of most local village schools. Over 20 percent of the population over the age of 15 have no schooling or did not complete the primary grades; only 38 percent completed primary school, and about 39 percent have had some high school or completed it. Only 2.5 percent finish some form of post-secondary education. China will have to overhaul its entire educational delivery system if it expects to sustain its skyrocketing economic growth, let alone the continued heavy foreign investment in its industrial expansion.

Table 4.1
Help Wanted
Despite what many consider a glut of graduates, multinational companies in China complain that a dearth of talented people is constraining their growth.

Company	Employees in China	College Recruitment	On Finding Talent
Coca-Cola	More than 500; including bottlers, 20,000	Began recruiting graduates and MBAs at top schools in Beijing and Shanghai this year. Aims to hire about 10 annually.	"The competition for talent is really intense. We don't expect it to be getting better in the next three to five years."
L'Oreal	3,000	Since 1998, has focused on top schools in Beijing, Shanghai and Guangzhou; hired 22 of 1,500 applicants this year. Also started recruiting in smaller locales.	"Because of the characteristics of the China market, the best results are with the people we grow from the beginning. We form them in line with out culture."
Deloitte Touche Tohmatsu	1,500	Since about 1997, has targeted to 10 colleges and cities where it has offices, such as Tianjin and Dalian. Hired 350 of this year's graduates, mostly as auditors.	"The main way we add people is through hiring college graduates.... We have to train them up from a blank piece of paper."

Source: China-based executives at the companies (*Wall Street Journal*, 2004).

Widely reported corruption is another surprising negative factor that distorts the work-readiness of the population. Norman Rogers, president of Z-World, a California microchip company, characterizes China as a "cowboy environment" in its attitudes toward the piracy of product designs and technology. "It has no laws whatever on regulating intellectual property," he states. Even Intel is not setting up a chip fabrication plant in China because the U.S. government will not allow it to transfer the necessary high-end production equipment because of fears over piracy or even the possibility that it could be utilized by the Chinese military. Need a B.A. degree? Within an hour of shopping, a Chinese customer can emerge with a complete educational makeover. Master's and Ph.D. degrees on forged official paper of almost every hue are available in rural fairs across China. Nearby printers will customize a diploma and transcript to individual specifications. The so-called secret market for counterfeit degrees is a booming business. China will find it will take more time to produce a well-educated population than to print one if it fails to rein in this bandit economy.

A *Financial Times* investigation (2005) revealed how "Factory managers in China are becoming increasingly sophisticated at falsifying worker time cards and payroll documents to disguise irregularities including under-payment, excessive hours, and inadequate health and safety provisions."

The New York-based organization, Human Rights in China, issued a 2005 report on the death of five factory girls who were under the age of 16, the minimum age for employment in China. Critics say that the government does little to enforce the nation's child-labor law. By some estimates, up to 10 million school-aged children are now part of China's low-cost manufacturing workforce.

The mind-boggling 8–9 percent annual growth rate of China's economy has placed China in an unending employment crisis. Skilled workers are in short supply. Even shortages of low-skill workers are appearing in some provinces. China's official one-child policy to control population growth means that by 2015 it, too, will experience a demographic squeeze. *The Economist* predicts that in the next decade, "China's rate of aging will be faster than that of any other country in history." Companies continue to throw masses of foreign capital at mechanization employing large numbers of cheap low-skill labor rather than trying to employ and train a high-tech workforce using advanced technologies. This looks like a repeat of past, shortsighted American industrial practices that have helped lead the United States to a 2010 skilled worker crisis.

These similar labor market symptoms of both China and the United States should offer an ominous warning to outside investors. Low-wage/low-skill workers may be in abundance, but China will be unable to sustain profitable, massive foreign investment without overhaul of its fragile, under-developed educational system.[15]

India's Third-World Workforce

Another major outsourcing destination, India, seems to be threatening to take both low-skill and high-tech jobs away from the United States and Europe. Yet, looking behind the sensational headlines, we are surprised to find a third-world workforce still struggling to attain basic national literacy.

In comparing India and China, the most telling difference might well be female literacy rates. According to the World Bank (2005) 87 percent of adult Chinese women are literate; in India this figure is about 45 percent. A better education for girls can help India in many ways: better health, a more productive workforce, and a boost to the fledgling high-tech economy. "An educated child," said Asian demographer Clint Laurent, "Does not want to plant rice." India's overall literacy rate rose from 18 percent in 1950 to 65 percent in 2001. This is a substantial improvement but not good enough.

Most Indians still live and work in rural villages. One-third subsist on less than $1 a day. Low-tech farming employs more than two-thirds of India's labor force of 430 million people. There, thousands of inadequate schools (often no more than mud-brick huts or porches) are failing to provide for the most basic educational needs of the people. Beyond its decrepit infrastructure, the blatant deficiencies of state schools explain why. For example, a 2005 study by Jean Dreza, a noted Indian economist, found that, on any given day, up to 25 percent of this country's elementary-school teachers are missing from their classrooms.

Like many other third-world nations, India boasts a fairly well-developed higher-education system. The government spends 4.1 percent (2003) of its GDP on education, with a disproportionate amount going to its universities. But Raghunath Anant Mashelkar, India's top scientific administrator, believes that there are few world-class departments at the country's 250 universities. They may produce 5,000 Ph.D. degrees a year, "but few of global standard," he says. Still, only low numbers of students (7.3 percent) complete both high school and post-secondary education. The vast majority (58 percent) has no formal education; only 7.2 percent even finish elementary school.

Kasturi Devi of Barehmora, India recalls her moment of discovery at age 29 that she could actually read the sign on the rickety local bus. She is lucky, for the hard truth is that this region of India's literacy rate for girls and women is lower than 30 percent.

For the first time since gaining political independence in 1948, India is accepting a great deal of outside help in order to bring literacy education to its neglected rural masses. The World Bank, the United Nations, and private organizations have thus far built 25,000 schools, including one in Barehmora, Devi's home village.

But Barehmora is not a model village. Only 300 of the 1,000 villagers are literate and women are only 15 percent of this small group. Just down the road, most villages have zero literacy.

The lack of a significant educational infrastructure in India raises many thought-provoking questions for overseas investors. Granted, low-skill/low-wage adult and child labor exists in abundance. But as India's domestic economy grows, where will this nation find adequate numbers of high-skill workers for their own high-tech economy? Rajiv Gandhi, India's prime minister from 1984–1989, estimated that 85 percent of the country's development spending in areas such as education for the poor was lost through "leakage"—bureaucratic inefficiency and widespread corruption. How will India find enough knowledge technologists to remain an attractive outsourcing destination?

Even if India's competitiveness in manufacturing and professional services continues to rely on low-skill/low-pay labor, such business still need well-educated managers and engineers to organize and supervise them. The biggest constraint on the growth of business in India many be the available talent pool. Ask Arman Zand, who manages the Bangalore unit of California-based Silicon Valley Bank. He is the go-to guy for American start-up companies. In Bangalore's hot business climate, Zand's services are critical. But even he has his limits. One of his major problems is recruiting qualified people in this city's tight job market.

As India approaches the 2010 crossroad, she must drastically expand the size of, and improve the quality of, her elementary and secondary school system. Whatever degree of success these efforts achieve will determine a major part of India's long-term economic role in a high-tech world.[16]

Japan—Where Are the People?

Japan's labor market more closely resembles that of Western European nations, rather than China or India. Unfortunately, this is also true of the aging of its population. According to a U.N. study (2002), Japan is graying so rapidly that it needs over 600,000 immigrants every year until 2050 just to keep its workforce stable. By then (if this happens), nearly one-third of Japan's population will be from overseas. But such massive immigration fills most Japanese with horror.

Once upon a time (until the 1850s), a foreigner trespassing in the land of the rising sun was likely to be put to death. Modern Japan welcomes tourists, but the people and its culture still remain very closed to the outside world. Though the Japanese buy American goods and love baseball, it has a miniscule foreign population compared to other industrialized nations.

Because of this demographic squeeze, Japan's booming information technology sector is already desperately short of younger, entry-level workers. Even though low wages in China and elsewhere are draining Japan of traditional manufacturing jobs, the future lies in producing high value-added technology and services, as is true of the United States.

Achieving that goal may prove difficult. The irony is that Japan has long been known for its excellent company worker-training programs. But its university system is a mess. Neglect of serious study has long been a feature of Japanese higher education. Even at the nation's top universities, poor student class attendance is epidemic. Professors' lectures are dull and student class discussion is rare. Business recruiters complain that the quality of recent graduates is declining.

Japan's 700 universities are constricted by labor laws that protect incompetent faculty. Too many administrators lack even basic management skills. However, part of the blame for falling standards rests with the business community that, until recently, has sought compliant workers who followed orders.

But now the world has changed. Can Japan's universities teach critical thinking and innovation? Will Japan be able to find more high-skill workers to keep its industries competitive? If Japan, Inc. is to survive, its universities must reform and become more creative to complement the success of the excellent technical training given by industry to workers on the job.[17]

EUROPE IN THE SLOW LANE

Unemployment and the lack of significant economic growth have plagued the 25 European Union (EU) nations and Russia since the beginning of the new millennium. As we have already seen, the demographics for EU retirement are far worse than America's. One reason is that the immigrant safety valve is not popular throughout Europe. A 2004 European Commission estimate is that between 2010 and 2030, at current immigration rates, the EU workforce faces an overall decline of 20 million people.

Unemployment is still very high (averaging over 8 percent) in the EU. Yet employers are increasingly looking for more highly educated workers. Those with poor skill levels are ill-equipped for the jobs being offered. There is a growing mismatch in European labor markets between job vacancies and the unemployed (See Table 4.2).

In France and Germany, this problem is becoming more acute. A contributing trend is the concentration of job openings in certain parts of European countries, while the unemployed live in other regions. This seems particularly true in Belgium, Germany, and Italy. To Americans who are now conditioned to move to where the jobs are, it may seem peculiar that European workers largely don't do the same, or that businesses won't relocate to where the workers are available.[18]

Italy: Twenty-two Barriers

Italy, the fifth-largest economy in the world, is a good example of why Europe is in the slow lane of economic growth. The birth rate is very low.

Table 4.2
European Competitiveness

Country	Competititveness Rating Scale Overall Performance *** Good, **Average, * Poor	
	Rating	Competitive Position
Germany	**	High budget deficit, unsustainable pensions, high unemployment, labor market rigidity, disappointing education, very poor record in implementing EU single-market directives.
France	**	High budget deficit, insecure long-term public finances, insufficient education and labor market reforms, energy market still not liberalized, failure to implement and abide by EU single-market laws
United Kingdom (UK)	***	Below average labor productivity, insufficient research, poorly educated workforce
Ireland	**	Poor environmental record despite skilled workforce gains, current below average spending on education and research, big price rises in recent years
Italy	*	Low employment rates, declining labor productivity, unstable public finances, poorly educated workforce particularly in the South
Spain	*	Highest unemployment in EU, Low female employment, no new pension reforms planned, disappointing education and worker training
Portugal	*	Big budget deficit, poor educational results
Netherlands	***	Weak labor productivity, declining research spending, education good
Luxembourg		Disappointing education, low employment rate among older workers
Sweden	***	High prices, declining labor productivity, weak competition in some sectors, little competition for public sector services, good education and workforce preparation
Finland	**	High prices, declining labor productivity, high structural unemployment
Denmark	**	High prices, big fall in IT spending, increase in school dropouts
Austria	***	Below average research spending, low employment of older women, good education
Greece	*	High government debt, low female employment rate, high long-term unemployment, poor education results
Russia	*	Improved economy, uncertain government reforms, poor labor productivity, declining educational system*

Sources: European Commission, 2004; Edward E. Gordon, 2004*.

The demographic meltdown of a rapidly aging workforce has combined with very restrictive immigration, below-standard education, and a lack of worker mobility to create serious skilled labor shortages.

From health care to high-tech industries, the number of unfilled jobs is growing (estimated at 160,000 in 2001). In an industrial suburb of Milan, new equipment to assemble auto components remains packed in crates. Overhead cranes are idle. "The machines are here," says Marco Zanaboni, the Franco Tosi Company's machining engineer, "The people are missing." The workers who are on the assembly line are older—in their forties and fifties.

In the past, 2.5 million southern Italians migrated north to these jobs. Now the low wages offered by northern employers, who struggle with high taxes for government welfare benefits, fail to tempt the south's chronically unemployed workforce.

Then there is the culture thing. "This is not just a country of north and south," explains Francesco Boccia in the Ministry of Industry. "We have 22 regions each with its own way of life. There is a reluctance to change cities, friendships, habits."

Though the Italian government offers tax incentives for business to relocate in the south, few are interested. Owners cite diverse reasons, ranging from the Mafia and corruption to poor road and railway infrastructure.

One other remedy for Italy's depleted workforce is immigration. Demographers warn that unless the birthrate increases, Italy's population could shrink from 57 million to 41 million by 2050. Yet the government is opposed to increasing the number of immigrants, who currently make up barely 3 percent of the nation's total population. This is the lowest proportion in Europe.

A spokesman for the Ministry of Labor, Guiseppe Mennella explains, "An immigrant is not in Italy for only eight hours a day. He is here 24 hours a day.... Our policies should not be determined by the manpower needs of businessmen. How will we integrate more immigrants?" Scoffs Gianpaolo Galli, chief economist for Confindustria, Italy's manufacturers' trade association, in reply, "Here you have a situation where industry needs immigrants, but society doesn't want them."[19]

Many of these same cultural issues prevail across Europe. In Finland, technology companies such as Nokia have been the biggest creators of jobs, but the sector now faces a shortage of skilled workers. This shortage across the EU has already begun to take its toll in declining productivity and a slowdown in GDP growth.[20]

Portugal is a good example. As late as 1970, 33 percent of its population was illiterate. By 1996 only one-third of the 25- to 34-year-old age group had graduated from high school. This compares unfavorably with the 75 percent average for the rest of the EU (Spain stands at 50 percent and Greece at 66 percent).[21] All these countries are still being held back by generations of education neglect. "The better educated a country's people are, the faster its economy can grow," *The Economist* (2003) concluded regarding its overall review of the current European economic situation.

Germany: Back to Basics

Signs of Germany's industrial decline are everywhere. Between 1990 and 2004 the manufacturing sector's output dropped from 130 percent of the value of total exports to only 90 percent. Over the same period about 400,000 manufacturing jobs were shed. Productivity continues to lag. This is curious because of the vaunted world-class expertise of the country's technical workforce.[22]

Germany, the world's third-biggest economic power, has long ranked near the top of international education surveys. Its career education program, the Dual-System, links local schools and industry to prepare, until recently, up to 70 percent of high-school-age youth for the world of work. Over 370 specific career-training programs are accredited for use across Germany. Government provides some funding, while industry offers hands-on-training. Schools are in charge of the theoretical and educational curriculum.

Most German business people, though envious of America's less-regulated capitalism, are satisfied with this system. Nikolaus Schves, CEO of a Hamburg shipping company, when asked whether there was anything about America he wouldn't import, mentioned only one thing: schooling. He thinks that Germany's system of comprehensive apprenticeship and classroom job training program is a plus. "In America," he said, "it is learning by doing. That is a disadvantage."[23] But there are dark clouds gathering on Germany's educational horizon.

Several years ago (2001), the PISA international comparison study (OECD) ranked the Germany, the so-called land of poets and thinkers, a shocking 21st out of 31 countries for the reading abilities of its 15-year-olds, and also 20th in math and science. Almost 25 percent of Germany's 15-year-olds could not read and understand a simple text! The top levels of reading ability were reached by only 28 percent of this age group. Finland achieved 50 percent, and over one-third were at this level in a dozen other OECD countries.[24] What has gone wrong in Germany?

After three years of study, several significant deep-seated problems surfaced:

- The education system is under-funded.
- Educational standards and approaches vary widely over the 16 regional German states.
- Non-German students (children of Turkish guest workers, who were only now included in the PISA data) have much lower academic standards. Many can barely speak German.
- Germany has large class sizes and a rapidly aging teaching force; two-fifths of all teachers are over age 50.
- In some German states a high proportion of students choose a college track and avoid the dual-system entirely. This, incredibly, has worked to lower math, science, and reading standards for many students. For the first time in many years, there are not enough apprentices to fill all the business occupational openings.[25]

For all its current shortcomings, mainstream German culture supports strong academic skills and career preparation for its children. There has been, until recently, a basic cultural commitment to try and make the content of elementary and secondary education more relevant to the changing career needs of children entering what I call the New Europe of the 21st century.[26]

Another major issue that will have a serious negative impact on the German economy is a serious demographic meltdown. As we saw earlier, the entire working population of Germany and the EU is falling because of escalating retirements and a declining birthrate. Though unemployment has remained stubbornly high (9+ percent), by 2020 Germany is projected to be short some 2.5 million high-skill workers. Just to keep its population stable, Germany will need about 487,000 immigrants each year between now and 2050, says a recent report by the United Nations Population Division. France will need 109,000, and the EU as a whole will need 1.6 million. Despite negative societal views toward admitting immigrants in Germany and most other European nations, with the dramatic fall coming in Europe's working population, immigration will become a necessity—not just an option.[27]

The United Kingdom's Workforce Decline

"Britain's pool of 7 million functionally illiterate adults is a disgrace, and it is not shrinking," proclaimed a *London Times* editorial. Sixty-seven percent of students across the UK leave school at age 16. Too many dropouts leave and never receive the skill qualifications for any meaningful career.

"We are far behind other countries in training students for the job market," remarks Hilary Steedman at the National Institute of Economic and Social Research."[28] The Ministry of Defense had to start a large remedial math program when it found that too many soldiers were baffled by fractions—they need this math to operate sophisticated technology. About half of UK universities have opened remedial math centers for students. In fact, so few students are majoring in math and science that King's College of London threatened to close its chemistry department because of its enrollment decline. This is the school whose professors discovered DNA.[29]

All of these long-term educational trends have had a major impact on Britain's competitiveness. There has been a steep decline in industries that once dominated the world. The manufacturing share of Britain's GDP fell from 31 percent in 1970 to only 17 percent in 2004. In 1978, 7.1 million people were employed in manufacturing. By the end of 2004, that figure had fallen to only 3.5 million workers. Today, biotechnology and pharmaceuticals remain two of the few bright spots in the battered remnants of British industry.[30]

For some time, government-sponsored studies have called for helping poorly skilled workers. The U.K. Working Group (1999) found that the nation's effort to improve adult literacy "is often marginalized." Why is Britain's manufacturing industry such a mess? Low literacy among 20 percent of the population "is one of the reasons for relative low productivity in our economy." This low productivity creates a vicious circle, says John Dowdy, author of an analysis by McKinsey & Company (2002), who notes that cash-strapped managers skimp on investment and training, causing profits to fall even further. Part of the solution in the UK is for business to offer their workers more and better training. Companies can also better collaborate with their local primary and secondary schools. Britain and Scotland are actually rather good at university/business education collaboration, notably at Warwick University in England and Glasgow and Strathclyde Universities in Scotland. As the UK approaches the 2010 crossroad, these examples needed to be replicated at a local level throughout the country to rebuild Britain's technical workforce.[31]

NORTH AND SOUTH AMERICA

Canada

Canada, like its U.S. neighbor, is aging fast. Though only one in eight Canadians is now over 65 (2002), that number will double by 2035. However, compared to the United States, the working population is better educated and will work longer. Canada's 2001 census claims that, "Canada is probably the best equipped among industrial countries" to deal with the world demographic and jobs crisis."

Unfortunately, that is only half of the picture. Canada has a relatively small population (31 million), unevenly distributed across a vast country. Its population is rising slowly. Studies now show that the country is facing a worsening shortage of key technological workers. As millions of baby boomers leave the workplace, Canada will have a much smaller and less-skilled workforce.

Canada is aggressively seeking new immigrants to fill its workforce ranks. Immigrants already account for over 70 percent of labor market growth, and according to Statistics Canada, by 2011 will account for all of it. Unfortunately, over 50 percent of these workers lack the skills needed to fill high-tech jobs.

Overall literacy rates in Canada are comparable to the United States. About 22 percent of all adults read at the sixth-grade level or below. Literacy ability is lowest in the poorest communities. In this group, 40 to 70 percent of the children will drop out of high school.

Canada ranked fifth in reading literacy and ninth in quantitative literacy compared to 20 other industrialized nations (PISA). Yet a 1996 Statistics Canada survey found that fewer than 5 percent of adults were in the top category for math skills.

"Numeracy is not just the ability to add or multiply numbers," says Ron Dunkley, director of the Center for Education in Math and Computing at the University of Waterloo. With so many potential employees being unable to grasp fundamental math concepts, there are tears in many Canadian boardrooms. Too often, companies can't find new workers, even university graduates, who can analyze consumer purchasing patterns or handle statistical process controls on an assembly line. Banks across Canada now provide remedial math training to employees, some of whom have MBAs.

Tim O'Neill, chief economist at the Bank of Montreal, considers Canada's pressing literacy issues as an "economic imperative." Building on the Conference Board of Canada's forecast of a million-person labor shortage by 2020, O'Neill concludes that, "Simply put, with a looming shortage of people, those individuals remaining in the labor force cannot afford to have literacy challenges.... The need to increase literacy levels among adult Canadians must be recognized not only as an individual and social problem, but also as a business and economic issue as well."[32]

Latin America's Culture Battle

Across Latin America, political leaders are promising big improvements in their citizens' basic education. To create stable democracies and spur economic development, there is a broad regional consensus about improving the quality and quantity of education. At the 2001 Summit of the Americas, the hemisphere's leaders pledged to ensure that 75 percent of their students will complete high school by 2010. School enrollment incentives under which poor families receive welfare payments if their children attend school daily have helped. Due to such programs, Brazil, Mexico, Argentina, Honduras, and Nicaragua have seen enrollments climb. Yet the region's overall school attendance contains huge disparities.[33]

In Peru, Elena Chamorro, a bright 13-year-old girl goes to school each morning. She wants to be a nurse when she grows up. But after school ends at 1:00 P.M., "There's no time for games or homework," she says. From 2:00 to 6:00 at night, she works in a brick factory with her parents.

Education is the first casualty of child labor. Thirty-three percent of Peru's 2 million children aged 5 to 17 do not attend school. They are at work. About 200,000 of these are younger than 12. In Peru's rural areas, 40 percent of the children work in subsistence agriculture.

"It's still not clear that Peru has either the resources or the political will to eradicate child labor," says Walter Alarcon, a UNICEF child labor expert. The government of President Alejandro Toledo, a self-proclaimed former shoeshine boy, plans to eventually eliminate all child labor. This will not be easy. Cultural attitudes will have to change drastically. Alarcon sees this problem as extremely deep-rooted. "Many middle-class Peruvians don't question child labor. It's tolerated that poor parents should rely on their children to help out," he said. You can see the results when over 12 percent of the people have no formal schooling, less than one-third finish elementary school, and only 36 percent complete high school.

Until this cultural indifference of the Peruvian people changes, Elena and millions of more children will trudge off to work each day. Her dream of becoming a nurse, or Peru's aspiration to compete well in a global, high-tech economy will remain just that—very unlikely fairy tales.[34]

Over the past decade Chile has done much better than most of its neighbors in ensuring that poorer children get better schooling. Today over 80 percent of its children complete high school. Chile devotes 7 percent of its GDP to education. The government aims at a 100-percent high school graduation rate by 2006. These are solid achievements and a worthwhile goal. Yet Chilean businesses still say they find it hard to recruit well-educated workers. Why?

In the past Chile, like other Latin American economies, had plenty of low-skill jobs based on mining its rich natural resources. Businesses have now invested heavily in technology to lower costs. Now they require large numbers of so-called knowledge technologists with far higher skills.

Nevertheless, 40 percent of the current Chilean labor force never finished high school. An OECD study found that four out of five adults do not fully understand what they read. Because of the educational shortcomings of the past, it is no wonder that technology firms complain about the difficulty in finding skilled adult workers. The government wants to expand career and technical education, including apprenticeship programs. But, as in the United States, many businesses complain that would cost them too much money. Until this business cultural issue changes, Chile will find it difficult to sustain job growth and economic development.[35]

Brazil and Mexico are by far the most important players in Latin America's economy. Yet in 2000, when the OECD published a 32-country comparison of 15-year-olds' math and reading abilities, Brazil and Mexico lagged far behind the pack.

The current president of Brazil, Luiz Inácio Lula da Silva, and two-thirds of his fellow Brazilian workers never finished their elementary school education. Brazil's 2000 census found that 13 percent of adults are totally illiterate; only 14 percent finish high school.

When Jan Wreford, a British education inspector, toured São Paulo schools, she was appalled. Classrooms were devoid of books and teaching materials. She found teachers overworked and ill-trained—many had no idea of what makes a successful lesson. School buildings were plagued by vandals and drug dealers.

It is no wonder that these conditions exist, since in Brazil public spending on education is skewed in the wrong direction. While only 2 percent of all students attend public universities, they receive 25 percent of all education funds.

Mexico's people fare little better. Over 13 percent of the adult population have never gone to school, 19 percent finish elementary school, and sixteen percent finish high school. A law passed in 1992 makes secondary education "mandatory," meaning that all students must attend school from first grade through ninth grade. Unfortunately, this is not happening today. On average, young Mexicans receive 7.7 years of total schooling (2002). This is a vast leap from only 1.7 years in 1940, but this is not nearly good enough.

By comparison, Poland and Hungary produce world-class pupils even though they spend only slightly more than Brazil or Mexico, says the OECD.

The differences are in the cultural expectations of Latin Americans. Funding is too often wasted on over-centralized and under-regulated school systems. Often, teachers are poorly educated on how to teach. Many educational systems suffer from an almost complete lack of accountability. There is little desire to improve student achievement, since no one knows what the standards are.

All of this means it is necessary to change the cultural expectations of parents, teachers, and business people. Unless Latin America shows more urgency in promoting basic structural reforms, the region will continue to suffer from underdeveloped economies. The glowing promises of the North American Free Trade Agreement (NAFTA) will remain largely a one-way street: Cheap goods will flow into Canada and the United States while Latin Americans buy little in return. If a sizeable middle class is to develop in this region, more high-skill/high-wage jobs must be created to expand these economies.[36]

GLOBAL FUTURES

Over the next 50 years China, India, and Brazil are poised to become much larger economic forces in the world. The key assumptions are that they will continue to develop the policies and institutions that will allow economic growth. However, they (along with much of the developed world) face severe labor development challenges tied to either higher skills or demographics or both. Education is not the so-called magic bullet that solely brings about prosperity. However, Harvard economist Michael Porter, in *The Competitive Advantage of Nations* (1990), sees it as decisive.

There is little doubt from our research that education and training are decisive in national competitive advantage.... What is even more telling is that in every nation, those industries that were the most competitive were often those whose specialized investment in education and training had been unusually great.... Education and training constitute perhaps the single greatest long-term leverage point available ... to upgrading industry ... [and] setting policies that link the educational system to industry and encourage industry's own efforts at training.[37]

Yet the world's culture is still far removed from heeding Porter's advice. Around the globe, millions of children lack any access to education. Even larger numbers of adolescents quit school before gaining adequate skills for any meaningful career, placing many nations at great economic risk in a high-tech international economy.

Twenty-seven percent of adults (887 million) in the world are totally illiterate; two-thirds of these are women (UNESCO, 2003). Though worldwide

Table 4.3
Adult Illiteracy

Country	Percent
Afghanistan	78
Angola	58
Eritrea	80
Haiti	65
Pakistan	62
Somalia	76
Tanzania	32
Togo	48

Source: Encyclopedia Britannica Almanac 2003.

this is an improvement, up to 3 billion of the world's adults still read so poorly that they are functionally illiterate for most high-pay/high-skill jobs. (This includes about 50 percent of adult Americans).

Despite some overall worldwide basic literacy gains, many regions lag far behind. In South Asia, adult literacy is 55 percent, in Sub-Saharan Africa it is 60 percent (See Table 4.3). This is well below the 73 percent average of other developing nations.[38] Worldwide, an estimated 120 million elementary school age children do not attend any school (UNICEF, 2003). The majority, 65 million, are girls.

Though more adults have achieved basic literacy, high school attendance and graduation rates are very low in many nations (See Table 4.4). High school remains an essential educational component for basic career skills. One quarter of the earth's population still lives in countries unable to achieve universal primary education, let alone secondary education preparation for more complex careers.[39]

How will large areas of Asia, Latin America, the Middle East, and Africa ever build modern, stable societies without first having their people reach 21st-century world education standards? For the world's leading economies, this remains a major question. Lack of skills severely impedes economic development for any country and hurts the global economy as a whole.

The "Education for All" campaign of the world's richest nations has been organized to achieve universal primary education by 2015. One hundred-eighty nations have agreed to try to reach this goal. "For half the price of a stealth bomber, the rich countries could each tackle the education crisis in seven of the world's poorest countries and get millions of children in school," said Oliver Buston at Oxfam, a UK think tank.

The World Bank estimates the total cost of universal primary education by 2015 at between $32 and 37 billion a year. Of this, the United States and other developed countries need to donate $5 to 8 billion. Compared to larger military expenditures, this seems a very small down payment for combating the ignorance and unemployment that are the major breading grounds for tyranny and terrorism around the world.[40]

From this global review we can see that the 2010 meltdown offers a variety of people and job challenges to the European Union, Asia, Africa, and the Americas. These challenges beg for massive cultural rethinking about education and work in every society. Each of these regions faces different dilemmas but the same underlying issues of the 2010 meltdown remain: the demographic shift, technology, globalization, and developing better-educated people. These socioeconomic forces require local and national cultures around the world to adjust, and the sooner the better for everyone.

Table 4.4
No High School Education

Students not attending high school	
Country	**Percent**
Afghanistan	98
Bolivia	85
Brazil	75
Chile	38
China	60
Cuba	70
Haiti	91
India	85
Iraq	88
Laos	90
Libya	94
Morocco	96
Pakistan	86
Sudan	98
Vietnam	89
Yemen	95
Zimbabwe	86

Source: Encyclopedia Britannica Almanac 2003.

CONNECTING THE DOTS

The first half of *The 2010 Meltdown* has explored how a new, far different 21st-century New America has arisen. By 2010, technology, globalization, and a major worldwide demographic shift will drastically change our workforce. These forces, combined with too few entry-level, skilled technologists, will produce ominous people-shortages in workplaces across America, the industrialized world, and the developing world.

The ramifications of the socioeconomic changes in the past hundred years are little understood or even discussed across America. If these problems remain unaddressed, they will eventually weaken most American cities and regions. A growing underclass of techno-peasants may begin to eclipse the middle class if more people do not have better access to local high-quality education that enables them to qualify for higher-paying jobs (See Table 4.5).

The current lack of serious efforts by most U.S. communities in this regard can be linked to the U.S. business community's declining commitment to keeping more high-skill/high-pay jobs and operations in America, rather than relocating these jobs to wherever in the world tech-savvy people can be found. No country can remain a major economic power if too many of its high-end manufacturing, industrial, and service jobs disappear. To some extent, one result of this accelerating process is the record U.S. 2005 trade deficit that threatens a serious devaluation of the dollar. The future economic fate of every region of the United States

Table 4.5
Jobs & the Economy: A Century of Transition

	"Old" America 20th Century	Transitional Events	"New" America 21st Century
I.	Baby Boomers 72M (1946–62)	Lower Birth Rates (1970–2010)	Fewer Workers 40 M
II.	Mass Production Low-Skill/High-Wage Jobs	1970s PCs Introduced	High Tech = High/Skill/High-Wage Jobs
III.	National U.S. Economy	1991 – Fall of the Soviet Union	Globalization Takes Off
IV.	Long-Term Business View	1990s Bubble Economy	Short-Term Profits King
V.	Creating Jobs	2002, Post-Bubble	Outsourcing Low-Skill & High-Skill Jobs

Source: Edward E. Gordon, 2005.

is inherently connected to these events. Over the long term, every region needs to change its people and job development infrastructure to sustain a dynamic, internationally competitive U.S. economy.

The second half of *The 2010 Meltdown* will explore some of the positive solutions already at work across the United States and the world. Local people are now coming forward to act as effective community intermediaries before it is too late. This is a new integration of the cultural forces needed in every city and town to propel people and jobs through the 2010 crossroad and beyond.

III

STRUCTURING RENEWAL

5

Signposts at the Workforce Crossroad

Chance favors only the prepared mind.

—Louis Pasteur

THE UNITED STATES

From Mickey Mouse to Microchips

At one time a popular mental picture of Orange County, California was a vacationland of verdant orange groves stretching to the horizons. Now it is a magical world of living cartoon icons, space rides, pirates, romance, and Americana—where everyone lives happily ever after.

What Orange County visitors seldom notice is the considerable number of high-tech and manufacturing businesses, such as PowerWave Technologies and Textron Aerospace Fasteners, are located in towns like Santa Ana. The good news is that over the past decade Orange County added 250,000 jobs to its highly diversified economic base. The bad news is that Santa Ana was not part of this trend, losing 1 percent of the county's job market share. Though Santa Ana has the second-largest cluster of small manufacturers in the United States and its industry productivity is increasing, it lost 20,000 jobs during that time period. By 2002, while U.S. unemployment was 4.5 percent, it was 7.6 percent in Santa Ana.

Employers Confront Crisis

The Santa Ana Chamber of Commerce, concerned about this growing trend early on, convened a task force of business and education community leaders in the summer of 1998. Their mandate was to discover the roots of the local downturn and develop a long-term, strategic action plan.

What they learned wasn't pretty. Santa Ana was suffering from the same labor–market disconnect that can be found today in most American communities: Employee skill levels were failing to keep pace with market demands.

The mainstreaming of technology throughout the workplace and the rapidly changing and highly competitive global marketplace had left Santa Ana workers behind and threatened employers' viability. "A lack of skills had undermined productivity and narrowed profit margins for many large and small businesses in Santa Ana," says Dale Ward, executive vice president of the Santa Ana Chamber.

Just to stay competitive, many Santa Ana companies had been forced to recruit outside the U.S. for IT talent. Also, businesses had begun to outsource more and more production overseas to IT workers in Asia, Mexico, and even parts of Europe.

Adding to the dilemma of this under-skilled workforce were the demographic facts that many older skilled workers would soon retire and could not be easily replaced. Even though the median age in Santa Ana (2005) is 24 (nearly 10 years younger than the county median at 33), the demographic shortfall of younger entry-level workers was projected to grow until about 2020. Immigration would only partially offset this problem, since most new U.S. immigrants lack the IT skills that Santa Ana industries demand.

These combined labor–market forces were about to cause a major human resource crisis in Santa Ana.

The chamber's task force also uncovered a major disconnect between the programs of training providers and the needs of the business community. For decades, product-driven training providers have been building programs around the skills of their instructors, rather than the workers. This traditional approach to workforce development contributed to the widening gap between the skills needed and the skills achieved.

The task force concluded that any initiative designed to meet the needs of a born-again-and-again marketplace, which was rebirthing almost every 18 months, had to be business-needs driven. Many executives were uninformed about the future skill demands of the marketplace, placing even greater importance on the need for good information. How should the Chamber and its task force of local community leaders respond to this crisis?

The Chamber decided to focus first on the workplace, as it is here that productivity and profitability are determined. Realigning the thinking of the product-driven training providers and the needs-driven employers would enable both to concentrate on meeting the skill needs of the workplace. It was this demand-and-supply approach at the workplace that laid the foundation for the task force to make the critical link between day-to-day Santa Ana labor demands and supplying the job training needs of local businesses.

The task force's next challenge was how to establish a sustainable program that would gather vital intelligence on economic development and then deliver successful job training programs to the Santa Ana business community.

Up to that point, the Chamber had funded its workforce turnaround initiative almost exclusively with member investments. It was clear that new, market-savvy players would have to be brought into the collaborative effort to enable the Chamber to drive a street-smart initiative that could successfully deliver market-specific data and market-responsive training.

Initiative Takes Off

Eighteen months after the first meeting of the task force, the Chamber was awarded a contract by the local community college district to design and test a research and development infrastructure that would be the building block for a unique, countywide, multi-industry job training initiative. The result was Bridge to Careers, a non-governmental organization (NGO) structured to break through the traditional county-level forecasting barrier and deliver block-by-block market data.

The Chamber commissioned the research center at Cal State University–Long Beach to conduct a market and occupation forecast of the nine-city central Orange County and Santa Ana economies. In addition, it contracted with the Employers Group of California–Orange County for a workplace assessment of 18 businesses in key industries to determine how market demand meshed with workplace supply.

Six months later, the Chamber focused its market-defining lens on the local Empowerment Zone, a geographical area in Santa Ana with approximately 55,000 residents and 10 percent of the city's businesses. The Chamber proposed a research and development project that would not only identify the business and workforce needs of the Zone, but also further develop its Bridge to Careers model.

The Santa Ana Empowerment Corporation responded by awarding funds to design and construct a labor–market research and development infrastructure that would pinpoint and track the needs of local businesses and the training needs of some of the city's most needy residents. To ensure success, the Chamber again expanded its collaborative outreach by contracting with the Orange County Business Council for the research component.

At this writing, the Chamber-led private/public collaborative initiative includes six colleges and universities, the city of Santa Ana, four non-profit business organizations, approximately 100 large and small area businesses (including aerospace, chemical, automotive, financial services, healthcare, business support services, real estate, and other sectors) and resident leaders—all engaged in the design of a process for conducting an up-close and professional assessment of the workplaces and the workforce of the Empowerment Zone.

Formula for Success

Bridge to Careers has two essential components: the Research Center and the Workforce Institute.

The Research Center was established to provide the market forecast system. It collects relevant labor–market intelligence on an ongoing basis by using multiple data-gathering methodologies, including electronic surveys, personal interviews, and quick-response touch systems. This street-smart information is correlated with existing county, regional, national, and global data to determine the impact on the Santa Ana economy. The data from the Research Center will direct follow-up programs of workforce development and training offered through the Workforce Institute.

The Workforce Institute is the training arm that links school curricula to the skill needs of the businesses. Training programs are customized and include both classroom and workplace learning. One example is a program in the Mater Dei High School intended to assist this private institution in its ongoing effort to build technology knowledge across its college-preparatory curriculum.

The Workforce Institute also focuses on the training of incumbent workers in specific workplaces. Seven industries are targeted: automotive, business services, construction, healthcare, logistics, transportation, and new media.

Specific Institute services include:

- Customizing training programs to the immediate production needs of businesses;
- Developing career advancement programs for workers and businesses;
- Consulting with learning organizations in the design of curricula and instructor training programs;

- Consulting with city staff and elected officials on public policy development.

According to the Chamber's Dale Ward, "Bridge to Careers has re-energized boardrooms, classrooms, and City Hall by taking market information from the abstract to the specific and thereby making it useable in the development of business strategies, school curriculum, and government policy."

Ward, a former HR executive, also said, "Bridge to Careers establishes a permanent collaborative community program that gives employers the option to offer a new benefit to their employees that will increase their skills for current and future local technology jobs."

What is really important is that the Santa Ana Chamber of Commerce's NGO model, Bridge to Careers, provides an important blueprint that can be replicated by other like-minded community business leaders anywhere in the United States. This NGO initiative illustrates that market- and workplace-specific information will drive ROI-specific training for world-class IT jobs in Santa Ana or anywhere else in the United States. It will also help Mickey Mouse get out of the orange groves and onto the information highway of the 21st century.[1]

How Fargo, North Dakota Restarted the American Dream Machine

Many American corporate executives have turned to outsourcing to keep their companies competitive and maintain or increase profitability. This has spurred calls for tariff walls to protect American jobs. Is there an alternative way of staying competitive and still keeping jobs here? Economist Robert C. Feenstra contended in a 2003 *New York Times* article that the quality of the U.S. workforce needs to be improved as low-pay/low-skill jobs disappear over the horizon. That way, America will be able to obtain higher productivity through comparative advantage (i.e., producing low-cost, high-technology and high-value goods and services made by high-skill/high-pay workers). This is already happening in communities scattered across the United States, like Fargo, North Dakota.

Mowing Grass Faster

Fargo, North Dakota was founded in 1871 with the expansion of the Northern Pacific Railroad and named after William G. Fargo, one of the founders of the WellsFargo Express Company. It may seem an unlikely spot for economic development that relies largely on a smart, reliable, well-educated workforce, but the Fargo–Moorhead metropolitan area was named one of *Business Week's* "Dazzling Dozen" cities in 2002. It was pronounced "America's fifth-best small city" for business and careers by *Forbes* (2003), and won *Expansion Management* magazine's eighth overall ranking. Fargo's unemployment rate has been around two percent since companies began scrambling to exploit its unique, highly competitive labor market.

Over the past 10 years, companies have been moving to the Fargo–Moorhead region, bringing the number of businesses located there to over 1,700. This includes Microsoft's second-largest campus in the United States, with over 1,000 employees.

Justin Andrist at the Fargo–Cass County Economic Development Corporation says that since they began to promote economic growth through relocation, 24,000 jobs were added over the past 10 years, with 90,000 people currently employed. Companies with facilities there include Aggregate Industries, Quest Corporation, American Crystal Sugar, Microsoft Business Solutions, U.S. Bank Service Center, Innovis Health, Hornbacker's Foods, Rosenbluth International, and a host of others. While other communities could be described as still mowing grass with a manual mower, Fargo projects a job growth rate of about 3 percent in 2005.

John Campbell, the recent president of the Fargo–Moorhead Chamber of Commerce, proudly describes the area's culture as one that sustains a great work ethic among its younger workers. In addition, Fargo businesses have a compelling interest in education fostered by the area's 11 post-secondary institutions. This includes a Skill and Technology Training Center that has helped local industry retrain thousands of older workers for newer high-tech jobs.

Established in 1995, the Fargo Skills and Technology Training Center is at the heart of this job machine. It is a joint venture among the region's two- and four-year colleges. Companies send their incumbent workers there for retraining. But college students, high school students, and even unemployed workers also use this fee-for-service education operation. Thirty percent of the people come from a 100–150 miles radius to use these educational services.

"It is absolutely essential to today's society and marketplace to stay up-to-date," says Mel Olson, the center's director. The 55,000-square-foot center trains more than 1,000 people annually in such diverse areas as health care, welding, computer software, sheet-metal work, truck driving, computer repair and networking, and many other career areas.

It Takes Activists

The Skills and Technology Training Center and the other regional programs to update people's skills and attract new business aren't just an accident. Olson said that "[A]ggressive people in this city made the difference." In other words, community activists at the grassroots level have helped turn Fargo into a pocket of prosperity.

North Dakota ranks highest in the nation, and neighboring Minnesota ranks fourth, in community self-help organizing activity called social capital. This is a measure of the social connections among a community's individuals and their inclination to work together to get things done that help each other.

In his ground-breaking book, *Bowling Alone: The Collapse and Revival of American Community* (Simon & Schuster, 2000), Harvard University professor Robert C. Putnam makes the case for the renewed need of this kind community engagement. His "Social Capital Index" rates a community's engagement in public affairs, volunteer activities, the number of non-profit groups, overall attitude toward others, and social trust.

Fargo–Moorhead demonstrates this community willingness to address the difficult twin issues of job development and related economic renewal. The two cities rely on the core value of community activism.

North Dakota's unemployment rate was 3.2 percent in 2004. "We grow problem-solvers here because of our culture. Many of our people have become titans of industry," say Linda Butts, North Dakota's director of economic development and finance.

North Dakota's investment in human capital is a dramatic shift from the recent past. The implications for the United States are very important. In charting a business's future economic success, increasing personal knowledge is becoming far more important than just buying capital equipment. Cities and regions across America can influence and even reshape their future pattern of comparative advantage through increased community activism.

Communities such as Fargo have come to understand that they can be liberated from the confines of their geography with appropriate career education that can transform their population's industrial and economic future. Fargo saw the need for a new breed of well-educated Americans who not only have information technology skills, but also are well-rounded in their general education.

The United States will continue to pursue a competitive advantage in leading-edge technologies. However, unless more American communities follow the Fargo and North Dakota model, this strategy will ultimately fail.[2]

Look at your own organization and your own community. What are you waiting for? Become a community activist today for the sake of your business, your job, and maybe even your family's future. If you don't, who will?

Needed: Another *Shawshank Redemption*

Seventy miles southwest of Cleveland, Ohio, the town of Mansfield in Richland County was the site of the popular prison film *The Shawshank Redemption*. The movie was filmed at the local Ohio State Reformatory. Built in 1898, the Victorian castle-style prison was operated late into the 20th century to house up to 3,000 juvenile prisoners.[3]

But the prison wasn't the only industry in Mansfield. Machine-tool shops, a booming local steel mill, and other manufacturers employed thousands of Ohioans in this industrial heartland.

By 2004, Mansfield was an ex-industrial town. It never recovered from the rust-belt meltdown of the 1980s. The entire county remains economically depressed, with only a few auto-parts plants and a small steel mill struggling to survive. Mansfield is ranked fifteenth-worst out of 3,150 U.S. counties for job loss, with an unemployment rate of 11 percent.

Ticking IT Time Bomb

In the late 1990s, Ohio was prospering with the seventh-largest state economy. It was the third-largest manufacturing state, employing 1.1 million workers. Ohio was the number one U.S. manufacturer of plastics, fabricated metals, and rubber and also was home to a $9.2 billion chemicals industry.

At the same time, though, Ohio was not doing too well in preparing for the new IT economy. It was ranked 33rd in the United States by the Progressive Policy Institute (2000) in its degree of progress toward an Information-Age economy. Ohio is ranked 48th among all the states in new business start-ups (2004).

This is graphically shown in how well Richland County is doing. In 1970, 51 percent of workers were employed in manufacturing. Today this number is below 30 percent. Then, there were 12 manufacturing establishments with over 500 workers; now there are only five.

Mansfield is not the only city suffering from this industrial decline. The other central business cities in Ohio have not kept pace in terms of job growth or personal income. Ohio's overall development is weak, as next-generation businesses are migrating out of the state.

One clear reason for this exodus is an undereducated workforce. Ohio ranks 35th in overall educational attainment and 40th in the number of

Bachelor's degrees. In Richland County only 24 percent of adults hold an Associate degree and 9.4 percent hold a Bachelor's degree. What this means is lower incomes and a lesser likelihood that new industry will find Mansfield an attractive relocation destination.

As older workers retire, the remaining small manufacturers are desperately searching for new, entry-level skilled workers. So far, local recruiting has produced dismal results. Most of the talented young people leave Mansfield, searching for better career opportunities elsewhere.

Finding professionals is even more futile. A local Mansfield engineering firm recently conducted an intensive recruiting campaign. It could find only a single civil engineer in the state of Ohio, one in Pakistan, and another in Indonesia who might even consider interviewing for this local job.

Training Redemption

But a new, broad, local coalition is now forming to revive the local economy. Robert Zettler, vice president of workforce and community development at North Central State College (a two-year technical school), and Douglas Theaker, director of Richland County Job and Family Services, are determined to mobilize their community. Upon their invitation, I spoke to local business and education leaders on "Winning the Skill Wars" to spur workforce development. Both Zettler and Theaker believe that there is great potential for local industry to develop people through training and to attract new businesses to the area.

"It is critical for this county's leadership to recognize that only the redevelopment of our human capital will bring back real economic growth," says Zettler.

Theaker takes this a step farther. "The retraining of local welfare recipients as part of Richland County's welfare-to-work efforts are vital if we are to find the necessary people for entry jobs that can attract new business," he maintains.

Measuring ROI Is Key

What will mobilize business support for these worker retraining programs? Other potential key players, such as Kevin Nestor, the president of the local Chamber of Commerce, and Christopher J. McKinniss, the regional coordinator of the Ohio Economic Development Office, recommend using return on investment (ROI) for training as a useful strategy to mobilize business support for these worker retraining programs.

McKinniss said,

The more progressive companies in our region already know the value of employee education and training. They are already attempting to manage their training investment by calculating their ROI for training. These companies are going to move forward with greater efficiencies, higher profits, and a workforce prepared for whatever the future throws their way. Those organizations that don't value an educated workforce are going to be washed away with the receding tide of lost profits, wondering where they went wrong.... The decision-makers in business and industry have been given the message. They have heard the forecasts. Our only hope is that they believe the message, take the time to calculate their ROI for training investment, and make the decision to education and train.

From all these individual perspectives, one thing is very obvious: There was nowhere to go but up, and they believed that investing in worker training and education-to-career programs could help to rebuild the human capital of Mansfield.

Whether these local leaders would find another *Shawshank Redemption* depended on their ability to collaborate through a local workforce-development board for organizing and subsidizing these programs.

Results

Since my initial visit in 2001, here's what Mansfield community activists have accomplished:

- A Skills MAX Assessment of high-risk youth who have the capacity to become viable workforce members was begun.
- North Central State College then merged this assessment with the Megallan Career Pathway Program that allows individuals to identify and explore specific careers.
- The first Integrated Systems Technology (IST) Program in Ohio was inaugurated.
- A collaborative effort of General Motors and the United Auto Workers established a new tool and die lab facility and regional training center.
- The Training Workers in Manufacturing Industries Program aims to retrain about 3,000 underemployed workers for the latest, high-skill technical industries. This program was developed through the collaboration of General Motors, the North Central State College, Richland County Job and Family Services, and other area businesses and governmental bodies.

As Goes Mansfield?

I have found basically the same issues on the road to the 2010 crossroad in almost every region in the United States. Community leaders play key roles in convincing business people that they can create more long-term, lasting value by investing in quality workforce education. What has begun in Mansfield needs to be done at local community levels all over America by family-owned businesses and employee-owned concerns, as well as the publicly traded corporations and local government.

With the entire United States clearly facing a demographic skilled-worker meltdown, what is needed is another *Shawshank Redemption* for every American in the workplace.[4]

You Get What You Ask For

The worldwide oil crisis of 2004 has once again highlighted the need to strengthen the U.S. oil industry. This is, in part, due to an unprecedented demand for oil partly fueled by China's emerging economy. We are only at the beginning of a new energy era. Consider this fact: For every 1,000 people in the United States, there are 997 automobiles. For every 1,000 people in China, there are 2 to 3 cars. With the potential of one billion new Chinese car customers, the emerging demand for energy over the next 20 years staggers the imagination. Petrochemical and refining companies such as British Petroleum (BP) and Shell are mainstay employers along the Texas, Louisiana, and Mississippi Gulf coasts. In that region, home to America's largest complex of petrochemical industries, over 250 chemical plants and 30 refineries employ more than 30,000 process technicians. These companies import the crude oil from around the world and refine it for a vast American market. More than two-thirds of the nation's petro-chemicals are produced in this region.

As is the case with most other economic sectors in the United States, by the early 1990s the projected high number of baby-boomer retire-ments began sending shock waves through the industry. For instance, BP projected that by 2012, 80 percent of its hourly and first-level supervisors would retire at its Texas City, Texas refining plant near Galveston. This is a real crisis. In 1994 only three U.S. community or technical colleges offered an Associate degree in process technology, a key education component for staffing the oil industry.

Dennis A. Link, BP South Houston manager of learning and devel-opment, said, "[T]he refiners and petrochemical manufacturers may be forced to leave the United States if they could not recruit and develop a local high-performance workforce." This was unacceptable to him. Since the mid-1990s Link, a community activist, has collaborated with other industrial and community leaders in an endeavor to find a job development solution.

A major breakthrough occurred in 1994, led by a partnership between local industry and the College of the Mainland in Texas City. With strong support from this college, local industry, and the community, an Associate of Applied Science degree (AAS) was implemented with a unique, industry-driven curriculum in process technology.

College of the Mainland's associate vice president Bill Raley, along with representatives from local Texas City petrochemical companies, and other community and business leaders, formed an advisory committee to iden-tify core competencies of entry-level positions in process technology. As it became evident that there was great variance in the competency outcomes of existing process technology programs, they formed a non-governmental organization (NGO) adjunct to the Process Technology Education Program (PTEC) as a meaningful, two-year education answer. Members included representatives from business, unions, community colleges, universities, high schools, and community action groups.

This PTEC partnership model got top executive buy-in, since it estab-lished clear goals, expectations, and outcomes that met real business needs. At the same time, the NGO's flexible governance structure ensured that students would receive high-quality career education. This achieved win-win results for all the stakeholders.

According to Bill Raley, a successful NGO partnership needs:

- Vision
- Creativity
- Persistence
- Determination
- Trust and respect
- Prudent risk-taking.

A key factor for the success of PTEC was industry commitment to hire program graduates. This makes it vital that local businesses be involved in every step of building the classroom programs and the hand-on internship/apprenticeship learning components.

In 1997 PTEC used federal vocational education funds to form the Gulf Coast Process Technology Alliance (GCPTA). In 1999 the NGO then partnered with the Center for the Advancement of Process Technology (CAPT) and won grants from the National Science Foundation and the U.S. Department of Education. This allowed GCPTA to expand and improve curriculum development for process technology degrees. The success of the GCPTA has spurred the formation of similar process technology alliances across the United States in Oklahoma, New Jersey, Alaska, California, and North Dakota.

Today 40 such programs are preparing the next generation of petro-chemical workers. Six partner alliances now support local NGOs that help bridge the worlds of education and industry. At the local level in Texas City, Texas, 350 students (2004), including many minorities, are enrolled in this program. Their participation in the program initiated by the local NGO is helping to guarantee that America's refining and petrochemical businesses are not going to move offshore.

When 8-year-old Amparo Garza took his first plant tour at the BP Chocolate Bayou Chemicals Plant, he never dreamed that one day he would be a process technician just like his father. Amparo only knew that the plant fascinated him. Years later, that impression influenced his decision to earn an Associate degree in process technology at College of the Mainland. Professor Mike Cobb found Amparo to be a good student, stating, "His projects were always well-researched and documented. Amparo demonstrated excellent process skills."

During Amparo's last semester, BP began an internship program at its Texas City plant. Amparo qualified on his first job assignment in a record 23 days, outperforming the plant average of 67 days. He found his degree invaluable, providing a sold foundation in science, math, and plant safety. Amparo stated that "knowing how and why the equipment and systems operate, and understanding how to troubleshoot processes" provided him the tools to excel as a process technician.

In nearby Houston, Candie Boderek's husband was injured on the job, and she needed to find a career that could support them both. On the recommendation of her father, a manager at a petrochemical plant, Candie decided to earn her degree at Lee College, a community college 20 miles east of Houston. "My teachers told me you can go to college for two years and within five years of employment be making $60,000 to $80,000 a year," she said. "With the shift schedule, you only work six months out of the year, unless you want to work overtime, and then you make even more money."

Dr. Charles Thomas, department chair at Lee College, remembers, "Candie was a very dynamic student who was dedicated to achieving her goal. Although Candie actually started the interview process with Marathon Ashland Petroleum, LLC before she graduated, she declined an on-site interview because she wanted to finish her degree. As soon as she graduated, they contacted her."

Candie explains, "Entering this field has been a huge opportunity for me. "Being an operator is not a stressful job. You are there to make sure things are running properly, and the company provides a lot of ongoing training on safety and unit-specific processes. Plus, everyone I work with is very supportive."

In 2004 the College of the Mainland began its Collegiate High School Program, serving junior and senior high school students who are college-bound. The first group of 16 students (both male and female) included African Americans, Hispanics, and Anglos who were in the upper 25 percent of their classes. Collegiate High School combines high school and college credit courses during the students' last two years of high school, including optional summer school attendance. They can graduate with both a high school degree and an Associate degree in process technology. Students will immediately qualify for a job with BP, Shell, or other petrochemical producers. Once hired, they will be able to continue working toward a four-year college degree through a company tuition assistance program.

"This is an important new program," says BP's Dennis Link. "As we approach the 2010 crossroad, we need to increase the number of new good people to take our place. The continuing technical upgrading of our facilities to make them more environmentally efficient requires us to find these highly skilled process technicians. Even though the numbers from these career education programs are increasing, we still need more smart people."

The complex U.S. petrochemical industry has not pursued the path of outsourcing as a solution for skilled labor shortages. Instead, they invested the required capital in technology, combined with human development and career education, to keep themselves competitive from a U.S. base. Many of these petroleum companies are now foreign-owned, with American managers. They could have easily moved production elsewhere but do not do so, largely because of local American leadership that had a long-term vision of their industry's training and education needs.

Other U.S. business sectors need to do the same. It's your community's future that is now on the global job firing line. Training/education NGOs aren't born spontaneously; leadership starts at the local level, with you. You get what you ask for![5]

Mayberry Wakes Up!

Mount Airy is located in Surry County, North Carolina. Because background footage for *The Andy Griffith Show* was shot here, it has taken on a second identity as the Mayberry of this popular television show.

Mount Airy is a place with gently rolling green hills, tobacco fields, and a history of small furniture and textile manufacturing companies, many of which were family owned. "Mayberry" had an almost ideal mixture of rural life—a family-oriented community with farming and light industry that employed many generations of residents. Until lately.

Globalization and new technologies have turned this whole region inside out. Many textile manufacturers have gone to Mexico to utilize the lower-wage workers there. The furniture industry also seems intent on outsourcing much of its business to China. German high-tech equipment, combined with low-wage Chinese labor, will make competitively priced furniture for the U.S. market.

The labor force in Surry and neighboring Yadkin County declined by more than 2 percent between 1995 and 2000. Younger workers are seeking jobs elsewhere. The tax base is also falling as the population becomes older. Since September 11, 2001, and the following economic downturn, a real sense of crisis has settled on community leaders.

But there is hope, too. "Small and larger sock manufacturers, such as Renfro Corporation and Sara Lee," says Tom Carter of the local State Employment Security Commission, "have introduced new technology and retrained with willing workers to operate it." In a cooperative spirit, sock producers banded together in a consortium to train workers and speed the development and use of new technology. The consortium's aim was to position U.S. plants as high-quality producers of socks and keep American jobs in North Carolina.

New wineries are springing up around the region, replacing some of the smaller tobacco farmers. "Mayberry Days" each year attracts tourists from across the United States, who might someday also seek diversion in potential winery tours, antique and craft malls, golf courses, hiking, and resorts with restaurants and hotel accommodations.

In December 2002, Angelou Economics was hired by the Northwest Piedmont Council of Governments and the Mount Airy Chamber of Commerce. It developed a strategic five-year plan to build on the region's strengths, as well as to change the culture regarding career expectations as this region's residents prepare for the 2010 crossroad. The overall vision offered by the report was that "Yadkin County's natural beauty, strategic location, dedicated workforce and infrastructure together create a great location for business development, tourism, and fine wines."

The strategic plan focused on economic development opportunities for the Mount Airy region in the following areas:

- Expand the viticulture industry (wineries)
- Develop a center for fine crafts and design

- Expand tourist facilities (outdoor recreation)
- Develop biotechnology education for the Winston–Salem Bio-Tech Center
- Enlarge health care facilities
- Retrain the growing Hispanic population.

To further these initiatives, in 2003 the Yadkin Center was opened in association with Surry Community College to create more workers for these targeted industries. This has meant a major expansion of the college's programs.

Yadkin County has seen an increase in its Hispanic population during the past decade. The strategic plan calls for a major expansion of the Yadkin Center, such as local English as a second language (ESL) programs. They will be tied into specific workforce training programs geared toward the Hispanic population.

The elementary and secondary schools of Yadkin and Surry counties had been overcrowded and using outdated curricula. The strategic plan envisions a strong tie-in to career education that will better prepare local children for tomorrow's job opportunities.

These are tough economic change issues. Mount Airy and the surrounding area have the potential to move to this next phase of its cultural evolution. As we all approach the 2010 crossroad, this community, along with many others, is faced with the same basic question: How much cultural willpower do local leaders possess to move their community on the road toward a New America, or will they be unable to overcome roadblocks and remain stuck in the past?[6]

Timing is Everything! The Philadelphia Academies, Inc.

In 1968 Philadelphia experienced some of the worst riots in the city's history. Economic stagnation, poverty, and soaring unemployment had planted the seeds of growing discontent. In tackling this crisis, community, business, education, labor and government leaders forged a new coalition. They decided to focus on the soaring high school dropout rate.

What was born from that collaboration was the so-called Academy Model for a schooling revolution. The first modern U.S. career academy was born the following year—the Electrical Academy at Edison High School, supported by the Philadelphia Electric Company. Thirty students were enrolled, who were promised employment upon their graduation.

Career academies are usually partially self-contained small schools within larger high schools. They differ from the public's perception of vocational education because they prepare high school students for both work and college.

Philadelphia Academies, Inc. gradually organized programs in 13 fields: automotive and mechanical science, aviation and aerospace, business, communications, environmental technology, health, information technology, fine arts, and other career areas. Today the Academy Model is flourishing in Philadelphia, with an enrollment of approximately 8,000 students in 24 high schools, 2 middle schools, at 33 academy program sites and 23 non-academy sites receiving career services.

These career academies educate students for a wide variety of careers in a given field. They provide a foundation that students can combine with more advanced, post-secondary education. What interests parents and students alike is how the career academy can combine this with a rigorous liberal arts curriculum that will qualify a student for admission to a four-year college or university. In essence, they have become what could be called a liberal arts career academy that combines the best of both types of education preparation.

The Philadelphia Academies have an independent board operating under one non-profit organization. This model has attracted wide business and community participation in the academies, while providing a management structure to interface with the public schools. Since these academies are financed by corporate contributions and foundation grants, they are neither tied to the local political culture nor to fluctuations in government funding. The Philadelphia Academies manage and finance these programs. The school district provides the teachers and classrooms. Long-term results have been impressive. About 90 percent of graduates continue in post secondary education or go to work. Academy students outperform their peers in attendance, promotion rates, and senior graduation rates.

"The Academies are a win-win proposition," says Connie Majka, director of Public Relations and National Partnerships. "Our graduates gain a brighter future, business gains a better-prepared workforce, and Philadelphia gains citizens ready for the New America of the 21st century."[7]

Gold-Collar Workforce

Like most American kids, when Chad Toulouse was growing up he was encouraged by his parents to go to college. His mother found a secretarial job at a nearby Pennsylvania college so that her two sons would qualify for a tuition break.

Chad struggled, like many of his friends, to identify a career interest, though he went to college for a year. He lost interest and dropped out.

Chad began working at a gas station while taking classes at a community college. By chance, he saw a television commercial about how to become a skilled machinist; a light bulb turned on. Chad signed up for an 18-week Manufacturing 2000 program at Duquesne University, sponsored by a consortium of local metal-working businesses. He got a job at graduation

Three years later, Chad works at Flowserve, Inc. in a bright, clean plant filled with computers as well as traditional metal-working machines, most of which are automated. "Some people find it hard to catch on to running machines, but its something I've always enjoyed," he says. "I'm not meant for an office or a cubicle." Chad, at age 24, is now a team leader and figures out how to divide the tasks for 70 other workers. He made about $45,000 last year. There are countless other students like Chad, but they never make the connection between their personal interests and aptitudes, and a high-wage/high-skill career that suits them.[8]

At the heart of the problem is an antiquated American culture that divides most of the workforce into two worlds: white-collar managers and professionals who are in the upper and middle American classes, and blue-collar manual laborers who mostly remain in the lower classes. Yet this leaves out a new class of worker—the skilled technology worker. These are well-educated people with a highly skilled, multi-disciplinary education. They combine the liberal arts education of the traditional white-collar career with advanced technical know-how across a range of careers. They are armed with a solid education in English, history, math, and science, as well as special career preparation. These so-called gold-collar workers are making major contributions to their employers, the economy, and themselves. Gold-collar workers are urgently needed in skilled technology careers across America and the world.[9] But how do we convince millions of parents and their children that this culture change is not only a new reality, but that it is also desirable?

Brave New World

From Santa Ana to Philadelphia, local community activists are struggling to bridge the jobs and careers culture gap between Old America and New America. They all feature specific local responses to meet growing community economic needs. Here are some additional snapshots of how many others are already building a brave new world of career opportunity.

- *Tulsa Tech Center* (Tulsa, Oklahoma). A partnership activated through the Chamber of Commerce brought about an expanding collaboration between business and education. Tulsa Tech has four campuses that offer 75 full-time and 150 part-time tech programs. About 1,900 public and private high school students are enrolled in four-year career programs: two years in high school, two years at Tulsa Tech, and an apprenticeship or internship job training experience. Also, 37,500 adults are pursuing studies to update their education and skills. Companies of all sizes use these career/ worker education programs: American Airlines, Kimberly–Clark, Nordan, Webco, Whirlpool, TriStar Aerospace, Boeing, and a host of others.[10]

- *The Met* (Providence, Rhode Island). The Met is a public high school composed of six separate buildings, each with a principal and about 120 students from diverse cultural, ethnic, and socioeconomic backgrounds. Its Learning through Internships Curriculum philosophy is to educate one student at a time within a diverse community of learners using many kinds of learning experiences. Each student has an internship site mentor, who also collaborates with the student's teacher on progress and learning. Through readings, meetings, and conference attendance, the student experiences the workplace as a community of learners. Parents sign an agreement supporting the teacher in understanding and educating their child. Parents must provide 10 hours of community service each school year. They participate in all formal curriculum-building activities for their child—developing quarterly learning plans and serving as panel members at quarterly student exhibitions. The non-profit Big Picture Company founded The Met, which also received support from the Bill and Melinda Gates Foundation.[11]

- *San Clemente High School Auto Tech Academy* (California). This academy is one of the relatively few high school programs that offer realistic preparation for high-tech auto repair careers. An important feature is that the program gives another chance to many students who have struggled in traditional classrooms and might have dropped out. Students at the auto academy do take a full program of liberal arts courses in math, science, English, and history. They also take increasingly complex auto technology classes four times a week. Dozens of local automobile dealers and repair shops provide internships. With entry-level jobs beginning at $30,000 a year (rising to $60,000 after five years), these high-tech students aren't grease monkeys anymore. Nationwide, the number of these tech jobs is projected to grow from 818,000 in 2004 to 919,000 by 2012, with about 32,000 jobs being created each year (U.S. Bureau of Labor Statistics).[12]

- *Biotechnology Academy and Biomanufacturing-Technology Academy, Minuteman Regional High School* (Lexington, Massachusetts). The Biotechnology Academy is the oldest on the East Coast. Its four-year program balances a liberal arts education with courses in bioethics, genetics, and honors courses in math, chemistry, physics, and extensive lab experiences. Coursework alternates between one week of liberal arts subjects, followed by one week of biotechnology courses. Students also are educated in related career skills. Almost all biotechnology students enter college, compared to 60 percent of all Minuteman Regional High School students. The sister program, the Biomanufacturing-Technology Academy, though less rigorous, prepares student for careers as laboratory technicians, quality control lab inspectors, manufacturing technicians, and other medical areas. Students in both academies can get college credit at local post-secondary institutions. Both programs also offer internships and job-shadowing with local biotechnology companies such as Biogen and Genzyme Corp. Other biotechnology academies can be found in San Diego, Seattle, the Silicon Valley, North Carolina's Research Triangle, Miami, and Baltimore.[13]
- *Construction Careers Center (CCC)* (St. Louis, Missouri) This center is a public charter school controlled by local construction companies and unions that combine the liberal arts with construction arts. Organized by local construction companies who are eagerly looking for racially diverse enthusiastic workers. The CCC tailors everyone a college entrance curriculum or entrance to union apprenticeship carpentry, masonry, electrical or plumber programs. Reggie Royers, 15, explains why the program attracted him, "I plan to go to college. But I like having this as back up support." Similar construction career academies have opened in Reno, Nevada, Philadelphia and Cranston, Rhode Island.[14]
- *Cristo Rey Jesuit High School* (Chicago, Illinois). The concept is to allow at-risk kids with the right attitude to use internships to work their way through a liberal arts college prep education. The reality is that 95 Chicago firms provide 130 jobs for 520 students every year. They earn about $6,250, with their parents contributing $2,400 a year. For example, Christo Rey High School is located in Chicago's Pilsen neighborhood—an urban area that struggles daily with poverty and gang violence. Students are bused once a week to internship jobs they share at Sidley & Austin, Madison Dearborn Partners, Loyola Medical Center, McKinsey & Co., B.W. Baird & Co., museums, and other business. Since 1995, Christo Rey has

combined challenging college prep courses, a personalized, supportive setting, and motivating curricula include internships. "It's bringing to America's poorest communities the three Rs: rigor, relationship, and relevance," says Marie Groark of the Bill and Melinda Gates Foundation that supports the program. Ninety-three percent of the students in this program begin college; in the eight years since its inception, 82 percent had graduated from college or were still attending a post-secondary institution. The Gates Foundation is also assisting other schools in Los Angeles, Portland, Detroit, and Austin, Texas using the Cristo Rey model. Plans are in the works for similar schools in Waukegan, Illinois; Cleveland; New York City; Boston (two); and Tucson, Arizona.[15]

- *Center for Advanced Research and Technology (CART)* (Clovis and Fresno, California). This charter high school in San Joaquin, California's Central Valley, combines a liberal arts curriculum with careers in the professional sciences, advanced communications, global business, and engineering. Eleventh- and twelfth-grade students from nearby high schools are bused to CART where they attend half-day classes in state-of-the art labs. This center is funded by companies such as Cisco Systems, Microsoft, Wells Fargo, Kaiser Permanente, SBC, Community Medical, and many others. Employees from these companies partner with teachers in class instruction. At CART, students team up to work on socially relevant projects such as investigating mock homicides, presenting research on local social issues, and engineering new products for the disabled. Physics, chemistry, English, or history are combined to provide comprehensive information for these projects. CART is designed mainly for average or below-average students. They are at higher risk of dropping out, and are not prime candidates for college and/or technology-based careers. CART offers systemic culture change through business–education collaboration that expands the future career opportunities for San Joaquin Valley students.[16]
- *New Technology High School* (Napa, California). Since 1996 about 650 graduates of New Technology High School have gone on to top colleges and internships with nearby Silicon Valley companies. Besides taking a liberal arts curriculum and technology courses, New Tech's 285 students must pass four college courses at Napa Valley Community College, complete 20 hours of community service, and serve a year-long, career-based internship. About half of these are technology-related, the others range from shadowing a professional pastry chef to assisting a physical therapist. Microsoft,

Hewlett-Packard, and others helped plan and support New Tech. The New Tech Foundation is at present helping eight additional northern California high schools adapt this curriculum and model to their local communities.[17]

Connecting the Dots

The more than 2,500 career academies in operation across America today are effectively bridging the gap between the current American popular culture and viable future careers for high school students.

As we have seen, the career academy model has been around for a long time, first appearing in Philadelphia. But parents want to know how successful these academies are as a way of helping their children on the road to reaching the American dream.

The answer may be in an eight-year review by MDRC, a nonpartisan education and social policy research group. They studied over 1,400 students at nine career academies during their four high school years and the four years after their expected graduation. What they found out about career academies should be of profound interest to parents and students alike:

- Academies are very good at preparing students for both college and personal careers.
- Career education produces "substantial and sustained job prospects" for students.
- Career academies are one of the few education programs that truly improve the job prospects of young men.[18]
- Students who attend a career academy are as likely as other, nonacademy high school students to enter two- or four-year college programs. Career academies can be designed so that the four-year college option is clearly left open.

"It does not need to be an 'either-or' proposition between academies and career-focused teaching," says James Kemple, the report's author. "We are seeing evidence that this choice need not be made."

At Santa Ana's Valley High School Global Academy of Finance, students clearly benefited from this program. It was one of four California schools that took part in this eight-year study. Many Santa Ana students face personal economic and learning challenges. These underprivileged academy students received a significant earnings boost with higher salaries than other high school students within four years of graduation, the MDRC study found.[19]

In New York City, the Manpower Demonstration Research Corporation completed a 10-year study of career academies. They discovered that only 21 percent of at-risk students enrolled in a career academy dropped out of high school, compared to 32 percent in non-academy programs.[20]

Yet critics have charged that these programs short-change students by focusing on practical skills instead of on a broader liberal arts education. Quality varies widely among career academies. Some programs have struggled with classrooms filled with a local company's cast-off equipment or obsolete computers.

Since their inception over 30 years ago, significant changes have gradually improved most career academies. To that end, the National Career Academy Coalition, the Career Academy Support Network, the National Academy Foundation, and Talent Development High Schools have collaborated on developing standards of best practice for career academies. Their intent is to place a renewed emphasis on melding the liberal arts with career education, thereby educating the whole child for a lifetime, not just preparation for a job. Remedial programs have also spread, since it is difficult to jump-start any high school student who is already far behind academically.

The career academy's smaller size and individual attention can also give a student substantial extra time to be coached on the mechanics of being a successful student such as meeting class deadlines or taking meaningful class notes. These basic, learning-how-to-learn skills are needed for higher education, future jobs, and for a successful, meaningful life in the 21st century. Career academies are better at teaching these skills because they are embedded in both a quality liberal arts curriculum combined with exposure to real career settings. Many students need this approach of taking the theory and putting it into hands-on practice. Career education gives many more students a greater feeling of personal academic competence and confidence in their future.

For almost everyone, career academies are a win-win situation. More students go on to start and complete college; students are guided to careers that better reflect their individual interest and aptitudes; and fewer students drop out of high school. They are better prepared by a more rigorous liberal arts education, by career-oriented courses, and by paid or unpaid career-related work activities to find high-wage/high-skill technology, professional, or business occupations.

Kevin Hollenbeck, at the W. E. Upjohn Institute for Employment Research confirmed these many positive results for most students. He believes that career programs built around a strong liberal arts curriculum can connect the important cultural dots for students and parents alike. They provide the vital link between individual life aspirations and the high-skill/high-wage jobs that need to be filled in every local American community.[21]

"Get 'Em While They're Young"

Sultan, Washington is an old lumber mill town just north of Seattle. In the late 1960s Boeing constructed a huge 747 plant in nearby Everett. High-tech industries serving the plant developed along Interstate 405. All this development brought major population increases to the area. At the same time, lumber production, fishing, and farming began to decline, economically depressing smaller communities like Sultan, Gold Bar, and Index. Local residents lacked the skills to work in the high-performance workplace and had little personal inclination or educational opportunity to change.

I traveled to Sultan (named after a local Indian chief), and met with local parents, students, and educators. We discussed what is happening in the American workplace and how to adequately prepare students with education for the high-tech careers of today and tomorrow.

In 1996, Boeing responded with its Tech Prep Program. This allows high school students to learn aircraft technician manufacturing skills through paid internship programs that earn college credits. The Boeing Tech Prep Program combines two years of a high school curriculum with two years at a local community college. These rigorous applied academics and technology courses lead to an Associate degree in manufacturing technology.

Boeing continues to experience the typical up and down cycles in the aircraft manufacturing industry. However, it still needs to address the compelling business need for younger knowledge technologists who can more competently build its 777s and new 787 aircraft.

Washington state and its business communities are trying to fill this knowledge worker shortfall. According to Carver Gayton of the Washington State Employment Security department, "Throughout the state, 60 high schools are using workplace standards developed in Washington to teach students in career programs the skills required for 21st-century employment."

Boeing has successfully hired more than 100 students through its Tech Prep Program. In 2004, about 62 students were participating in three states with Boeing manufacturing facilities.

Rick Stephens, vice president and general manager of Boeing Space and Communications, says there are three phases required to establish and maintain a successful career education program:

Phase I   Share data and start collaborative discussions
Phase II   Develop a common language among players (e.g., business, schools, unions, government)
Phase III   Highlight and promote programs. Facilitate and collaborate efforts inside and outside of business, schools, unions, government agencies, community organizations.

"Boeing is involved in career education because it needs a solid foundation for a diverse, skilled and motivated workforce within its manufacturing business," says Stephens.[22]

More companies are beginning to reluctantly understand the severity of future skilled labor shortages they will face at the 2010 crossroad. Savvy businesses also expect declining HR returns from past solutions—outsourcing, foreign direct investment (FDI), or H-1B visas for temporary guest workers. Therefore, more and more employers are investing in career programs for students. Some begin with students in elementary schools in a quest to lock in a long-term, skilled workforce. They hope to stimulate student and parent interest and awareness of exciting career opportunities. Such programs might be termed HR insurance policies that will help secure a continuous future flow of qualified, high-skill job applicants.

A liberal arts career academy corresponds to business support that began one hundred years ago for the system of tax-supported public schools. Both then and now, these actions are not prompted by philanthropy, but are prompted by very real business interest—survival!

Liberal arts career academies are no longer isolated programs. More employers will migrate in that direction to retrain their own workers. Even *The Wall Street Journal* reported as early as 1999 that, in response to their inability to recruit knowledgeable, new entry-level workers, "farsighted companies are helping high schools across America teach today's skills instead of yesterdays."[23]

Intel is one of those companies. In 2001 Gordon Moore, one of the principal founders of Intel Corporation, pledged $600 million to the California Institute of Technology. This is by far the largest donation ever given to a U.S. college or university. Moore, a Cal Tech alumnus, contributed the money because, he said, "I've seen their needs develop over the last several years . . . opportunities that they could not pursue because there wasn't the money."

This was at a time when Intel Corp. was eliminating 5,000 jobs. Yet an important company long-term goal still remains in place: To ensure that its new plants in Colorado, Massachusetts, or elsewhere in the United States and around the world can find enough knowledge technologists.

To that end, in early 2001 Intel sent 5 executives and 12 community college presidents and deans on a three-day tour of four model community colleges in New Mexico and Texas. This trip occurred because Intel had learned at the height the 1990s tech bubble that skilled workers to operate chip plants are scarce. Training programs can't be turned on and off like a spigot. "If we don't invest now, the students won't be there when we need them," says Intel's Keith Baumgardner.

The job just hadn't been done by previous Intel education initiatives— sprinkling scholarships across the country, hiring some interns, and donating new or used tech equipment to schools. In other words, typical corporate educational charity and standard industry practices weren't enough. This past level of business culture support failed to ensure Intel an adequate supply of highly skilled workers. "We just sort of figured we hire whomever we could hire," said Roger Cook, a manager at the Albuquerque plant.

But times have changed. Intel's unskilled jobs went overseas or were automated out of existence. Today most new hires must have at least two years of college, higher math, physics, and chemistry.

Intel sees the supply of skilled workers as critical. It has expanded its career education programs to help supply a stronger human capital knowledge foundation upon which the entire company depends. In chief executive Craig Barrett's view, "There are certain things that Intel does that provide returns to the company on a long-term basis." The same point of view goes for the rest of the country.[24]

Here is a representative cross-section of business-sponsored "get 'em while they're young" career programs across America:

- Hewlett-Packard supports about 70 U.S. school districts with an enhanced math and science Scholar Program. This is part of a larger career initiative called Diversity in Education wherein HP offers jobs to students right after their freshman year of college. Says HP's Cathy Lipe, "The summer internships and working with HP mentors are the key to their retention in their major."
- Advanced Micro Devices (AMD) provides $1.1 million to education institutions in communities surrounding its sites. The Math and Science Summer Academy at the Del Valle Independent School District in Texas, is a six-week program for 700 students

incorporating hands-on learning and field trips to AMD and other local companies.[25]

- Citigroup's investment banking arm has curtailed outsourcing to Bangalore, India by hiring Boston-area college undergraduates as interns. It gives talented students a crack at entry-level banking experiences. The bank has hired about 100 college-student interns— many from MIT.[26]

- The Higher Education and Advanced Technology Center (HEAT) in Denver, Colorado is a collaborative career effort between local community colleges and corporations including Cisco Systems, Intel, Lucent Technologies, Miller Electric, Haas Automation, and Parametric Technology. These companies provide state-of-the-art facilities on the new technologies they use every day to educate future gold-collar workers in such technologies as electronics manufacturing, laser troubleshooting, precision joining, electron-optics and fiber optics, vacuum systems, biotech manufacturing, and digital film and video production. HEAT also trains K–12 teachers on how to offer their students classroom instruction in these new technologies.[27]

- ExploraVision is national science and math competition for elementary and high school students. The focus of this contest is to project new technologies that might be used 20 years from now. Toshiba Corp. sponsors the year-long competition of student teams, and it is administered by the National Science Teachers Association. The contest encourages students to discover and learn science while envisioning its future applications. One winner was the "Nanoclotterator" (La Jolla High School, California), an injectable blood-clot-eating robot of microscopic proportions that could be used to prevent blood clots. Bill Schlotter, a 1998 first-place team winner, is now in Stanford University's Ph.D. program in applied physics and is working on the engineering of walking robots (2004). Student members of the four first-place teams receive $10,000 savings bonds; -second-place winners receive $5,000 bonds.[28]

- Achievement Counts is a career education initiative of the Maryland Roundtable for Education, sponsored by corporations such as Kaiser Permanente, Legg Mason, Infinity Broadcasting, State Farm Insurance, IBM, Verizon, Lockheed Martin Corporation, and many others. Achievement Counts offers interactive, informational programs including Maryland Scholars, a Speakers Bureau, Teen Web, and Parents Count. Maryland Scholars helps students make a realistic connection between what they learn in school and their future ability to go to college and get a good job. Business volunteers go into eighth-grade classrooms just prior to when students will select high school courses, and again in ninth grade. All students are encouraged to enroll in the Maryland Scholars Course of Study throughout high school (four years of English, three years of math and science, 3½ years of social studies, and two years of a foreign language). The Speakers Bureau places more than 1,200 business volunteers before ninth-graders to bridge the gulf between classroom learning and what the world expects. Hearing from a person outside the student's immediate world can have a dramatic and lasting motivational impact. Teen Website is a teen-oriented website devoted to career information. Students helped design the Web site so it's edgy and fun. It demonstrates the kinds of skills a career requires, relates career stories of young workers, and provides college, scholarship, and job information. It also gives students a chance to ask questions and get straight answers from career experts (see www.mbrt.org/teenweb). Parents Count reaches to parents through their workplace e-mail, news-letters, local newspapers, school bulletins, and a Web site. This information program gives practical, useful, down-to-earth point-ers on child learning, staying in school, homework, achievement, careers, and much more. The basic message is that parents begin the cultivation of the learning seed, schools nurture the plant, and adulthood is where careers bloom.[29]

• *FIRST* (For Inspiration and Recognition of Science and Technology) is a non-profit group founded by Dean Kamen (the Segway inven-tor) that sponsors programs to motivate young people to pur-sue careers in science, technology, and engineering. The FIRST Robotics Competition is an annual event that attracted 928 high school teams in 2004—over 20,000 students from across the United States, Canada, Brazil, Mexico, Ecuador, and the United Kingdom. They worked with professional engineering and business men-tors to design and build a robot and compete in 26 regional and international championship events that measure the effectiveness of each robot and the strengths of each team. Business spon-sors include John Abele/Boston Scientific Corporation, Baxter International, Inc., DaimlerChrysler, Delphi Automotive Systems, General Motors, Johnson & Johnson, Motorola, Xerox Corp., NASA, and many others. FIRST students are eligible for over $4.9 million every year in scholarship funds. FIRST is much more than a contest; it's building a student team synergy and motivation through exploring new, exciting ideas. Twelfth-grader Andrea Triba of Wilmington, Delaware played varsity soccer until it become monotonous. Then she joined her school robotics club. "It's more of a challenge than sports," she said. "You're always learning."[30]

Why should companies get involved in career education? Lynn Olson, senior editor of *Education Week*, in her book *The School-To-Work Revolution* (Addison Wesley, 1997), listed eight major reasons relevant to any small business owner, corporate executive, or just business people concerned about the future of America and the business in which they work. Such involvement can produce the following benefits to businesses:

1. Reduce "the cost of identifying, screening and training candidates."
2. Provide immediate, short-term benefits, since young workers can be productive and contributing employees.
3. "Increase the pool of qualified applicants and fill labor shortage in high-demand fields."
4. "Ensure that applicants meet their needs by working more closely with schools on education and training." Local businesses can directly influence the quality of the schools by constantly communicating what they need.
5. "Increase the diversity of their workforce" by recruiting young women and members of minority groups into underrepresented occupational areas.
6. "Directly teach the work ethics and employability skills that they want."
7. "Enhance the skills and the morale of their existing workforce." Many employees frequently find their own enthusiasm at work and learning lifted by mentoring and coaching young people.
8. Help support an education revolution. Companies complain about the schools' inability to provide enough entry-level workers. Here is a chance to get really involved "where the rubber meets the road" and do something about fulfilling your HR needs.

Supporting career education is partly a community service activity. However, the potential ROI of career education for almost any business can be considerable if it becomes a serious, consistent effort. "Corporations can't ignore education forever," say Nancy Shiels of Children's Hospital in Boston." Since government hasn't been adequately preparing students for real jobs in the rapidly changing workforce, I think it only makes good business sense for the business community to step in.... So why not invest their resources sooner, where it's really going to count?" Business people will each have to ask that vital question for themselves.[31]

Workforce education initiatives are also being developed around the world. Here are some highlights from Asia and the European Union.

ASIA

South Korea Tops Out

In 2000, South Korea for the first time led the world in its investment in education as a percentage of gross domestic product. Its 7.1 percent surpassed the United States (7.0%) and many other wealthy industrial nations.

South Korea also seems to get more bang for its educational buck. It vaulted ahead (2002) of America in the proportion of its younger population that has completed at least high school and entered post-secondary educational institutions.

Only 49 percent of South Koreans who are now aged 45 to 54 finished high school. Nevertheless, it has bolted to the leading nation spot by now having 95 percent of its younger citizens (aged 25 to 34) completing high school. In comparison, the United States dropped from 1st to 9th place for the same age group (See Figure 5.1).

South Korea's culture has also supported other impressive gains. In the percentage of its people completing a college education, it moved from

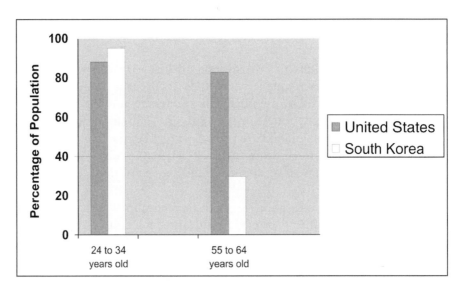

Figure 5.1—Secondary School Completion Rates, United States and South Korea
Source: OECD, 2002.

17th a generation ago to 3rd place (2003). Norway now has the top spot, nudging the U.S. into second place.

Barry McGaw, the OECD's director of education, commenting on South Korea's impressive gains, said that these changes will have a long-term impact because "[T]he biggest contribution to a nation's economic growth comes from increases in the skills of its labor market."[32]

Southeast Asia Banks on Education

The leaders of southeast Asia fear their nations might lose foreign direct investment unless they produce more skilled workers. Few cultural issues are more important to them than education.

From a policy standpoint, it was widely believed that, before the region's 1997 economic downturn, education largely had created the so-called Asian Tigers and was propelling their breakneck economic growth. Today it is still the cultural icon that politicians believe will fuel economic expansion.

For good reason, then, two-thirds or more of all children in Singapore, Malaysia, Thailand, the Philippines, and even Vietnam attend high school. Singapore's students regularly are at the top in international comparisons of students' math and science knowledge.

Thailand has extended its compulsory education from 9 to 12 years (most U.S. states require only 10 years). Thailand is considering providing up to 15 years of free education! Malaysia has targeted 40 percent of its students for university enrollment by 2010, and Vietnam has embraced private education to help fuel expansion. Twenty-three private universities have opened since 1993, enrolling more than 100,000 students.

Singapore has gone on a step farther—billing itself as a global school-house. It invited the University of Chicago and France's INSTEAD to establish local branches of their business schools. This is in addition to nine other foreign university affiliations with Singaporean educational institutions. By 2013 the city-state hopes to attract 100,000 foreign students to its shores, borrowing an economic driver from the U.S. playbook. On the horizon are Singapore's plans for expansion of private high schools as well as culinary academies and arts schools.[33]

EUROPE

Bridging Europe's Skills Gap

Most Americans will be surprised to learn that the European Union (EU) long ago (1998) surpassed the United States as the world's biggest trading block partner. That year, the EU garnered a 19 percent share of world trade versus the United States at 16 percent.[34] Stronger exports are at least partially the result of Europe's response to career education. In an earlier book, *Skills Wars* (Praeger, 2000), this author gave a rundown on the strengths and weaknesses of individual national career education programs.[35]

Since then, the Europeans have continued working on the better integration of each others' career education efforts by allowing more people access to cross-border programs. And for good reason, since Europe's demographic meltdown has begun producing local skills gaps. When asked about the causes of high unemployment, 64 percent of Europeans cited lack of training and education; 87 percent thought improving these opportunities was a high priority for combating unemployment.[36]

At their 2000 Lisbon summit, EU leaders acknowledged that future competitiveness depends on a renovated education policy and lifelong workforce training. They committed to:

- Increase the percentage of GDP investment in education.
- By 2010, halve the number of 18- to 24-year-olds who do not enroll in post-secondary career programs.
- Define the new European "basic skills": IT skills, foreign languages, technological culture, entrepreneurship, and social skills.[37]

In the New Europe, efforts are now being made to overcome the cultural barriers to labor mobility between countries (see Chapter 1). Between 1987 and 1999 more than 1 million students, teachers, and trainers used the EU's Socrates, Leonardo da Vinci and Youth programs to experience life in another country. There they learned foreign language skills and took advantage of international career education opportunities.[38]

Employment agencies in 17 EU countries now share information about job openings through a network run by the European commission, called Eures. This helps provide the bridge from areas where jobs are scarce to where they are plentiful.

This was certainly the case when 37-year-old Gerd Niebelschutz finished his hospital residency in Germany. Instead of joining the ranks of some 10,000 other unemployed German doctors, Dr. Niebelschutz migrated to Norway. There he joined more than 100 other physicians from Germany, France, and Austria who had relocated to fill a local health-care shortage.

"Over the last decade or so there's been an increase in the number of young people moving within Western Europe," says John Salt, head of the

Migration Research Institute at University College, London. "A lot of this sort of movement is for career development."[39] Let's take a brief swing through Europe and see how individual EU members are preparing for the 2010 crossroad.

Germany's Silicon Saxony

In 1999 Advanced Micro Devices (ADM) opened a semiconductor plant in Dresden (see Chapter 1). "This is our largest investment and most important operation worldwide," said Hector Ruiz, ADM's chief executive. After searching across the United States for a suitable plant site, they were drawn to Germany because of what Ruiz described as a "high skills base and good work ethic in the local labor market."

In 2004 German Chancellor Gerhard Schröder led a ceremony marking the partial completion of a second ADM semiconductor facility. It isn't every day that a U.S. company will invest another $2.5 billion in eastern Germany. At least 11,000 people are now working in Saxony's semiconductor industry. ADM didn't come here for a low wage base but, rather, for highly qualified, entry-level workers.[40]

The German Dual System is commonly identified as one of the most successful career education systems in the world. A key element is the participation of companies of all sizes that provide both practical and financial support to local programs. Technical, craft, and service careers all involve extensive classroom instruction and applied apprenticeships within businesses.

The Dual System's chief strength is an emphasis on broad, cross-curriculum learning, not narrow job training. This avoids education for a single, straight-line career path that is worthless if certain jobs become obsolete.[41]

At first glance, Germany's workforce looks very promising. In fact, the government has committed up to almost $5 billion in additional funds for its national education system. This is to address two nagging issues: the recent fall of German student test scores compared to other EU members, and a labor shortage of highly skilled workers.

The OECD's 2002 PISA study has spurred a flurry of school reforms to tackle the first problem (see Chapter 4). The second issue is complicated by high unemployment rates of low-skilled workers, and massive retirements by a rapidly aging German population.

Germany's long and bitter debate about immigrant labor was finally brought to a close in 2004 by creating Europe's most comprehensive immigration policy. This liberal immigration program aims at replenishing

Germany's pool of skilled labor by allowing people to enter if they possess skills in certain understaffed fields such as engineering, information technology, or the sciences. The need is immediate. About 20,000 German high-skill jobs remain vacant despite a national 11 percent unemployment rate (2005).[42]

Due to population aging and a low birth rate, Germany's labor force may shrink from the current 42 million to about 30 million by 2050. Over 7 million foreigners already live in the country and it seems apparent that more are on the way. However, worldwide, there exists only a finite number of people with the desired high-tech skills. Simply importing people is not an answer to Germany's problem, any more that it is in the United States. German culture will have to adjust to produce more home-grown skilled technologists. There will clearly remain an increasing worldwide demand for such workers over the next 100 years.[43]

The Celtic Tiger

For much of its modern history, Ireland was known as a land of emigrants. In an economy dominated by farming, the potato famine of 1845–1850 led to joblessness and despair. That now is ancient history.

Today, Ireland's high-tech economy is referred to as the "Celtic Tiger." American multinationals have set up headquarters here, and from 1993 to 1998 Ireland's economy grew by an astonishing 51 percent. Unemployment in Ireland is among the lowest in Europe. What happened to produce the so-called Irish miracle?

In 1968 the government took the economic long view. It made a commitment to a world-class education system and began investing heavily in universal high schools, then community colleges and improved technical training. Today, the nation ranks near the top among advanced countries in the share of national income devoted to public education.

In the 1980s, says John Fitzgerald, a professor at the Economic and Social Research Institute in Dublin, only 33 percent of men and 42 percent of women in Ireland had a post-secondary education. By the latter 1990s this had climbed to 42 percent for men and 52 percent of women and is still rising.

American tech companies have come flocking in—Intel, Dell Computer, Microsoft, Digital Equipment Corp., and a host of biotech and chemical companies. The workforce grew by approximately 40 percent, with high-tech and financial services growth creating skilled jobs that tend to pay better. American tech firms and their Irish partners employ over 100,000 people. Microsoft alone said its exports accounted for 2 percent of Irish annual economic growth (2001). A typical requirement for such entry-level jobs now is one or two years of education at one of the new Irish technical colleges

Ireland combined investing in its people with massive infrastructure improvements and low corporate tax rates. So what pulled off the Irish miracle? "The market didn't do it alone," says economist Robert Kuttner. "Clearly economics helped ... but so did massive investment in education.... Score one for social outlay." Ireland is winning the skill wars; it has changed the cultural expectations of its people. Now Ireland needs to export this success story to the entire world.[44]

Britain: Bridging the Great Education Divide

In the World Cup of education, Britain's scores have recently gone way up. An OECD survey (2000) of 15-year-olds from 32 countries tested reading, math, and science abilities. Britain's rankings were well above average: reading, fifth; math, eighth; and science, fourth. Britain did very well in comparison to other European countries, beating out both France and Germany (and even the U.S.).

On the other hand, British adult workers' skills came in far behind. Only 28 percent of the country's working age population had educational skills at the apprenticeship, technical, or craft levels (compared to 51 percent in France and 65 percent in Germany). Another OECD report placed Britain 14th out of 20 other industrial powers.[45]

British industries as a whole suffer from low productivity. Part of the problem is a low-skilled workforce, starting at the bottom and extending all the way up to senior managers. One result is that manufacturing cannot deploy the latest technologies because of a shortage of knowledge technologists. Nor can many British firms make the most of new lean manufacturing techniques because people lack key managerial skills, says John Dowdy from McKinsey & Co. Between 2000 and 2004, the British government began two new national initiatives to address these issues—the raising of overall adult worker skills, and enlarging student career education programs.

Skills for Life is a national government initiative for improving adult reading and math skills; a government Minister for Lifelong Learning oversees its implementation. Free basic adult education courses in literacy, numeracy, and language skills are being provided at a new national network of about 2,000 fully equipped learning centers at workplaces, schools, and colleges. Since 2001, 2.4 million adult learners have enrolled in 4.8 million courses, including unemployed persons, prison inmates, parolees, public sector workers, adults in low-skilled jobs, younger workers, recent immigrants needing English as a second language (ESL) training, and welfare recipients.

In December 2004, Britain celebrated the attainment of a national goal set three years earlier – 750,000 adult learners in the Skills for Life program had reached the national literacy standard. This national commitment has been expanded to 2.25 million adults by 2010, with an interim target of 1.5 million in 2007.[46]

In 2004 Charles Clarke, Britain's Education Secretary, announced a new career education apprenticeships program. "It will mean that motivated and able pupils could spend up to two days a week learning 'on the job' skills in the workplace. This will be an exciting prospect for any pupil wanting to pursue industry-specific vocational programs on top of the core national (academic) curriculum," said Clark.

Students, starting at age 14, can participate in this career education program. An age limit of 25 years was also abolished for older workers wanting to become apprentices. Gordon Brown, Britain's Chancellor of the Exchequer, believes that these moves demonstrate the growing importance of education training and skills to the future of the British economy.

Ivan Lewis, the Minister of Lifelong Learning, said that the academic–career divide was a "bogus choice," and insisted that higher-achieving students will also enroll in career programs. Britain had to tackle its "uniquely snobbish attitudes" to career education, he believes. Yet many of these same cultural feelings also persist in the United States.[47]

Another notable career program is the British Gas Engineering Academy that opened (2002) a £2 million apprenticeship training center. British Gas (a public utility) has been hit by the skills shortage, and an aging work-force. A report by the Gas and Water Industry Training Organization predicted a shortage of 34,000 UK gas technicians by the end of 2004 because of declining recruitment.

British Gas will expand its apprenticeship programs to recruit more women and older workers. One career education programs is for students aged 17 to 23; the other trains older adult apprentices.

In another career education initiative, Francesca Norris, age 14, is enrolled in a food technology career program at Tring School in Hartfordshire. Her ambition is to become a chef or to work in the catering industry. "My friends and I think career subjects are great because they are more likely to help us to get a job," she says. "But I am still happy to do liberal arts subjects such as history, English, and French. Just because I want to do something practical does not mean I am stupid."

Another 14-year-old, Haleema Williams at Thomas Tallis School in south-east London, wants to become a lawyer. "But I am still going to take business career studies because I think the skills we learn will be relevant to everybody, whatever we do," says Williams. "I don't think it is right to label young people as either academic or career. Most of us want to do a mixture."

Even Prince Charles has become personally involved in career education. In October 2002, he was shocked to discover that the custom woodwork reflooring at Buckingham Palace in London and nearby Windsor Castle was being done almost exclusively by Australians because there is a shortage of skilled carpenters in the UK.

The Prince's Trust, together with UK Skills, sponsored a celebrity-backed career show in Manchester that exposed students to wide variety of careers. "We want to make these young people proud to enroll in career education courses, and need to make them as prestigious and desirable as a degree in the classics or anthropology," says Tom Shebbeare, chief executive of the Prince's Trust.[48]

To further these education reform moves, in 2004 the British government began a new effort to change the public high school curriculum. The Labor Party has started to retreat from its core education policy of one-size-fits-all comprehensive high schools. Charles Clarke unveiled a five-year plan that encourages local high schools across the UK to tailor their curricula to best meet the career needs of their students.

This British version of the career academy complements earlier tech education moves. It gives the schools greater latitude in collaborating with businesses to develop meaningful career programs for students over 14 years of age.[49]

The British government is looking for help from outsiders to run so-called contract schools. Sponsors from business or the charitable sectors will be allowed to run some departments in the new schools. These contract schools can then modify the curriculum to teach specific academic specialties such as the classics, or to establish career-oriented programs.

By 2005 about 40 percent of all British secondary schools will have become career academies. In addition to offering a liberal arts curriculum, they will focus on at least one or two career areas such as technology, business, engineering, or advanced math and science. "We need to break away from the narrow definition of the less able and try to encourage more bright youngsters to go into more technical professions," says Paul Carter, a Kent County cabinet member for education.[50]

THE AMERICAS

The Workforce Ghosts of Nova Scotia Awake

Roy Plickie of Cape Breton, Nova Scotia, was a steelworker for 40 years at the Devco Foundry. There he made the iron, brass, aluminum, and lead castings required for the machines at the nearby Dominion Coal Company.

These mines extended many miles under the Atlantic Ocean. They are closed now, and so is the Devco Foundry that employed 350 workers. On the day in 2002 when this author arrived in Sydney, Nova Scotia to meet with these steelworkers, the last of their steel mills was demolished.

As Roy watched the last buildings collapse, his reaction was, "To me, they are not tearing down old buildings. They are tearing down the ghosts of central shops." But the workforce ghosts of Nova Scotia are rising again as new occupations in new industries begin transforming this part of Canada.

The Canadian Province of Nova Scotia lies 50 miles east of Maine, across a beautiful arm of the Atlantic called the Bay of Fundy. There, slightly more than 900,000 people have traditionally worked in occupations that rely mainly on natural resources.

Nova Scotia also possesses important educational resources: twelve universities, colleges, and community colleges located across the province. This is one of the chief reasons that 63 percent of Nova Scotia's workforce has education beyond high school.

As Nova Scotia's timber, fishing, and mining resources diminished over the years, unemployment has remained at above 10 percent. All of Canada's maritime provinces have likewise suffered, as even the important shipbuilding industry gradually vanished.

Nova Scotia has particularly benefited from a burgeoning tourist industry. Supported by expanding career education programs in its post-secondary schools, tourism has grown throughout the province. This is true from the picturesque little towns along Nova Scotia's long shoreline, to Halifax, the principal city and provincial capital, and at the Louisburg National Historic site on Cape Breton.

But the 2001 discovery of the Panuke oil field under the Atlantic, midway between Nova Scotia and Newfoundland, has also changed the potential career equation. This has proven to be a major economic benefit and is the focus of retraining the Nova Scotia's unemployed coal, steel, and forest product workers.

Education and training are essential components needed for a highly skilled workforce. "Companies are looking for workers who have multi-tasking ability, due to the advances in workplace technology," said Stephen Foran, oil and gas training manager for Nova Scotia Community College (NSCC).

With over 90 technical education programs related to this industry, the college is one of the province's major career training partners with petrochemical companies. NSCC provides career pathways for younger students as well as re-education for mature workers moving into this industry.

The Centre of Excellence in Petroleum Development at the University College of Cape Breton (UCCB) is another major workforce-education retraining partner. Shell, Mobil, Imperial, and West Coast oil and gas companies have invested heavily in the Centre's programs and facilities. Without a local workforce base of knowledgeable technicians, these petroleum producers would be unable to construct and develop either the offshore platforms or the onshore receiving hub for raw products.

UCCB offers students and older workers a three-tiered Petroleum Career Education Program: certificate programs in Petroleum Development and Petroleum Operations; a diploma in Petroleum Engineering Technology; and a Bachelor's degree in Technology, Petroleum. Lucia Mac Isaac, the Centre's director, believes that "Industry has indicated a growing and very significant need for applied research and education infrastructure."

Canada is a vast country, rich in natural resources and talented people. The workforce ghosts of Nova Scotia will rise again as a new workforce of knowledge technologists forged through these career and worker re-education programs.[51]

DESIGN FOR CHANGE

Why is there a worldwide demand for more knowledge?

- All countries confront the same challenge of preparing a higher percentage of the school-age population with the skills needed to succeed in the knowledge-based careers of the 21st century.
- Countries that in past decades invested heavily in quality elementary and secondary education are now experiencing a higher rate of economic growth than in the past (examples, South Korea, Ireland).
- The fall of the Soviet Union and the rise of democratic aspirations there have driven globalization and made more education universally available.
- Though education for all has increased the quantity of educational opportunities, very few nations have reached the quality and equity levels needed by the demanding world of technology.[52]

In light of these conditions, how many readers will seriously argue against the statement that education, now more than ever, is an important foundation stone for personal advancement in the world of work, and for the wealth of nations in the global high-tech marketplace?

But the devil is in the details. Moving this cultural football farther down field will prove difficult. Education and popular culture are like fire and ice—they don't mix well. If you say to many students "You need more education," or mention "life-long learning" to a typical adult audience, there will be a stampede for the exits!

Nevertheless, the age in which we live has a clear line drawn in the sand: Less education now means a lower standard of living for everyone. There will be few exceptions!

After studying these issues across the United States, I don't think that education will ever be joyfully embraced by mainstream American culture. I want to be proven wrong. The 2010 crossroad is offering people a stark lifestyle choice to motivate more people around the world to speed up the process of reinventing schooling and learning as we now know it. "This is not just a personal tragedy for young people who get sold short on their futures," says Hilary Pennington, CEO of Jobs for the Future. "It continues a crisis for the entire country because our collective future rests on the future employment and civic engagement of *all* our young people.[53]

Here are some of the guiding principles that we can expect to emerge at the 2010 crossroad:

- Every person must be given the opportunity to receive a rigorous liberal arts education and relevant career courses based on a variety of teaching and learning strategies.
- Every person needs to achieve high school graduation and 12th-grade-level abilities in reading, writing, and math skills.
- Every person needs to develop critical thinking or critical competency skills to analyze, evaluate, organize, access, and present information.
- Every person, from childhood through adulthood, needs access to broad, community-based career information to make a lifetime of informed career decisions and job changes.
- Every person needs to achieve the basic acceptance that "learning is for life."
- Every person, in every part of the nation, must have access to educational systems that are flexible enough to respond to rapidly changing societal needs.[54]

I understand that, to skeptics, these seem lofty goals. Yet if we do not aim high, will we ever overcome the mediocrity and even outright failure that often typifies the average American's educational experience?

The New System

What can we learn from the above program case studies? To begin the development of a liberal arts–career academy model, we need to consider the following ten major developmental activities:

1. Assess community labor market needs and climate to determine the feasibility of career learning programs.
2. Select career areas for work-related learning.
3. Hold numerous community meetings to provide information on the proposed liberal arts–career academy programs. Listen carefully to feedback. Recruit interested parents and business, education, labor, political, and community representatives.
4. Recruit businesses and non-profit service organizations to provide career education sites for students.
5. Use appropriate community representatives to work with professional program staff to design a program that meets local needs.
6. Seek broad funding support throughout the program planning process from state, federal, corporate, foundation, or other sources.
7. If required, submit state program applications.
8. Provide ongoing training and education to teachers and career workplace instructors and mentors.
9. Develop program administration materials and an evaluation plan.
10. Prepare public relations materials, including a Web site, and keep them up-to-date.

The Big Picture

The 2010 crossroad demands that America must begin to assume greater shared responsibility for those social issues that transcend national boundaries. Whether we like it or not, the ignorance of other people has an impact on life inside the United States. Isolationism will only breed greater worldwide chaos.

Across America, the cultural solutions for the people and jobs issues we have reviewed are broader in scope than just liberal arts and career academies. In the next chapter we will look at the other half of the demand for change—workforce development and lifelong learning.

6

The "Sixth Discipline"

Training less to save money is like stopping the clock to save time.

—John Tobin
CEO/President, Siemens Corporation

HAVE WE WRITTEN THE OBITUARY FOR THE LEARNING ORGANIZATION?

Not long ago I read the obituary for the learning organization. The *Chicago Tribune* (2001) ran an article titled "Learning Never Stops for Successful People," written by the senior vice president of an American energy company. This top executive told business people that "There is a compelling need for individuals to continue their development and the acquisition of knowledge over time.... The people I see succeed are increasingly people who commit to lifelong learning."

Well said and very true. The pace of the marketplace, technology, and global change compels all of us to continue learning more in order to adapt and grow our careers.

That vice president then counseled readers to assess themselves and their careers, get feedback from peers and friends, identify what new skills they will need, develop a game plan, and "go to it." In other words: You're on your own, baby! There was no mention of either the learning organization or any organizational commitment that develops the intellectual capital of its employees. I guess that when a major U.S. newspaper places such statements on the front page of its Working/Employment Marketplace Section it's now officially the wisdom on the street.

Has the early 1990s workplace learning revolution, which began with Peter Senge's book, *The Fifth Discipline* (Currency Doubleday, 1990), run its course? Many organizations are abrogating their responsibility for employee development by empowering people to figure out what new knowledge they need and encouraging them to just "go do it." Who has time for classroom training any more? "E-learning is faster and eliminates training staff and lost job time. Employees can do it when they want to. Overall, it is cheaper. What more can you ask for?" so the argument goes. However, this employer do-it-yourself training method is now backfiring as a management cost-cutting strategy. Employees are actually learning less through e-learning, particularly those who lack the basic required skills, training, and education to become smart people—knowledge workers.

Why is do-it-yourself training now dominating so many organizations' cultures? Businesses often engage in a financial levitation (i.e., they try to make bigger and bigger stacks of money from companies that are barely growing). Their magic art includes mergers, acquisitions, cost-cutting, squeezing staff, slashing training, and eliminating everything except their core business operations. They outsource everything else, and this often this includes the training department.

Table 6.1
Training and Development Expenditures by U.S. Business

Year	$ (Billion)	+/− % (Rounded)
1990	45.5	—
1995	52.2	+15
1996	59.8	+15
1997	58.6	−2
1998	60.7	+4
1999	62.5	+3
2000	54.0	−14
2001	56.8	+5
2002	54.2	−5
2003	51.3	−5
2004	51.4	—

Source: "Annual Industry Reports," *Training Magazine* (March, 2004).

The predominant culture of American management today is that businesses exist only to drive up stock options and enrich shareholders as fast as possible. As "Chainsaw Al" Dunlap, former CEO of Sunbeam Corporation, put it, "The point of business is to make a profit. The responsibility of the CEO is to deliver shareholder value. Period."[1]

It looks like Chainsaw Al is getting his way. In 1990, businesses invested $45.5 billion in training and development. By 1999 this had risen to $62.5 billion (a 37 percent increase), only to drop by 2003 to $51.3 billion (an 18 percent decline), and it remains flat in 2004. This decrease is even more significant since more Americans are now at work (138 million in 2003 versus 133 million in 1999).[2] (See Table 6.1.)

NEEDED: A SIXTH DISCIPLINE

For many U.S. managers, training is just another piece of useless jargon, the latest fad of senior management, university professors, and publishers. Where have all the CLOs (Chief Learning Officers) and CKOs (Chief Knowledge Officers) gone?

The fact is that training remains a dirty word in management articles, more so if employees are paid while being trained. Jeffrey Pfeffer, a professor of organizational behavior at the Stanford University Graduate School of Business, observes that "Particularly in the U.S., most companies cut training because they view it as a luxury. That distinguishes them from companies in Europe and Japan."[3] What drives this American prejudice? There seem to be several strong cultural issues.

Training departments, corporate universities, employee learning centers, or any learning-focused divisions, draw unsympathetic management scrutiny during any business slowdown because they don't directly produce revenue. As non-core business functions, they are prime targets for cost-cutting.

Another major issue is the widespread belief among most managers that training usually doesn't do that much good anyway. The infamous, often-quoted McKinsey & Co. Consulting study (1990) is that "80 percent of training and development is never used back on the job!"[4]

Avron Barr, a principal of Aldo Ventures, a software consulting firm in Aptos, California, personifies this so-called knowledge on the street. "We feel that the best people are born that way," Barr says. "Our belief is that they can't, in general, train people who aren't very good into people who are very good." So forget it.[5]

Yet most business managers will still argue that, in general, they support training their people. We have seen how the above data undercut their contention. Just the opposite is now happening in the majority of U.S. organizations.

What businesses need is what I call a Sixth Discipline—striking a balance between investing in the long-term development of employee skills and meeting reasonable short-term quarterly profit goals.

Executive development, sales training, advanced technical training, and continuing professional education are indeed still happening. Nevertheless, about 66 percent of all training and development provided by U.S. businesses is invested in these areas for about only 25 percent of the workforce. That leaves the majority getting less and less. "They are not investing enough on training," says Jim Hinds of Marakon Associates, "and what they are investing is often directed at the wrong places."[6]

Even though executive education has been one of the hardest-hit areas for recent training cuts, an Educational Testing Service (ETS) study (2002) found that employees in the United States were ten times more likely to receive new training from their employer if they were already well-educated and holding a management, professional, or advanced technical job. This was in comparison to other employees with limited educational backgrounds and holding non-managerial, executive, or professional jobs (See Table 6.2).[7]

A separate OECD study of corporate training confirmed these results and also showed how many other countries offer non-executive employees much more training. American business cannot continue to treat employee education as an unnecessary long-term investment without facing dire, long-term economic consequences.[8]

Click for Brains?

Some readers might object to the above conclusion since e-learning and the worldwide Web have many ardent disciples. This author attended a business seminar not long ago on the future of training. A new, university based e-learning system was featured at this meeting and debated by the participants. One senior business executive offered a stunning observation: "I am greatly relieved that because of e-learning the oral learning tradition will once again become the dominant form of learning in business, and will replace reading." In light of the recent surveys on the decline of Americans reading, might this even be a dominant cultural viewpoint? If so, there are dire consequences for America's ability to compete with other nations.[9]

The steadily increasing enthusiasm for e-learning has created a vast virtual learning industry. Companies using this new technology are now

Table 6.2
Lifetime Training (Mean Training Hours). Comparison of U.S. Employees to Other Nations. Training expectancy is the accumulation, over 5-year age intervals between the ages of 25 and 64, of age- and education-level-specific estimates of mean training hours.

Country	All Levels	Drop Outs	High School Grad	Some College	College Grad
Belgium (Fland.)	478	111	623	877	1194
Canada	2109	1115	1420	2863	5444
Germany	1833	1397	2361	2027	2668
Ireland	1259	813	1818	1859	2081
Netherlands	1512	780	1768	0	2086
New Zealand	2627	2099	1993	3046	5443
Poland	391	199	417	1115	1077
Switzerland (Fr.)	217	56	180	403	446
Switzerland (Ger.)	353	8	344	638	1155
United Kingdom	1666	926	1937	3331	3339
United States	1403	364	1116	1575	2523

Education Level spans the columns High School Grad, Some College, and College Grad.

Source: OECD and Statistics Canada, International Adult Literacy Survey, 1994–95.

being pressed to measure the real benefits in terms of time, reduced cost, and increased people performance.

"What we are now discovering is that one-time savings in labor and travel isn't worth it if the online learning initiative doesn't lead to ongoing measurable business benefits," says Donna Goldwasser, senior editor of *Training*. In other words, if little employee learning occurs, what value has e-learning given to the business? As Jack Hupple of Idea Connections observed, "Six months on the Internet will save an hour in the library."[10]

Innovation in a company is not just about technology. If we lose sight of this, we will lose the ongoing skill wars in our workplace. Remember what Pablo Picasso once said: "Computers are stupid; they only give you answers." Too many businesses don't want to admit this because they had invested serious money in e-learning courses only to find out that employees are dropping out in record numbers.

"We're coming to the end, thank God, of a lot of hype about e-learning," says Martyn Sloman at the Chartered Institute of Personnel Development in the United Kingdom.[11] The results of workplace-based research on e-learning are now coming in loud and clear. Here are what they say:

- Employees clearly prefer training in a classroom context rather than either computer-based self-directed or independent e-learning.
- Blended learning (classroom and technology) of text and visual programs increase learning.[12]
- A 2004 survey by the American Society for Training and Development found that 70 percent of respondents considered classroom training to be the best training investment.
- A study by *Information Week* found that 85 percent of its respondents considered classroom training most effective.
- Another study by *Information Week* of the training of 2,700 Tucson, Arizona city workers found that neither e-learning nor video-based training was as effective as classroom training. The report observed that "people need to be able to ask questions and participate in discussion to learn most effectively."[13]
- A 2002 survey of 502 British companies by the Institute of Personnel Development found only about 30 percent using e-learning. Seventy percent of these said they relied "only a little" on the approach.
- Jim Stewart, professor of human resource development at the Nottingham Business School, cites a study of very basic computer training in a financial services company. Although staff performance was initially enhanced, the improvement was not sustained in the long term. Bottom line: "There is too much confidence in the technology," says Stewart.[14]
- A 2003 survey was conducted on distance/e-learning by the London-based Association of MBAs. They found that distance and part-time learners experienced significantly more dissatisfaction with their chosen mode of learning than did full-time classroom learners.[15]
- A major Harvard University study found that well-educated adults who were employed or actively seeking jobs were among those most likely to benefit from e-learning and distance learning.
- By comparison, the same Harvard study showed that individuals least likely to benefit from e-learning were adults with less education, poor reading comprehension, and weak computer skills.[16]
- *The Review of Educational Research* (2004) published a major analysis of 232 studies that addressed the effectiveness of distance

learning compared to classroom instruction. While some applications of distance learning did well, "many performed more poorly,"
the analysis concluded.[17]

A good example of a successful e-learner is Susan Mills, the director
of human resources for the city of Palm Springs, California. She decided
to earn her Master's degree in organizational management. Mills got her
degree without ever walking into a classroom. "It was always online," she
says. Her graduate program was offered by the University of Phoenix. Mills
found the experience both challenging and rewarding. "The assumption
was it would be easy, but you have to be really committed to completing
the work," she found. Mills fits the profile of a successful e-learner—a person who already is well-educated, and is a driven self-starter who thrives
on independent projects with light supervision.[18]

For technical or new product training, e-learning has proven its value
for subjects that are heavy on facts, if the personal learning ability prereq-
uisites mentioned above are also met. But in other areas, where learning
depends on the social interaction of students and instructors, blended
learning is usually superior.

E-learning and distance learning, for all their helpful benefits, will never
replace some of the most important characteristics of learning that take
place when people assemble as a group in one physical location to acquire
skills and knowledge and improve personal thinking. Indeed, learning is
not the one-dimensional, all-inclusive commodity suggested by digital hype
in recent years. Learning to think is an important component in the current technology revolution. It is about how we better facilitate the curious,
unpredictable thinking of people both inside and outside the classroom.

Stanford University professor of organizational behavior and strategies
management Joel Podolny offers this observation: "One of the things I've
been increasingly struck by is how much in the classroom there is a sub-
text going on which is unrelated to the content." Even the best e-learning
courses lack the immediate, stimulating social interaction, verbal jousting,
debate, exploring the edge between social collaboration and competitiveness. This is what e-learning can never have. "It is a very dry, unmotivating
experience," Podolny says.[19]

Past predictions that e-learning would replace classroom learning have
proven overly optimistic. In reality, e-learning is only a small component
of how most Americans are trained. Blended learning combines the best
features of e-learning with other classroom training methods. In fact, the
blending of instructional methods has always been the way that most
training and education has been provided. It still makes sense today.[20]

Striking a Balance

At a recent corporate university conference (2003) that the author hosted, leaders from Intel, McDonald's, American Family Insurance, Capital One, Harley–Davidson, and the Defense Acquisition University (U.S. Department of Defense) discussed their organizations' programs. The ongoing negative impact of socioeconomic forces beyond their control and how these have constrained the business learning community was particularly striking. At best, training is a lagging and largely reactive indicator of how these forces have played out across the U.S. and world economies.

The puncturing of the bubble economy in the late 1990s created a fierce downturn for workforce education. The continued emphasis on short-term profit-taking runs counter to the long-term development of an organization's most important asset—its human capital. But a change is in the wind. Not only were these corporate university leaders adamant in proclaiming their essential contributions to performance and productivity, many other business leaders at the conference were thinking about replicating these corporate university models. This may at least be partially explained by a major business culture shift now underway across American businesses.

There is increasing evidence that senior executives are beginning to realize that they can't just buy technology to cut costs and expect to automatically generate big productivity and benefits. Recently Anne Mulcahy admitted as much. "It's no secret that technology alone is not enough," says the chairman and CEO of Stamford, Connecticut-based Xerox Corp. "Technology requires changes in the way humans work, yet companies continue to inject technology without making the necessary changes," she added.

There are no rules set in stone on how to evolve a company's culture and its learning systems. Learning in a so-called living company happens as a normal offshoot of daily business activity. Morgan Witzel, author of *The Living Company,* (Nicholas Brealey, 1997) believes that "Learning organizations learn as entities; effective learning is shared, not locked up in individuals." To work, this requires that all employees have a chance at workplace learning.

As the corporate university conference continued, an unspoken question bubbled to the surface. Is it more important to cut costs or to increase learning? Each corporate university leader used technology to cut costs, but they all considered improving learning as their highest goal. Most of these presenters believed that in the present and future, blended learning methods provide the optimum means for reconciling these two objectives.

Jeanette Harrison, director of Intel Knowledge and Learning, Santa Clara, California, offered a particularly striking case study. Of Intel's employees, the engineers were among the most vocal in demanding classroom instruction rather than e-learning because, she said, "they place a high value on social learning."

Most of the other speakers agreed that they place a premium on the spontaneous classroom interaction between learners and instructors that can drive creativity. These corporate university representatives try to have e-learning constitute 25 percent of their overall course offerings.[21]

It may seem obvious to most readers that these leading U.S. companies owe at least part of their success to continually letting their employees learn, test, and use new skills. "Training is what keeps companies competitive, particularly in a down business cycle," say Jeffrey Pfeffer at Stanford University's Graduate School of Business. "It helps get work results," believes William J. Rothwell, a professor of workforce education at Penn State University, "whether orienting new hires to know why they should do something, helping current employees prepare for promotions, and having everyone upgrade skills as technologies and other conditions change."

Too many companies fail to do this. But the organizations at that corporate university conference provided many excellent case studies of how they integrated training into the context of how to run a business. They practice the difficult Sixth Discipline—improving employee skills by balancing the needs of business to both invest in the long-term development of people while meeting reasonable, short-term quarterly profit goals. They are not alone. Let's look at how other organizations are changing their cultural outlook by using the Sixth Discipline.[22]

THE NEW BREED OF WORKFORCE EDUCATION

In 2003, William Rothwell probed CEO expectations on what results they wanted from corporate education. To be most effective, he found, corporate education must focus on helping the organization cope with six challenges: technological change and innovation, the knowledge explosion, global competition, recruitment of a productive labor force, customer satisfaction, and financial health.

It is obvious from this all-inclusive shopping list that people need many kinds of knowledge and skills to accommodate all the competitive demands made on a typical 21st-century business. This includes being better able to learn new information, as well as improving communication skills, problem solving, and creativity. All these areas are pretty advanced for many Americans, who are often shortchanged by our dumbed-down public school system. To reach the needed knowledge and skill levels, many Americans now working in offices or plants need remedial education. The longer they go without it, the higher the price America will eventually pay in limited economic growth. Let's look at how organizations have become more successful by first addressing the basic educational skills of their employees.[23]

People "Make It or Break It"

In 1985 Donald J. Ehrlich created Wabash National, a truck trailer manufacturing company, in Lafayette, Indiana; he started with a card table and three folding chairs in a downtown office. While Ehrlich began building a customer base, he enlisted Purdue University for employee training. "The philosophy was that the people at Wabash were either going to make it or break it and needed all the skills we can give them," says Tim Monaghan, Wabash executive vice president of human relations.

Wabash began employee training with ESL classes for recent immigrants and technical training classes for workers to become welders. But Wabash went beyond the basics to give workers the big picture. When an employee complained to Ehrlich that the company was wasting his profit-sharing on paving the parking lot, Ehrlich added a course in business basics. Now everyone can learn the difference between a capitalized expense (parking lot improvements) and an operating cost (purchasing a load of parts).

All workers and managers have the opportunity to improve their basic skills and then receive training in how a business works (systems). This all leads to education for so-called critical competencies—problem-solving, decision-making, and team-building. In Wabash's culture, the future depends on its workers understanding how a company makes a profit, and how constant change and rapid growth will keep it profitable. Ehrlich says that at Wabash, "We're constantly trying to help workers to think about building better trailers."

One practical result has been over 160 worker teams that have implemented product improvements, such as the air brake stroke and free-play adjustment teams. These groups of workers have been trained to help the company save hundreds of thousands of dollars through their thoughtful, practical production innovations.

Does Wabash support a more educated workforce? At Wabash, Jerry Ehrlich thinks that "Three Einsteins would be no match for a factory full of workers attending classes and contributing ideas." This is the essence of the learning organization and the payoff for a business investing in its human capital.

In 2002 Wabash went through a major restructuring and expansion. Bill Geubel took over as president and CEO, and continued to expand a culture supporting learning and change. Since then, Wabash introduced lean management and continuous improvement teams. "We have reinvented our manufacturing activities," says Wabash's Tim Monaghan, "and are beginning to collaborate with Ivy Tech to increase our technical training for our people." This continues a 20-year commitment of investing in people at Wabash, and the employees have responded. "I've never seen a group of people so highly motivated to learn new things and accept training as a natural part of day-to-day change," states Monaghan.[24]

Doing Something about It

Many companies have learned the hard way about the real cost to their business when employees lack basic educational skills. Companies such as Ames Rubber Corp. in Hamburg, New Jersey and Bimba Manufacturing in Monee, Illinois discovered that their total quality or ISO-9000 programs were going nowhere because "The people don't comprehend what we're saying," and "Because they couldn't read or write very well," according to company representatives. They then invested in these worker skills program. According to the Conference Board, U.S. business loses over $60 billion in productivity every year because employees lack these basic skills. Yet, on the flip side, the Conference Board found that when companies like Wabash National begin educating their workers, the quality of work increases, error rates fall, absenteeism is reduced. These were among the many other benefits gained by the organization (See Table 6.3).[25]

Why don't more businesses invest in these basic skill programs? For one reason, there is the old saw of an excuse that if you improve workers' skills, they will then leave and take better jobs somewhere else, and you will have wasted your money. This is true if you don't give workers who increase their skills a chance at a better job, or offer other pay incentives that are linked to better personal productivity. But there may also be deeper, hidden motivations that curb many managers from supporting training and development in general.

Jay Thiessens is a self-made man. He built his B&J Machine Tool Company from a Mom-and-Pop operation into a $5 million-a-year enterprise. He did it the hard way, and his secret was that he couldn't read.

When Thiessens was in first or second grade, he recalls, "A teacher called me stupid because I had trouble reading." Though he somehow graduated from high school, for the rest of his life he suffered from the stigma of being labeled a dummy in school. He obviously compensated and was

Table 6.3
Read 'Em and Reap. Organizational Benefits Gained through Basic Skills Training Programs

Benefit	Percent of Employers Reporting
Improved employee morale/self-esteem	87
Increased quality of work	82
Improved capacity to solve problems	82
Better team performance	82
Improved capacity to cope with change in the workplace	75
Improved capacity to use new technology	73
Higher success rate for promoting employees within the organization	71
Increased output of products and services	65
Increased profitability	56
Reduced time per task	56
Reduced error rate	53
Better health and safety record	51
Reduced waste in production of products and services	49
Increased customer retention	42
Increased employee retention	40
Reduced absenteeism	33

Source: The Conference Board, "Turning Skills into Profit: Economic Benefits of Workplace Education Programs," 1999.

able to succeed in his business. Only at the age of 56, through a local CEO support group, did Thiessens hire a tutor to work with him for an hour a day, five days a week, on learning how to read.

This may seem to be a remarkable story, but this author has witnessed it many times. Senior managers in many fields—banking, accounting, law—often possess very poor basic skills in reading, writing, or speaking. They get by, and even advance, because they are obviously brilliant in their specialized business knowledge. But the do it the hard way, against long odds.

My point is that many business people have had bad experiences in school. For whatever reasons, they will pointedly talk about "the year they got out"—not out of prison, but out of school. These personal anti-education viewpoints reflect a broad cultural undercurrent that dominates the contemporary American business scene.

There is also the simplistic reasoning that in America the so-called self-made man or woman, through hard work and self-sacrifice, can become a success in the world of business. To prove this contention, they point to all the current business high-rollers who are college dropouts, including mega-billionaire Bill Gates. Education just isn't that important, they argue, particularly for the non-executive or non-professional worker.

These anti-education attitudes are deep rooted across Old America's popular culture. They help account for the major skills train wreck now in progress in New America's businesses. Times have changed. Business culture must also change in the face of new, 21st-century realities.

Jay Thiessens hopes his story will encourage other Americans to learn more. "There is no shame in not knowing how to read," said Bonnie Thiessens, his wife. "The shame is not doing anything about it."[26]

Riding the Rails into the Future

From 1988 through 1996, the U.S. Department of Education's National Workplace Literacy Program collaborated with businesses and unions to help increase the number of workforce literacy programs in U.S. companies. The objective was to develop model programs and best practices. This information would then be widely disseminated throughout the U.S. business community. Companies would then have strong models to begin or expand these essential training and development programs. At least 40 percent of America's workers need these training programs because of their limited reading, writing, and math skills. In a study of the program, Mathematics Policy Research, Inc. found many compelling business reasons why employers and unions gladly participated in these workplace literacy partnerships (See Table 6.4).

These company-based training programs benefited both the participating workers and, in turn, the employers. Improved personal literacy skills led many of these adults to change their career and educational plans. This led to promotions within the workplace and/or workers assuming greater job responsibilities, resulting in higher productivity and higher pay. These results provided a great incentive for many businesses to continue their workplace literacy training after the federal grant ended. In 1997 nearly 66 percent of these 37 local programs were continued using company training funds. This included businesses in the retail, hotel/hospitality, healthcare, industrial, and manufacturing sectors.[27]

Many other businesses both large and small have begun to treat their workers' educational needs more seriously. They are encouraged by this federal effort and other state and local government initiatives, as well as

Table 6.4
Reasons Why Employers and Unions Participated in Workplace Literacy Partnerships

Reason	Employers (%)	Unions (%)
To reduce errors and waste	61	58
Organizational innovations	54	47
Changes in production/operations	48	58
Improve skills of limited English speakers	45	68
New technology	41	47
Changes in the available workforce	25	21
Worker requests	25	18
Other reasons	13	29
Meet health and safety standards	11	13
Attract new workers	8	3
Agreement with labor organizations	5	11

Source: Mathematica Policy Research, Inc. (1997).

by the research findings published by American Society for Training and Development, *Training* magazine, the Conference Board of Canada, ABC Canada, and other professional business and education publications. One of the most interesting programs was begun by METRA, Chicago's commuter rail authority.

The Northeast Illinois Metropolitan Transit Railroad Authority (METRA), provides commuter rail services for the six-county Chicago metropolitan area. Begun in 1982, METRA is the second-largest commuter rail system in the United States. It generates over 300,000 trips on an average weekday, using rail lines radiating north, south, and west of downtown. METRA wants to utilize the latest technological innovations to expand passenger railway service throughout this region.

America's railroads dramatically changed during the 1980s and 1990s. Now, profits are up, personnel requirements are down, and high-tech railroad applications are mushrooming throughout day-to-day operations. Computers now drive a new generation of diesel locomotives, eliminating the little red caboose on most trains. Fewer but better-trained maintenance-of-way (rail-track) workers are required to maintain steel rails for greater safety and operating speed. A key ingredient to implementing all these high-tech rail applications is a new management commitment to employee training.

Railroad employees live in an increasingly high-tech world. The application of their educational skills to computerized technology has already started and will continue to accelerate. Nationally, the number of railroad employees has declined because of the increasing use of these technologies. Railroads need workers to be better trained and educated than in earlier years because of the increasing complexity of these jobs.

Microprocessors are now in every locomotive, and computers operate advanced signaling devices. High-speed, high-tech trains are now operating daily in Europe and Japan at speeds of 125 to over 200 mph. The ever-greater suburban sprawl could make this an attractive future technology for a railroad that wants to increase its ridership by offering shorter travel times compared to expressway alternatives. METRA's vision of the future prompted much research and its decision, in 1992, to begin training their employees in order to fulfill their long-term goals.

METRA's workforce education program is designed to train current workers who have educational skills below the 10th-grade level. This "people program" gives an older, well-established workforce the opportunity to improve their reading, math, and communication skills (such as English as a second language). Employees participating in the program are specifically interested in improving current job skills, gaining promotion to a new job at METRA, or entering union apprenticeship training programs.

Classrooms were located in the METRA railroad marshalling yards scattered throughout the Chicago metropolitan area. This placed the training programs near the individual employees' daily work activities. In the briefing sessions held for all employees before the program began, workers were told, "This program is like a floating crap game. It can go wherever you want it to go." From the beginning, a key concept was building the entire training effort around what METRA's training manager described as "on-the-job trust."

In the two years prior to the program, METRA stressed its commitment from the top down. The executive director made a major commitment to the concepts behind this workforce education effort. Fifteen unions were briefed and lent their support to beginning the program. Question-and-answer presentations on workforce education were made during general management and small committee meetings.

An information campaign was then begun for all 2,100 METRA employees. Flyers were distributed to all employees and information was published in the METRA newsletter. Even more important, face-to-face briefing sessions were held in METRA rail yards for all employees, who attended on a voluntary basis. METRA's workforce education program is offered to all employees who wish to volunteer for the training classes. All program test scores are kept confidential. Progress reports on each worker are given to METRA's human resource department rather than to the employee's immediate supervisor.

At its inception, approximately 200 METRA employees volunteered for the program. Maintenance-of-way personnel, coach cleaners, engine machinists, and workers in many other job classifications were tutored in groups of five, using a rapid-learning-program curriculum. Every effort has been made to use realistic, on-the-job training materials and other instructional materials applicable to the employees' personal interests or daily life.

The Workforce Education Program became a viable source of job readiness for employees seeking to improve reading comprehension, math skills, and language skills, including ESL. More than 180 employees participated in this voluntary education program, with minimum commitments of 10 weeks (40 instructional hours); the majority participate in 20 or more weeks of instruction geared to meet specific individual needs. This program annually provides over 800 classroom hours of instruction at several METRA work sites.

An Apprentice Prep Program became a subset of METRA's overall workforce education effort. This optional program was offered to internal candidates for the Mechanical Department Apprentice Program as a means of improving individual math and/or language skills. There were several success stories involving 10 out of the 28 apprentices, who, through enrollment in workforce education classes, subsequently met the verbal and math requirements after 10 to 20 weeks of classes.

Between 1992 and 2005, hundreds of METRA employees have successfully participated in the Workforce Education Program. They have increased their overall on-the-job productivity, and some employees have passed job proficiency examinations that qualified them for promotions.

Beginning with a workforce literacy grant from the state of Illinois, METRA has for almost 14 years has made a long-term budgetary commitment to do whatever it takes to meet all the educational requirements of its high-tech workplace for all employees. The METRA workforce educational program is a serious, long-term commitment to broaden the availability of training and development services for all workers.[28]

A Core Business Value

METRA is by no means alone. Here are some snapshots of what other U.S. and Canadian organizations, both small and large, are now doing to raise their employees skills.

- *Allied Signal*, aerospace manufacturing (Arizona, California, Connecticut, Maryland, New Jersey). Worker retraining program to upgrade the skills of defense workers for a high-performance workplace, including quality, customer relations, technical, and occupational training.

- *Cameco*, uranium mining (Saskatoon, Canada). The world's largest uranium miner has sites spread across remote northern Saskatchewan. Half of the employees who live in aboriginal communities are tutored one-to-one in learning centers. Cameco made long-term commitments for employee training through a consortium with other mining companies, the Multi-Pay Training Program (MPTP), as well as with local and federal government support for education and training.

- *Dofasco, Inc. (Hamilton, Ontario, Canada).* One of Canada's largest steel producers, Dofasco provides customers throughout North America with high-quality flat-rolled and tubular steel. To maintain and increase the company's ability to remain competitive in the global market, Dofasco launched its Essential Skills Program in 1997. Based on the assessments, requests, and goals of the participants and instructors, the program provides more than 40 employees per year with opportunities to learn the essential skills needed to make the best contribution they can in the workplace, home, and community. Winner of the Conference Board of Canada's 2004 Workplace Literacy Award.

- *Dudels Manufacturing*, metal fabricating (Chicago, Illinois). Workforce education in ESL, shop math, measurements, and recordkeeping for statistical process control (SPC).

- *Elmsdale Lumber Co.* (Nova Scotia, Canada). Developed in partnership with the Nova Scotia Department of Education, its training program helps Elmsdale manage change and keeps the company on the leading edge of its industry. An on-site program team runs learning programs for employees covering communications for staff and supervisors, academic upgrading, written communications, and basic computer literacy. The program has benefited the organization economically and socially, as employees from mill workers to the owner become more efficient and apply what they have learned to new ways of harvesting, processing, and selling lumber. A winner of the Conference Board of Canada's 2004 Workplace Literacy Award.

- *Hampden Papers*, paper products (Holyoke, Massachusetts). Skills training program in ESL, GED classes, and tuition assistance for technical schools and college courses related to the workplace. One and one-half percent of its payroll is budgeted annually to send its workers to school.

- *Hardy Industries,* automobile accessories (Portland, Oregon). Teamwork and educational skills training in reading, writing, math, algebra, participatory skills, quality, problem solving, and company-paid tuition courses.
- *Institute for Career Development,* steel industry (Indiana). More than $24 million invested by 14 steel companies in worker basic skill enhancements, technical skills training, personal development, and tuition assistance.
- *Lumonics, Inc.,* lasers, laser-based systems (Kanates, Ontario, Canada). In 1990 Lumonics implemented an ESL program. Its Workplace Language Program addresses oral communication, team participation, problem solving, reading, and writing. Quality program leadership training is also offered.
- *MacLean–Fogg Company,* car parts supplier (Mundelein, Illinois). This company's BASE Program enrolled about 8 percent of employees in reading, writing, math, and ESL classes. Every employee also receives 20 hours of job training per year (approximately 400,000 hours of training). Tuition reimbursement is given for college courses.
- *Methodist Medical Center,* health care (Peoria, Illinois). Education programs have been a long-standing tradition at this hospital. Programs include ESL, math, reading, and GED.
- *Minas Basin Pulp & Power Company, Ltd.* (Nova Scotia, Canada). Produces linerboard and coreboard from 100%-recycled paperboard products using the latest in computer technology. Minas Basin recognized that in order to evolve and compete in the global market it needed to raise its employees' standard education level and improve basic literacy and work skills. In response to this need, the first GED upgrading program was started in October 1999 with 10 participants. To date, over one-quarter of its 177 employees have participated in workplace education programs. These programs include: preparation for GED diplomas, oral communication, document literacy, using computers, and math skills upgrading. It has as a Development Centre with a computer lab to provide training for all employees. A 2004 winner of the Conference Board of Canada's Workplace Literacy Award.
- *Navistar International,* truck components (Waukesha, Wisconsin). Since 1998 its Education Center has offered instruction in educational skills: writing, reading, ESL, math, and computers; site-specific training: blueprint reading, personal enrichment; career education: GED, college prep.

- *SCC SoftComputer,* software manufacturer (Palm Harbor, Florida). Recognizing that some of its employees from foreign countries needed extra help, SCC started a volunteer English tutoring program in which volunteers are assigned to employees who sign up for the program. The pairs meet during breaks, lunches, and off-hours for tutoring sessions in English. SCC also offers training called Living in America for foreign nationals who have come to the United States for the first time. The program teaches skills such as how to shop in grocery stores, behave in the workplace, and interact with Americans.
- *Palliser Furniture* (Winnipeg, Canada). Two-day hiring course to assess each employee's potential, followed by courses in ESL, math, reading, computers, totaling 30 ten-week-long classes. Two-hour classes, employees paid for first hour, second hour on their own.
- *Smith & Wesson,* firearms manufacturer (Springfield, Massachusetts). All 676 front-line workers were assessed in math and reading. For more than three years, classes were held on company time to improve attendance. Each class of up to 15 employees met four times a week for an hour each day. ESL classes were also provided. The results? Smith & Wesson sees a continued need to ensure that new workers are able to read and use state-of-the-art manufacturing techniques (See Table 6.5).
- *Warner Lambert Company,* confectionery manufacturing facility (Rockford, Illinois). One-to-one skills tutoring programs for workers. Established in 1989, it has been expanded each year.
- *Will-Burt Co.,* auto parts, metal fabricating (Ohio). Since 1985, a company-wide workplace education program offers courses in blueprint reading, geometry, leadership, creativity, self-esteem, logic, a mini-MBA program, and many other quality training areas.
- *Verizon Telecommunications* (across the United States). As one of the country's largest employers, Verizon is among a number of organizations supporting programs to ensure a skilled workforce. In 2005, the Verizon Foundation, the company's philanthropic arm, will invest $15 million in workforce development projects run by non-profit organizations. The Verizon Foundation is committed to helping people and communities make progress every day, and will invest another $19 million in literacy initiatives and $75 million overall. The foundation supports a variety of programs that focus on improving basic and computer literacy, creating a skilled workforce, enriching communities through technology, and bridging the digital divide. The foundation also

Table 6.5
Smith & Wesson Workforce Education Program Results

In support of the claim that basic skills classes have helped them do their job better, students wrote the following comments in response to the question, "What is the most important thing you do better at work because of this class?"

- I can read charts on the boards that I couldn't understand before.
- I read the ISO book better.
- The most important thing I do better is read the bulletin board more often.
- I feel more comfortable about writing notes for second shift.
- I can write work orders and better communicate with people.
- I can use fractions and decimals better.
- Helps me feel more comfortable speaking at the meeting I have every morning.
- It's easier to talk to my team.
- Better communication with my supervisor.
- I use the computer a little better.
- I've learned how to write about machine problems.
- I'm not afraid to write a note because my spelling got better.
- I can chart statistical process control better.
- Better problem solving with math.

Source: Adapted from ASTD Technical Writing (1998).

supports Verizon Volunteers, an incentive program that encourages employee volunteerism by matching employee gifts of money, time, and talent with foundation grants.[29]

While this compilation of business employee basic skills programs seems impressive, why do only about 5 percent of U.S. companies currently see this as one of their core business values? Many offer the excuse that employee literacy is a public school issue, or say they "don't own the problem." Outsourcing has become the favored substitute for this training. However, as technology becomes more complex across the entire business spectrum, the education bar of what is considered basic reading, math, and writing skills will be continually raised. More employees will need these basic skill programs. Only at great peril can any business choose to ignore this skills issue and not get involved in the re-education of the current workforce.

Reading, writing, and math skills are only the foundational blocks that support worker knowledge. Let's look at how some businesses are using training and development to encourage innovation and improve their competitiveness.

"You Gotta Take.... Quantum Leaps"

Jim Kelly, as chairman of United Parcel Service (UPS) was interviewed in 2001 by the *Harvard Business Review* on "reinventing" a company. When asked about the short-term thinking that is over-focused on stock prices, he replied, "We think our share owners should get treated well and should get a fair return, but ... we've always thought that the long term was the important thing. If you were to start dancing for the folks on Wall Street because they expect something in the quarter, it would be counterproductive."

Kelly's focus is clearly on how to continually reinvent UPS through a culture that, as Kelly says, encourages employees to be heroes. "But around here, we don't think of ourselves as individuals doing too much on our own. We think of ourselves as people working together to get things accomplished.... When your culture causes people to engage in heroics on behalf of the company, you certainly don't want to damage it. A lot of our routines—like training—allow the culture to perpetuate itself. We invest $300 million a year in training (1 percent of UPS's gross sales), much more than most companies do," he said.[30]

How many heroes are there left in global training, you may ask? Many more than you might think. Each year, *Training* magazine conducts extensive research to rank the "Top 100" companies in this context. Each year more than 160,000 applications are distributed and over 500 organizations respond. In a comparison of year-to-year results, some companies drop off this list and others move up or down in the rankings. Yet, most remain committed to high quality training as a part of doing business. During an economic phase (2003) when many organizations slashed training budgets, the Top 100 invested over $6 billion, offering 65 hours of training for each of their employees. In the big numbers department, IBM scored with the largest annual training budget ($700 million). Pfizer ranked #1 in terms of training as a percentage of payroll—15 percent (See Tables 6.6 and 6.7).

Companies used numerous metrics to measure training's quantifiable impact, ranging from retention of employees to innovation and product development. As a result, these organizations were better able to demonstrate to their leadership the critical links between training, performance, and business results. Among the Top 100, leadership development heads the list of training and development programs designed to increase the critical competencies of employees. All of these formal training programs show how these Top 100 balance the short-term versus the long-term needs of business. According to Tammy Galvin, editor of *Training Magazine*, they prove that workforce education has been positioned "as the key ingredient

Table 6.6
2004 Top Training Budgets (Does not include NFP companies)

Budget (million)	Company	Rank
$700	IBM	#1
$350	Lockheed Martin	#9
$336	Intel Corp.	#17
$324	Dept. of Defense: DAU	#50
$260	Hewlett-Packard	#81
$225	United Airlines	#92
$144	Dow Chemical Co.	#68
$135	Verizon Comm.	#71
$113	Continental Airlines	#96
$102	Wachovia Corp.	#27

Best 10 Total Budget: $2.7 billion
Top 100 Total Budget: $6.6 billion

Source: Training Magazine, "Training Top 100" (2004).

Table 6.7
2003 Training as a Percentage of Payroll (Does not include NFP companies)

Percentage	Company	Rank
15	Pfizer	#1
14	Century 21	#81
10	Ritz-Carlton	#9
9	KLA-Tencor	#5
8	Ohio Savings Bank	#16

Best 5 Average: 11%
Top 100 Average: 4.6%

Source: Training Magazine (2002).

in solidifying corporate cultures ... that continually foster and reward both the creation and subsequent application of knowledge, not only for the betterment of the company's near- and long-term financial success, but for the betterment of the individuals that constitute their workforces as well."[31] (See Table 6.8.)

Table 6.8
2003 Top 100 Highlights (Number of companies with the following formal programs...)

- Leadership Development: 99
- First-Line Supervisors: 93
- Mentoring: 85
- Career Counseling: 82
- Executive Coaching: 82
- Succession planning: 79
- Job Rotation: 63
- Job Shadowing: 61

Source: Training Magazine.

Chuck Parke, a Maytag washing machine plant manager, puts it more plainly. "The key to the whole thing is you can't perform at the level that you're currently performing at, or even at some incrementally better level. You gotta take major risks and quantum leaps to make this thing work," he said.

The honest answer to the 2010 crossroad challenge is for every business to create more smart people to redesign jobs and work processes. They will create more high-value-added products and services at lower cost and higher profit. "If we're going to save manufacturing (and more high-wage U.S. jobs) in this country," Parke says, "we have to be more creative. There's a solution on the table, but it's hard work."[32]

You bet it is. Following the short-term herd mentality will lead many businesses over the cliff. Going against the grain is never easy. Ask Nestlé's CEO, Peter Brabeck, and he will tell you.

Nestlé is about people, production, and brands—that's it.... We have never managed for the maximization of short-term shareholder value. It doesn't make sense.... I am not going to run a company based on what the market wants at any given moment and make mistake after mistake because I told the analysts one thing one day to make them happy.... To grow and learn, people have to collaborate. It won't work if a few people have all the information and power and the rest do not.... Those who lack the skills I can take care of more easily; they can be trained ... but the truth is, in business, you can win the war without killing off half the army.[33]

Perhaps the learning organization isn't dead after all! Both companies across the United States and Canada and an influential Swiss CEO have discovered the Sixth Discipline. America might just be able to still avoid an HR train wreck at the 2010 crossroad if we follow their advice and carefully invest in more smart people.

WHERE'S THE BEEF? TRAINING ROI

Alan Greenspan said, "Clearly, investing in human capital to complement physical capital is perceived by many businesses as adding to shareholder value."[34] How applicable is this statement to American business in general? Does the average American business manager believe that investing in human capital (his or her people) through training and education will result in a more profitable company? U.S. businesses are spending as much as 10 times more per employee on information technology (IT) as they are spending on training. Ironically, these IT investments are made on faith with little specific proof of a payoff. Yet investment in human capital for education and training is held to a higher standard. They must prove their worth.[35] So be it. Let's see how to do it well.

In looking at the Training Top 100 companies described earlier, 67 percent measure training effectiveness through return on investment (ROI). Accenture Consulting developed their own ROI calculator to analyze all the training for 261,000 employees over the history of the company. Their analysis factored out the effects of inflation, market cycles, experience, and employee levels to isolate the training effect on each person. Accenture determined that for every dollar invested in training, there was a return of $3.53 in net training benefits. They also found that their better-trained employees had a higher number of billable client hours and stayed with the company longer.[36]

Companies around the world, both large and small, are today measuring training ROI. The International Corporate University Xchange Excellence Awards (2003) were given to organizations such as Intel Ireland, European Aeromatic Defense and Space Company (EADS), and Old Mutual. All clearly used ROI "because that's the determining factor in future training investment," says Crystal Shaffer, one of the judges from les Fontaines, a Cap Gemini Ernst & Young company. Successful training now needs to affect the company's bottom line.[37]

Here are three ROI case studies of smaller companies, showing how it works:

I.   Trident Precision Manufacturing (Webster, New York) is one of the smallest companies ever to win a Malcolm Baldrige National Quality Award (1996). Over a period of six years, they invested

4.7 percent of their payroll educating their employees. This custom-product, sheet-metal company taught workers blueprint reading, trigonometry, and ESL. Product defect rates fell from 3 percent to 99.994 percent defect-free; turnover declined from 41 percent to 5 percent per year; revenue rose from $5 million to $19 million, and revenue per employee shot up 73 percent.

II. Otto Engineering is an Illinois supplier of switches and electrical assemblies for Motorola products. Over a period of four years, Otto invested in its human capital by training 185 employees in statistical process control (SPC), blueprint reading, other technical classes, and ESL. Field returns dropped dramatically, and scrap caused by worker errors was substantially reduced. Thirty-one percent of productivity improvement came directly from training, 32 percent came from structural capital improvement, and 37 percent from management operational changes not specifically tracked.

III. Equimeter Company in Pennsylvania invested in its human capital by providing a group of engineers with a Kaizen team training program in order to improve the quality and productivity of a gas meter assembly line. They achieved a 16 percent productivity improvement, a 22 percent space savings, a work-in-process reduction of 10 percent, and they solved three safety issues. The estimated ROI of this training program was 31.6 percent.[38]

But how do you do the calculations? To get you started, there are many free training ROI worksheet tools available on the Internet. EmployeeBenefitNews.com offers a variety of these calculators on the "Measuring Training's Return on Investment" page on their Web site. One of these tools, a Human Capital ROI Worksheet, was developed by the author and a team of experts. Since its introduction in 2000, thousands of businesses around the globe have used this spreadsheet. You can access the worksheets' latest, upgraded versions free of charge at www.imperialcorp.com.[39]

An OECD study on this issue seems to have been governed by three major concerns: time spent in learning, the depreciation rate, and the business investment rate. The evidence from many companies suggests that the exact content, duration, and quality of training will clearly affect its outcomes. "Modest benefits are the result of modest investments," concluded the OECD. Training ROIs are driven by how well an organization targets and designs education programs around the participants' performance needs that are clearly linked to productivity.[40]

A more accurate training ROI calculation will help in the second step of wider business culture change—the pressure from Wall Street stock analysts to make the numbers for each quarter. "Our analysis has shown clearly over the years that ... privately held firms make larger investments in the training of their people than do publicly traded ones," says Laurie Bassi of Bassi Investments, Inc.

However, from what we have already seen, this seems to be changing as the culture of Wall Street begins to rub against the relentless forces of the 2010 crossroad. Even Bassi reports there are now more publicly traded companies that are making "significant investments" in employee learning, including Applied Materials, Inc., Capital One Financial Corp., Dow Chemical Co, FedEx Corp., General Electric Corp., Intel Corp., KLA–Tencor Corp., Lockheed Martin Corp., and Microsoft.

These and other publicly traded companies—large and small—are investing in their workforces for the long term and are improving their rate of return. An earlier ground-breaking study by the American Society for Training and Development showed that companies that made large investments in employee development between 1997 and 2001 had an annualized rate of return on invested capital of 16.3 percent compared with the 10.7 percent average for the S&P 500.[41]

Human capital investment and the discipline of training ROI need to be as rigorous as possible. "By training workers," says Michael Moskow, president of the Federal Reserve Bank of Chicago, "we can take full advantage of the gains from technological advance and international trade.... We should invest in programs for which research shows the benefits clearly outweigh the costs."[42]

THE NEW FRONTIER: THE FUTURE OF TRAINING AND DEVELOPMENT

The pace of technological innovation is likely to continue accelerating as more open global markets vie for the world's consumers. Yet most companies have not yet fully exploited the potential of their existing IT.

The ability of businesses to organize themselves more efficiently is dependent on their smart people. But according to an OECD economic study, between 33 and 50 percent of all adults in the United States "lack the kinds of literacy skills that are needed to function well in modern societies. However, many of these same adults have graduated from high school, or even college and still need additional human capital investment to become productive." If we add on the dearth of technical skills and critical competencies, one begins to realize the true scope of the 2010 meltdown.[43]

The dam of current management neglect is about to burst from its vain attempt to hold back a rising tide of poorly educated workers. A flood is already washing high-skill/high-wage jobs overseas under the banner of short-term profit. If the flood becomes a torrent of these jobs going overseas, organizations that do little training will not survive. Learning through training and education is a invisible process. It is internal and often takes time, and therefore, it is often ridiculed and undervalued by many people.

Ian Cunningham of Strategic Developments International, Ltd., sees four current organizational responses to the Sixth Discipline. Three of the four are negative:

Apathetic/Antagonistic. Neglect or hostility toward supporting and funding training. Many small businesses fall into this category. The boss is convinced that money and time given to training is either wasteful or harmful. "If you need training, get it on your own."

Reactive. Employees might receive funding for an external course, but only if they push their managers. Training is not systematic or evaluated.

Bureaucratic. The organization has a training budget for internal or external courses that are standardized. Line managers see little linkage of training to on-the-job needs and do not consider training effective. Evaluation is weak.

Strategic. The owner or senior management is committed to training and education programs in which there are direct links between business needs and specific learning activities. Flexible business responses are based on the careful evaluation of individual program results.

Why should business owners or senior management move in the strategic direction? "Companies should be trying to create environments where performance is enabled," says Tom Davenport, author of *Human Capital: What It Is and Why People Invest in It* (1999). When employees have the social tools to perform, "the proper training, coaching and feedback from the boss, and recognition for good work—they do a better job, and feel better about themselves and their company." So many businesses today talk about empowering their workers to achieve better results. Why not move on to increasing their mental power to innovate and create the new ideas for future growth?[44]

The Secrets of Innovation

Q. What is a skilled person? How do these critical competencies grow?

A. People's skills develop from the controlled, corrected repetitions of an act for which someone has some aptitude. Skill is the byproduct of education, experience, criticism, and thinking. Between the amateur and the expert there is a difference, not only of degree but in kind.

A skilled person, within the scope of particular sets of parameters, has the ability to integrate thinking, behaviors, or muscular activities in different ways. The skilled person has specialized responses of great complexity. He or she has carefully tuned faculties for screening information, acceptance or rejection, analysis, evaluation, and selective adjustment. These patterns of appraisal are both conscious and unconscious. The performance of a golf pro, a brain surgeon, a carpenter, an auto mechanic, or a customer service representative may look automatic, but it is really based on internal self-criticism and a wisdom developed over time. From this performance, innovation may spring.

Q. When does innovation happen?

A. Innovation happens when the power of combinational logic is used to meld various, often divergent ideas into something new and successful.

Q. How does innovation happen?

A. Most modern business issues are multi-dimensional, usually involving a wide variety of disciplines. An innovative person learns how to network different disciplines into new, interdisciplinary answers. This is neither easy nor quick. Education can help activate a person's mental reasoning abilities, by first providing information, then imparting broader knowledge and, finally, by fostering in-depth wisdom. This is a gradual transformation process. The process also relies upon the person's capacity to network by locating other experts with partial answers, who are willing to collaborate in crafting real breakthrough, new solutions.

Innovation is difficult because the skilled person must overcome the cultural biases and language barriers that divide the worlds of business, the sciences, academe, and education one from another. Innovators must really become knowledge brokers who can remain above the fray, acting as arbitrators who keep their eye on the prize—delivery of a truly new idea that solves a vexing problem, introduces a new service, or invents a new product or procedure (See Figure 6.1).

Orthodoxy be damned! The human narrow-minded, reactionary, self-protective nature of any specific discipline needs to be ignored if skilled people are to successfully craft answers to the What if?—Why not? breakthrough questions and answers that will lead America and the world to the new, innovative ideas of the future.[45]

Broadly speaking, this is what these Top 100 companies hope for when they invest $50+ billion each year in employee training, development, and education. They are following the advice of the great sage of management, Peter Drucker, who warned that rapid change puts a premium on

HOW INNOVATION HAPPENS

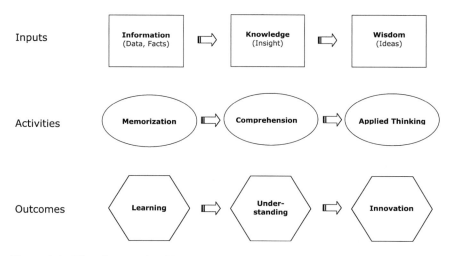

Figure 6.1—How Innovation Happens
Source: Edward E. Gordon, 2005.

innovation: "[Innovation] means first, the systematic sloughing off of yesterday. It means, next, the systematic search for opportunities ... to aim at creating new businesses rather than new products, or modifications of old products ... to set up innovative ventures separately, outside the existing managerial structure." Whether or not these innovations happen is usually a matter of degree, rather than absolutes. Often, it happens in stages.

Richard E. Dauch, chairman of the Manufacturing Institute, believes that it is vitally important for business owners and senior executives to understand how the productivity process happens. When they consider training and education, they should not leave out the needs of ordinary workers in the office, plant, laboratory, or elsewhere. They all need to constantly upgrade their skills so they can master ever-changing technology, its applications, and potential innovations.[46]

Tapping the Treasure Trove

In the New America, jobs morph to suit the rapid pace of change. This new arrangement works well, but only if the company has skilled workers. The less-skilled people, or the ones with the wrong skills for the new jobs now being created, are simply being squeezed out by automation or global competition.

In high-wage Japan, Canon and Sharp show how it is still possible to reap impressive profits from manufacturing if such production requires high technical or production expertise. Kenwood, a maker of home and car electronics and wireless equipment, went a step farther by moving production back to Japan from its low-wage Malaysian plant. The secret was its highly skilled Japanese workforce, which was termed "a treasure trove" by Kazuhiro Sato, the managing director of Kenwood Yamagata.

Mr. Sato and his team changed the layout of the factory in Japan. They used highly skilled workers to speed up rehandling, improve inspection, and reduce inventory, which was the largest element in overall costs. The improved efficiencies achieved through highly skilled people meant that seven Japanese workers could produce the same portable mini-disc player that formerly required 22 Malaysian workers.[47]

In the United States, Toyota, Honda, and Nissan are following the same Sixth Discipline strategies with their local American workforces. In 2004 they increased their combined share of the U.S. automobile market to over 30 percent. True, their non-unionized plants in the South and West are not burdened with Detroit's legacy pension and health-care costs. But the secret of the Japanese car makers' success story is their relentless focus on training their U.S. workforce for higher quality, production flexibility, and product innovation.

In South Korea, Yuhan-Kimberly (YK), a company which is 70-percent owned by U.S. Kimberly–Clark, was threatened by increased competition from China. Instead of cutting staff members and costs, it took a counterintuitive approach—starting lifelong learning classes twice a month. Instead of working more than 50 hours a week, employees now work a maximum of 42 hours. YK has instituted a four-days-on, four-days-off schedule. Employees now work up to 12 hours a day, but fewer hours overall. They can choose to study on their days off for extra pay. The company's expanded 1,700-person workforce spends an average of 300 hours a year in classes covering a wide range of information—from the Chinese language to e-learning and work-related technologies. YK's changes have tripled its factory's capacity, raising net income almost 18-fold over the past ten years. Labor costs amount to around 15 percent of the company's expenses. Almost a quarter of that amount is invested in its lifelong learning program.

This approach might seem anathema to U.S. business culture, but YK executives take an opposite view. "We are making real productivity gains, and that will help us keep our competitive edge," states Moon Kook-hyun, YK's chief executive. He also takes pride that "employee satisfaction and safety have greatly improved."

Other South Korean companies, including Pulmuone, a mid-sized food company, and Kookmin Bank, South Korea's largest lender, have adopted a Sixth Discipline culture. "We are strengthening our employees' abilities, and their concentration on their work is increased by balancing work and life," says Kookmin executive, Choi In-suk.

This business culture outlook will help South Korea keep the cheap labor threat of China at bay, thinks YK's Mr. Moon. "To keep ahead, we should move towards a knowledge-based rather than a labor-intensive economy," he states. "In every sense, China is bigger than Korea, so we can't continue to enjoy the advantage we had up until the late 1980s."[48]

At all employment levels, U.S. businesses also need to offer these development opportunities, and workers need to embrace them if the majority are to survive and thrive, as did 56-year-old Jim Willard at Lincoln Electric in Cleveland and Jesse Mercer, age 49, at Blackhawk Automotive Plastics in Salem, Ohio. Both agreed to participate in extensive new training for new jobs at their companies. "Some people resent being moved," Willard says. "You accept it or you don't. It's good for the company. Sometimes it's good for the employees. You still have a place to go."[49]

A study published in the *Harvard Business Review* by the Boston University School of Management and the University of Pennsylvania's Wharton School studied 400 mid-level executives in a wide range of industries around the globe. It found that employee commitment can be enhanced through training. Organizations that give executives more skills through training "can actually induce them to stay and remain committed, even when their jobs aren't guaranteed." the study reported.[50]

Predicting the Future

In my search for enlightenment on the future of training and development, I have repeatedly found that the chief challenges that a business needs to overcome are not so much technical, demographic, or financial, as they are cultural. Here are some of the more thought-provoking predictions I have found:

Peter Drucker, consultant

The only comparative advantage of the developed countries is in the supply of knowledge workers. It is not a qualitative advantage: the educated people in the emerging countries are every whit as knowledgeable as their counterparts in the developed world.... To convert this quantitative lead into a qualitative lead is one—and perhaps the only—way for the developed countries to maintain their competitive position in the world economy. This means continual, systematic work on the productivity of knowledge and knowledge workers, which is still neglected and abysmally low.... It is likely to become the decisive factor, at least for most industries in the developed world.[51]

... The great majority of executives will not stay with their present employer or in their present line of work until traditional retirement age.... They will go back to school, one way or another—at least every three years. And I don't mean just read a book, and I don't mean just go to a seminar—I mean *go back to school*. I think those changes are predictable and certain, and very few of the executives I know, whether in business or in nonprofits, are prepared for them.[52]

Michael Gelb, author

How to Think Like Leonardo da Vinci (Dell, 2000)

Don't talk about creating a learning organization unless you're serious. I've worked for big companies that are doing great things. They get to a point where people are starting to think more creatively, more like Leonardo, then the stock price drops and they pull the plug on training. I don't hear from them for a year or two, then they call back and say, "We're desperate. We need creativity." And I have to start over again. That's the dark side of this.

I try to tell them it's better not even to talk about creativity and creating a learning organization unless they're serious. If you're not committed and not prepared to walk your talk, you're just going to build more cynicism and alienation. It's better to say, "Look people, we don't care about learning, we don't care about creativity, and we don't care about you. You're lucky to have a job, now go back to work." It's better to be honest than to say, "We're going to change and create a culture that supports development because people are our most precious resource," then lay off 40 percent of your workforce.[53]

Arie de Geus, business change and learning guru

Although the priority is the survival of the organization, the challenge to executives, "is not to just strip people out of the equation." The critical production factor has shifted to people: human talent is the key to competitive success. The challenge to companies is to shift from managing capital to get the best out of human talent to attain an ever higher quality of output: This requires time, longer than the next quarter. You may cut employees to improve the quarterly bottom line but that short-term gain risks the consequences of long-term death.[54]

Michael H. Jordon, chairman and CEO of Electronic Data Systems Corp.

I contend it makes more economic sense to focus on, say, a three-year investment horizon, versus a quarterly obsession. And for companies whose future prospects are tied to technological advances, multi-year plans should look out a decade or more into the future.

I'm convinced that more market patience will go a long way in allowing corporate leaders to manage their businesses in a more productive, collaborative way,
for the benefit not only of shareholders, but of economy as a whole.[55]

Thomas Petzinger, author

The New Pioneers (Simon & Schuster, 1999)

It would be ludicrous to imply that all companies or business people, or even
most, have abandoned the old command-and-control ethos.... But while the
old order persists, the new order is rising quickly and is poised to overtake it....
In an era when change arrives without warning and threatens to eradicate entire
companies and industries overnight, organizations can survive only by engaging
the eyes, ears, minds and emotions of all individuals and by encouraging them to
act on their knowledge and beliefs.[56]

We can boil down all this expert advice to five tactics that any business
can use to achieve the Sixth Discipline:

1. Use appropriate training and education as a tool to help implement core business needs.
2. Offer a blend of both classroom and technology-based training.
3. Partner with educational institutions to broaden education
   options for employees.
4. Measure the training ROI to determine the value of these programs.
5. Budget training and education to balance the human capital and
   financial capital objectives of the business.[57]

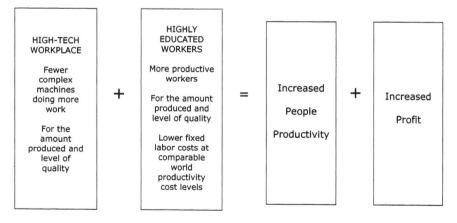

Figure 6.2—Results from Adopting the "Sixth Discipline"
Source: Edward E. Gordon, 2005.

There will be high rewards for those companies that have the vision and leadership to adopt the Sixth Discipline. In the short term (2005–2010), business must also increase its support of stronger, community-based career education programs that will create more next generation knowledge workers in every local community. "In a global economy it is education, not location, that determines the standard of living," says Albert Hoser, president of Siemens (See Figure 6.2).

American business has long been a consumer of smart people. The business community and the rest of American society must work harder at creating more smart people. After considering these future trends, do we have any choice?

7

Beyond the 2010 Crossroad

In the transition between eras, the obsolescing precepts of the old order can be leveraged toward bringing about the new.
—Holman W. Jenkins, Jr.
The Transitional Generations

We all know how this story is going to end. Sometime in the future, the U.S. labor pool will catch up with the realities of New America. But history teaches us that nations are wiser to defuse such anxieties with incremental change rather than waiting for the big bang.[1]

There are major policy makers who understand what needs to be done. "We need to foster a flexible education system," says Alan Greenspan, chairman of the Federal Reserve Board, "one that integrates work and training and that serves the needs both of experienced workers at different stages in their careers and of students embarking on their initial course of study."[2]

Yet the *big questions* remain unanswered:

- How will the majority of workers acquire the higher skills necessary to become part of New America?
- Where will we find the smart people for the New America?
- What can we do to alter a popular culture that holds back change?
- Why have most politicians turned a deaf ear to systematic remedies?

- Where can local communities begin this transition process?
- How do we motivate more people to become involved in their communities?

These are some of the central issues explored throughout *The 2010 Meltdown* that need clear answers.

At the end of the Second World War, the United States and the Soviet Union emerged as the world's two great superpowers. At that time, John Colville, Winston Churchill's private wartime secretary, observed, "We are the transitional generation, who have climbed to the watershed and will soon look down the other side, on a new world."[3]

Today, America and the world are staring at a new transitional era of powerful socioeconomic forces that will that will shape a very different 21st century. Between 2005 and 2020, about 20 million new, high-skill jobs will be created in the U.S. economy (U.S. Department of Labor, 2004). In comparison to her competitors, America's diverse population and creativity are major advantages in filling these high-wage jobs. Yet America's relative strengths cannot paper over its major weakness—the need to overhaul U.S. cultural attitudes about education, careers, and lifelong learning. Most Americans continue to live in a mythical world of the past that defies the current realities. "It is like trying to research and do business in the 21st century in a culture that wants to live in the 19th," says a noted scientist at the University of Illinois.[4]

Despite over two decades of numerous expert studies, endless public debate, and sweeping government policy initiatives, very little has changed. Instead, small business owners and corporate executives have begun circling their wagons. Some are starting to give up on American education, in general, and the American worker, in particular.

A valiant few are still trying to collaborate with community partners. As we have seen, islands of successful change do exist today across the United States. But a general cultural indifference has gradually settled across the land. Token programs, empty rhetoric, and broken promises are all too typical responses to the realities of New America that have stalled solutions to the U.S. jobs, education, and careers revolution.

The first white flags of potential surrender and retreat are now being run up by major U.S. IT players such as Hewlett–Packard, Intel, Microsoft, and other members of the Computer Systems Policy Project (see chapter 2.). "As the United States encounters new global realities, policy makers face a choice: We can compete in the international arena or we can retreat," says Craig Barrett, Intel's Chairman.

Multinational U.S. companies have no intention of surrendering their market dominance. If they cannot find large enough numbers of entry-level (aged 22–32), well-educated workers in the United States, they will expand their use of outsourcing and foreign direct investment, retreating more and more overseas. There they hope to thrive by finding the smart knowledge technologists that American society cannot or will not produce in sufficient numbers. This process is now accelerating. An example: Over 100 companies have now established R&D centers in India. This includes General Electric, employing 1,600 overseas workers, and Microsoft having established its largest software center outside of the United States.[5]

"The lack of basic skills throughout much of the workforce, and the growing shortages of workers with specific skills that are increasingly needed, create a danger that the American economy will drift into what economists call 'low skills equilibrium,'" says the report, *Learning Partnerships: Strengthening American Jobs in the Global Economy*, issued in 2004 by the non-profit Foundation for Democratic Education in Washington, D.C.[6]

This drift has already begun. The United States is now permanently losing many high-pay/high-skill jobs, and perhaps even the IT world dominance we now take for granted. In this vital area, our popular culture seriously lags in recognizing the demands of a global, 21st-century labor market.

The 2010 Meltdown has explored these interconnected issues leading to both a New America and a wider New World. What can we expect might happen over the next 15 years?

Until 2010, growth in the workforce may be sustained as the so-called echo-boom generation (the children of the baby boomers) reach working age. However, by 2010 labor-force growth will begin to drop to near zero and remain so past 2020. Under a business-as-usual scenario, labor shortages will begin to appear across the country in a broad range of employment sectors (see Chapters 1, 2 and 4). This, in turn, will lead to a rise in wages as employers compete for the fewer skilled workers (the knowledge technologists) available in each business arena. Organizations are likely to encourage employees to postpone retirement by offering more flexible employment, such as part-time positions, job sharing, or work-at-home arrangements.

Companies using immigration to fill their ranks will be forced to offer better incentives as global competition heats up for the same shrinking pool of knowledge workers. Technology programs that encourage more productivity per worker will become essential for every business as the labor force contracts. This might produce a catch-22 skills scenario that we have discussed in preceding chapters.

RESOLVING THE ISSUES: CULTURE— EDUCATION—PEOPLE

In essence, the United States today faces this central socioeconomic question: How do we provide the right content and quality levels of education to the young,, and training to current workers so they can thrive in the changing, knowledge-based environment of a new age? Three key issues need to be addressed if this process of people and jobs development is to be successfully resolved:

- Issue 1: Changing the Culture
- Issue 2: Igniting an Education Revolution
- Issue 3: Finding the People

Let us now examine each issue in turn and explore potential action and policy plans.

Issue 1: Changing the Culture

Depreciating People

We are all living in a time where the workplace rules our lives. Remember the promises of how technology would set us free? The work week would be shortened. We would all have more time to think and innovate while the machines performed repetitive tasks. What a fantasy that prediction has proven to be! Once there was a time when strong unions negotiated strict hourly limits on the workday. This ironclad culture was reinforced by law. In today's workplace all such strictures have been warped out of shape.

The culture gets bent when companies put blue-collar workers on 12-hour shifts in order to reduce costs by running a plant around the clock. To keep the payroll down, hospitals overwork nurses, thus attempting to contain health-care costs. Companies wipe out jobs and then load up the survivors with enabling technology such as cell phones, Palm Pilots™, BlackBerries™, wireless laptops, and so forth. They empower you to do the work for two or maybe three people.[7]

"These are not corporate pioneers," says Stephen Franklin of the *Chicago Tribune*, "They are thieves who steal workers' time. That is why, for some time, the average annual hours worked in the U.S. have led the world."[8]

Most employees feel stuck in the middle. They loyally work punishing hours for companies that could dispense with them tomorrow. In the past 20 years, most businesses tore up their implicit contract to provide people with secure employment if they worked hard. Now many companies can't even be relied upon to pay the pension they promised. How many more male and female executives do I have to interview to confirm that even many 35-year-olds are already sick of the long hours and no family life?

If you lose your job, it will not because you spent too few hours in the office. It will be because new technology put your industry in decline or a competitor had a better business plan that forced your company to downsize. Or maybe a big corporate honcho, facing criticism from stockholders, devised a draconian right-sizing solution so he could survive.

There are companies that allow people time to be with their families. They do so because it assists them in recruiting and retaining irreplaceable workers. As the 2010 crossroad approaches, watch for more employers to adopt this practice, as more and more companies struggle to find smart people. Those organizations will institute policies that allow their employees to balance both meaningful work and a life outside the workplace.

At present, many Americans feel burnt out and personally defenseless in tackling, let alone solving, work, life, and education issues with their own personal action or fresh thinking. These personal feelings of helplessness are driven by the collapse of community solidarity and community activism throughout much of the nation. People feel overwhelmed by the divisive rhetoric of politicians and segments of the media that portray these social change issues as being larger-than-life situations that only the so-called experts can solve.

So we disconnect. We wait for the president, governor, mayor, or just somebody else to solve these quality of life issues, because we feel we cannot. Are there really any other alternatives?[9]

Community Activism

Our arrival at the 2010 crossroad will not automatically readjust the workforce and global society. We need some new culture-change venues inside organizations, and collaborative efforts among groups at the community level. There is very strong resistance to culture change in the United States. Why? British journalist Michael Skapinker of the *Financial Times* thinks it is because " ...No other country has believed in itself so fervently or for so long, or been able to give its people, established or newcomers, such a clear idea of what it expected of them."[10] It is an interesting perspective on why it is difficult for American to rethink work, community, and education connections.

Most Americans know that something bad is going on in their communities. There is a growing sense of cultural disintegration. Robert Putnam, in his book *Bowling Alone: The Collapse and Revival of American Community* (2000), was struck by the current decline in all manner of social and civic involvement in America. In today's social order, relations tend to be superficial, the restraints imposed by public opinion on unacceptable personal behavior are weak, and a sense of a common cause with one's neighbor has begun to wane.[11]

Yet we have gone through much of this before. The Progressive Era was a time of mass social unrest and change across the United States. Putnam says grassroots community organization " ... inventiveness reached a crescendo unmatched in American history, not merely in terms of number of clubs, but in the range and durability of the newly founded organizations.... Their diagnosis of social change led to prescription, not despair." These local community activists saw "society's ills, poverty and the rest, as reflecting societal and economic causes, not individual moral failings," according to Putnam. The Progressive outlook "was activist and optimistic, not fatalist and despondent."

Most historians agree that these decades saw a veritable boom in association-building as the cultural norm. Society was reformed on the foundations of a massive new structure of civic associations. The so-called club movement, emphasizing a culture of self-help, swept across America. Ordinary people—amateurs—became involved in alliances across class lines. This was both top–down and bottom–up at once, as popular debate about local issues became part of America's culture.

New types of associations multiplied, chapters of pre-existing groups proliferated, and associations set up national, state, and local groups, including Chambers of Commerce, the Rotary, the Better Business Bureau, the Parent–Teacher Association (PTA), the Boy Scouts, the Girl Scouts, 4-H, the Society for the Prevention of Cruelty to Animals, and numerous other organizations.[12]

Today every community still contains dozens of people who do want to create something—people with ideas and ambitions for a better future. But they need information and contacts, as well as getting obstacles cleared out of their way. Author Ernesto Sirolli coined the term "enterprise facilitation"—a technique that has generated hundreds of new enterprises and thousands of jobs in the United States, Canada, Australia, and New Zealand. Enterprise facilitation starts with the idea that much of social and cultural development is something that people should do for themselves.

These are the people America needs as we enter a new era of responsibility for businesses, families, and individuals. We are ending an era of entitlement as government regulation declines. This opens a new window of opportunity for organizations of all types to again see themselves as stewards of social responsibility, allying with local community activists to pursue "capitalism with a conscience."[13]

The so-called Return on Responsibility for all these groups is far greater than the defunct ideology of unrestrained, laissez-faire capitalism. Do we really wish to glorify a new breed of robber barons, the speculative manipulators, as some in the media would lead us to believe?

"To some degree, the market will sort this out," says Jerry Rubin, vice president of Jobs for the Future. But without more intermediary alliances with community groups, as workforce expert Nancy Dunne points out, "It will take a long time, during which U.S. competitiveness will diminish."[14] Government (with a small "g") will remain, not as the initiator of change, but as another partner in the overall change process.

Culture change in America remains no simple task. In the first decade of the 21st century, the United States, for better or for worse, has begun to face a galvanizing people and jobs crisis. Chapters 5 and 6 of this book have shown how intermediary groups of ordinary citizens have been establishing new community organizations (NGOs) to bring about this culture change. Now let's see how these groups were successfully organized.

Non-Governmental Organizations (NGOs)

NGOs worldwide have grown from 1,400 in 1975 to over 30,000 today. Peter Drucker has referred to them as the "third sector of society." NGOs are accomplishing what business and government together have failed to do. Through their collaborative power, they have had a significant cultural impact on corporate and government strategy and decision-making.

NGOs can be broadly defined as independent voluntary associations of people acting together on a continuous basis for some common purpose. What they are now doing across the United States is bypassing the empty political rhetoric at the top to shape the debate at the local level about the goals and aspirations of the people.

Knowledge is power. NGOs, by marshalling that power, are beginning to transform the political agenda, first at the local level, then extending to the state level, and eventually nationally.

No one said that this will be easy, quick, or cheap. One hundred years ago, during a similar time of social crisis, community groups organized across the United States and fundamentally altered the jobs, people, and education culture of America. The time has come to do it again.

In the coming years, we can expect local NGOs to evolve from unofficial non-profit associations to major culture-change players in the restructuring of New America.[15] Why? It is because their collective leadership has a greater conceptual capacity to digest the increasingly complex masses of information that top leaders must comprehend. NGOs have greater ability than solo organizations to view, understand, and act instead of surrendering to gridlock, which only preserves the status quo.[16]

"NGOs, when adequately funded," says Jessica T. Mathews, a senior fellow at the Council on Foreign Relations, "can outperform government in the delivery of public services.... And they are better than governments at dealing with problems that grow slowly and affect society through their cumulative effect on individuals."[17]

This may be one of the reasons that, in recent years, traditional foundations have moved their charitable giving into more sustainable partnerships with NGOs in support of a range of education and training initiatives. For example, the Bill and Melinda Gates Foundation, the Chicago Community Trust, and the Carnegie Corporation of New York are all supporting new, not-for-profit, grass-roots efforts in education and training. "If you're going to tackle education, you have to have a concerted approach," believes Hugh Jagger, a strategic adviser to Cisco Systems. "The private sector doesn't have the resources to do the whole job, but it certainly has the capacity to help put the right models in place that the public sector can scale up."[18]

Much has already been written about organizing a successful NGO. Table 7.1. boils down some of these essentials into a five-step planning process.

As Chapters 5 and 6 illustrated, NGOs come in many organizational formats and have diverse purposes. Often, a well-known nonprofit community group or activist takes the lead to begin discussing jobs, training, or career issues. A roundtable series of discussion ensues, with early, more serious players coming forward. From these meetings, task forces take on the examination of the specific problems that the NGO might target for solution. Then an NGO board of directors coalesces around a mission statement and a funding plan.

Such NGOs establish a system for continuously gathering local information on labor-market needs and the careers they encompass. Multiple ways are found to circulate this information to parents, students, the community's workforce, and the for-profit as well as non-profit business communities. The NGO builds clear links between student and worker development and the wider community's economy and quality of life.

Table 7.1
Establishing an NGO

Step1	*Build a Framework*

- Mission Statement
- Board of Directors = Community members who:
  A. know the issues
  B. are connected to the NGO's mission
- By-Laws of the Board
- Conflict of Interest Statement
- Financial Management Practices

Step 2   *Program Planning & Evaluation*

- Describe the problem to be addressed
- Identify strategies to address the problem
- Describe the individual activities for each strategy
- Establish monitoring procedures to determine if a project is on track or if revisions are needed
- Plan periodic evaluation of NGO programs

Step 3   *Coalition Building*

- Develop partnerships with other community players
- Adopt coordinated long and short term programs
- Look for common activities with other groups
- Determine if a coalition is temporary for a specific issue or permanent if missions and interests are compatible

Step 4   *Development of Sustainable Benchmarks*

- Early Transition (Examples)
  —Develop clear mission and strategic plan
  —Dialogue with key players: business, government, unions, schools, etc.
- Mid-Transition (Examples)
  —Clearly define the roles of the board and staff
  —Lobby and advocate at local and state levels
  —Develop a diversified funding base
  —Fully involve community and staff in strategic planning
- Consolidation (Examples)
  —Attract public support and engage decision-makers though clarity of vision and purpose
  —Enlist the board in fundraising, public relations, and lobbying activities
  —Adapt the strategic plan to ongoing changes

(*continued*)

Table 7.1
(continued)

Step 5	*Fundraising*

- Diversify activities and donor base
- Build partnership with donors
- Ensure a continuous process of grant seeking

Adapted from: Peter Willets, "What Is a Non-Governmental Organization?" Encyclopedia of Life Support Systems, 2002; Olena P. Maslyukivska, "The Role of Non-Governmental Organization in Development Cooperation." Research paper, UNDP/Yale Collaboration Program, 1999. Research Clinic, New Haven, 1999; and *The Handbook on Good Practices for Laws Relating to Non-Governmental Organizations.* International Center for Non-Profit Law. Washington, D.C.: World Bank, 1997.

The NGO develops plans for workforce education. It identifies training service providers, and a system is established to get these services into businesses and/or to establish a local training or education center.

Student career education and overall education quality standards are developed that meet local business needs and more global career-requirement standards. A diversity of curriculum models are developed by public and private educational institutions collaborating with local businesses through the NGO.

The reasons the NGOs we have reviewed have been successful seems to hinge on five organizational strengths:

1. They are specifically organized around a strong mission that they stick to.
2. They represent the leading authorities of the community.
3. They develop the power to implement their vision.
4. They are consistent in their community programs.
5. They are stable forces for long-lasting change.[19]

NGOs are springing up around the nation to help students, workers, employers, and communities cope in the wider global arena of people and jobs. They act as intermediaries, enabling people to come together to fill a vacuum that is undermining community vitality. NGOs tend to be scrappy and entrepreneurial in their efforts to cobble together breakthrough program models and finding the funding to make them work. NGOs offer America the chance to again release forces for self-help in a drive to boost the nation's skills, education, and career bases and reinvent the American dream machine.[20]

Issue 2: Igniting an Education Revolution

What Is the Purpose of Education?

Across the United States, over 15,000 local public school districts and tens of thousands of private elementary and high schools now enroll more than 60 million students (U.S. Department of Education, 2004). The question "What is the purpose of schooling?" is now being debated with increasing vigor.

One answer has come from the passage in 2001 of the No Child Left Behind (NCLB)Act. It has become the cornerstone of a movement promoting accountability and standards in education. NCLB was passed because many states receiving massive federal Title I funding for at-risk children had failed to set standards for achievement levels and/or the means to determine whether these standards were being met.

NCLB has set high academic standards and requires all public schools receiving federal funding to test students and report their progress in reaching these goals. The results of this high-stakes testing triggers a number of measures if a school is determined to be not making adequate progress and, ultimately, can reduce future levels of federal Title I funding for a school district or an entire state. As a result, a great deal of classroom time is now being spent "teaching to the test" (i.e., trying to improve student test scores, rather than teaching the school's curriculum). This is an "earthquake that has rearranged, maybe deformed, the American education landscape," says Howard Gardner, a professor at Harvard University.[21] Testing alone will not achieve better results unless what schools teach and how they teach are changed.

Standards-based reform "assumes that high standards and a challenging academic curriculum are for all students, not just an academic elite," states Washington writer David Broder. But testing systems are not ends unto themselves, but the means to an end.

An accountability system needs to include a substantial, school-wide plan for assisting low scorers that encompasses both parents and teachers. For example, in Pennsylvania report cards on student and school test performance produced by the Grow Network are customized for parents and teachers. The parent reports give suggestions for home reading and math activities that parents can do together with their child to improve academic performance. Coaching suggestions are given to parents for better communication with the child's teacher. Parents are also alerted to other local community resources that will enrich their child's education. Such informational, coaching, and collaborative strategies are far more productive than just giving parents test scores alone. It places more emphasis on the importance of the parents' role in raising a child's achievement, whereas just furnishing a test score may be viewed measuring a child's fixed innate ability or IQ. Tutoring by subject-expert, experienced teachers can help. However, unless we change what goes on in the classroom and at home, the standards-based movement will achieve little more than reporting additional low test scores.[22]

The other major part of the accountability movement seeks to answer the question: How much does it cost to provide every American child with a quality education? The answer is called the adequacy level, but who knows what that level is? School and school district figures are all over the map. For example, in Kenilworth, Illinois, an elite suburb north of Chicago, 93 percent of its public school students passed a state achievement test. The annual bill: $10,676 per student. Contrast this with Western Springs, in southwest Cook County, Illinois, which had the same test results. The bill in this district was $5,917 per student.

More money doesn't always guarantee success. After 15 years and spending $2 billion, Kansas City, Missouri became the first big-city school district ever to lose its accreditation. "Kansas City is a very, very sad story," said Gary Orfield, a Harvard sociologist, who has studied the district for years. Students come to school exhausted, hungry, or afraid. There is often no one at home to get them up in the morning or see if they have done their homework, Orfield found. "Basically, we have a huge social crisis, and schools really can't solve it by themselves," he concluded.

Some states, such as Arkansas, have taken a different approach to the adequacy issue. In 2004 the Arkansas Supreme Court ruled that $1.8 billion in state funds had been unfairly distributed, with not enough going to local schools. Legislators proposed merging small districts to make schools more efficient and to increase per-pupil expenditures. However, research shows that bigger schools generally produce less student learning.[23]

In the debate over the purpose of education, there are advocates for public schools who see them as almost mythological places for democratic discourse about our society and its education. Yet, do our local schools really offer this large, common vision of America bound by a common heritage, common economic and political institutions, and a common core of knowledge? One of America's greatest strengths has been its diversity. The United States is a large nation with many different regions and a vast mosaic of small communities. That is one of the compelling reasons that local school boards were established by their individual states, not by the federal government.

After decades of talk about education reform, there remains a surprising lack of recognition by many in business, government, and education that "Parents have the primary responsibility for their own children," as stated by Robert J. Taggart, a professor at the University of Delaware.[24] This cultural oxymoron actually emerged at the beginning of the 20th century, with compulsory public schooling. Measuring how well students learned needed to be school-based rather than family-based. This has led us down a long, slippery slope of, at first, giving the schools the primary, and more recently, almost exclusive responsibility for guaranteeing student learning. Strengthening family life and offering coaching to parents in the home-learning environment has only recently come onto our radar screens, largely as an afterthought.[25]

One of the earliest and most influential studies of parental influence and educational results was done by James Coleman at the University of Chicago (1987). He looked for the causes of lower dropout rates and the more effective teaching of reading and math of private high schools in comparison to their public counterparts. What he found was surprising:

- Schools success was not due to the filtering out of the troublesome students whom public schools must accept.
- School success was due to the culture dominating the school. Parents were the major factor insulating the school from pressures to water down its curriculum and to provide the social resources for its at-risk students.[26]

Other educational researchers tend to agree. Anne Henderson and Nancy Berla have summarized a large number of studies that show:

- Parental involvement in their child's education helps the child and school do better.
- Children with involved parents tend to succeed not just in school but throughout life.[27]

In the broader context of this debate over the purpose of American education, another viewpoint is the traditional argument that schooling is to educate the mind in the broadest sense, to expose as many students as possible to the cultural touchstones of civilization. Other people believe that education is to provide the qualifications necessary for a successful career. Education must be useful, and to do that it must be streamlined. Out go the liberal arts—history, music, literature, art, and so forth—in favor of technology, business, sports, science, and computing. Education, according to their argument, needs to be discussed in terms of outcomes, productivity, and usable skills. The school has become a factory, and the classroom a production line.

According to Frank Levy, an economist at MIT, and Richard J. Murnane, a Harvard economist, living a meaningful life today requires a more sophisticated solution than either of these two alternatives. On the low-wage end of the American economy, there has been growth in the number of service-sector jobs that almost any person can do, but computers cannot. On the high-wage end, there remains growth in the numbers of technical, sales, professional, and managerial jobs that computers don't do well, but that smart people can do very well.

The jobs that have declined are those involving repetitive, rule-bound tasks that can be easily programmed on computers. These include administrative support, manufacturing, and production jobs that pay relatively well and support a large segment of the middle class. Many of these traditionally employed people never entered or completed any type of post-secondary education, such as a certificate program, a two- or four-year degree, or a graduate degree. They currently comprise about 70 percent of the U.S. adult workforce.

Today's great education divide between future individual success and failure exists between students who can use a computer and other technology to do valuable work versus those who cannot. What is valuable work and what educational preparation is needed for it? Valuable work requires a variety of intellectual capabilities. The list includes critical thinking skills (or what business people call critical competencies), engaging in sustained reasoning, managing complex tasks, testing solutions, collaborating well with others, and communicating well verbally and in writing. These are all abilities that are developed by a good liberal arts education.

For all these reasons, our goal as a nation needs to be the blending of a traditional liberal arts education with an appropriate career or technical education that most closely meets each individual student's aptitudes and interests. We need to aspire to equip the majority of our students with this more comprehensive educational foundation. Most average students will reach these standards if they receive the right educational preparation.[28]

To bridge the education chasm currently dividing America, let us consider three major obstacles that are currently blocking a successful education revolution: discipline and parental involvement; the creation of a real education profession; and the development of a greater diversity of local schools.

Discipline and Parenting

As a cultural phenomenon, discipline problems are not minor irritations for most teachers across the United States and Canada. Jean Johnson, senior vice president at the non-profit research group Public Agenda, paints a dreary picture of the state of school discipline in the study *Teaching Interrupted* (2004). Ninety-seven percent of teachers agree that good student discipline " ... [i]s a prerequisite for a successful school," reports Johnson. Almost eight in ten teachers say they would be better teachers if disruptive students didn't take up so much of their time. In fact, over four in ten teachers admit they now spend more time keeping order than teaching in the classroom!

Though most schools have addressed outright dangers such as drugs and weapons, a culture of ill-discipline prevails. Almost 80 percent of teachers report that students say "they have rights and their parents can sue." Almost 50 percent have been accused by a parent of unfairly disciplining a child. Unless this litigation-tinged cultural attitude of contempt for a teacher's authority is changed, how will America ever upgrade the teaching profession?

There are no easy answers to this discipline problem, but it must be taken seriously. Parental authority is paramount. Principals also have a leadership role in setting firm rules and making teachers, students, and parents feel that they are working together as a team. As Kathleen Parker recently wrote, "Human beings respond to ... an absence of caring or of anyone being in charge. In the absence of authority—the symbolic adult—children tend to behave badly. Order breaks down. Civility disintegrates."[29]

Teachers are also stressed out by trying to fill the roles of educator, social worker, and parent. Too many children have family-related breakdowns, making the children unready or unwilling to learn when they arrive in school. And the situation seems to be getting worse. A survey by the Canadian Teachers Federation (2001) reports that 56 percent of instructors now spend more time with the personal problems of students than just two years earlier. This was echoed loudly in a 2003 study of Chicago teachers which found that large numbers of teachers are quitting because of disruptive student behavior, little parent involvement, and lax administrative support. "We are in the midst of a crisis and think we really need to sound the alarm bell."[30]

Parents play a critical role in motivating their child to learn. A 2002 Minority Student Achievement Network survey asked students why they worked hard. Sixty percent of African American, Hispanic, and white students said they do so "to please or impress parents." Unfortunately, "[T]oo many parents believe education stops once a child leaves the schoolhouse gate," states a 2004 *Chicago Tribune* editorial, a lament frequently echoed in the press.[31]

Paul R. Lehman, a professor at the University of Michigan, strongly criticizes parents' cultural attitudes toward schooling.

Despite all our talk about the importance of education, in speaking with kids, adults regularly give the impression that school is more a minimum-security prison than the staging area for a successful life. We can't pretend that school is all fun, but education remains the most valuable asset that any kid can have.... We can't afford to allow the nation's young people to share the typical adult live-for-the-weekend mentality we see all around us, when they will soon be competing in the marketplace with eager students from around the world who realize the importance of education and work hard at it.[32]

The entertainer Bill Cosby became a searing social critic of African American family culture that contributes to black high school students graduating an average of four years behind white students in their basic academic skills. "They think they're hip. They can't read; they can't write. They're laughing and giggling, and they're going nowhere," Cosby told a shocked audience. Attacking street slang, he said, "You can't be a doctor with that kind of crap coming out of your mouth."[33] His comments have been harshly criticized by some, but the real problem is that his message is far too narrow. It's not just black parents who are failing their children with low cultural standards—it is American parents in general.

Maybe you think I am being too harsh or attaching too much importance to the parental influence over children's educational aspirations and attainments. I think not. Research conducted in the United States and a number of other nations supports this conclusion. In a 2000 study sponsored by the National Science Foundation, Larry E. Suter found that parental involvement had a stronger potential influence on a child's school achievement than the school (curriculum, teacher, principal, class size, and so forth). This was particularly true in reading achievement, while more complex subjects such as literature, math, and science, respond more to the school's curriculum and the quality of teaching.

For their study, "Learning to Love Reading" (2004), researchers Linda Teran Strommen and Barbara Fowles Mates surveyed students in the sixth and ninth grades to determine what factors influenced their development of a love for reading. They found that "students surely benefit when teachers recognize the need to motivate them to read." However, their basic conclusion was "The ongoing dialogue about books that takes place between parents and children seems to have a particularly important role in the development of a child's love of reading.... To this end the child's immediate culture, the family, must invest itself in the process to demonstrate the pleasure reading affords by ... providing a model for children to emulate."[34]

Ask George C. Albano, principal of the K–6 inner-city Lincoln Elementary School in Mount Vernon, New York about the importance of involving parents more closely with their children's education. In 2004, 99 percent of the school's fourth-graders made it over the achievement bar that New York State sets for English, math, and science. "If children grow up in an environment where they see their parents involved, they will follow suit," says Albano.

When he first became principal, few parents were coming to school for parents' night or other activities. So he decided to make them show up: "If you want to see your child's report card, come to school to pick it up … from six in the morning to any time at night."

Albano broke the rules. People complained. "The school told me to change, and I was even threatened with lawsuits." In the beginning, 25 to 30 percent of the parents did not come. But now, "If we have one, two, or three parents who don't come, out of 800-plus children, it's a lot," he says.[35]

Ask Ray and Rose Chávez of Albuquerque, New Mexico about parent involvement. "We understood that education could make a life better," said Ray. Both he and his wife had only a high school education. They refinanced their home six times to pay tuition for all five of their children to attend a parochial school, the Albuquerque Academy.

At one point Rose took a night job so she could be home full-time with her children. She tutored, coached, and encouraged them. They all learned to read before they started school.

Ray and Rose are not rich people. "We've always had just one car," they said They seem indifferent to status symbols, except for the plaque on the living room wall signed by a dean of Harvard University. It reads: "To Ramon and Rosanne Chávez—Harvard expresses its respect, admiration, and thanks for the gift of their five extraordinary children." The dean conferred this on the Chávez parents when their fifth child had followed her older siblings by graduating from Harvard University.

An unusual story, you might say. But there are many other American parents like Rose and Ray who are struggling to provide their children with an excellent education so they can achieve the American dream. Why not more of them?[36]

There are many ways for schools and other agencies to increase parental involvement. Here are a few examples:

- Even Start and Early Head Start are federally funded, early education programs that send teachers and other educators into the homes of parents with infants and young children. They coach parents on how to provide reading and other cultural activities as their child grows up.[37]

- In Mecca, California, teachers from Saúl Martinez Elementary School visit their students' homes to coach parents in areas they need to work on with their children. The home visit program also gets more parents involved in out-of-school activities.[38]
- Healthy Families First in Santa Fe County, New Mexico, provides parents with trained home coaches to promote positive parenting practices that can enhance child health and educational development. This is one of 441 programs across the United States and Canada designed to strengthen family–child development.[39]
- Practical Parenting Partnerships (PPP) provides a system of training and home visits to build strong home–school relationships. PPP operates through 530 Missouri schools and more than 200 schools in 11 other states and Canada. Parent development workshops have also have been provided to many additional schools.[40]
- The Commonwealth Institute for Parent Leadership is an intensive, three-weekend program designed to help Kentucky parents improve their local schools. Since 1996, over 1,100 parents have been trained to plan and execute projects in their local school districts. The aim of these projects is to involve more parents with schools in ways that have lasting effects.[41]
- The Imagination Library program aims to distribute one book a month to every child under the age of five in Tennessee. This effort is a collaboration between Dolly Parton's Dollywood Foundation and the state of Tennessee. "It has been my dream since we first stated my Imagination Library programs that my home state would help us inspire the love for reading in every family," explained Parton. In 2004, her Imagination Library programs distributed more than 1.2 million books to 288 communities in 36 states.[42]
- A *Parent Reading Guide* in English and Spanish was distributed free in 2004 to families in Los Angeles, Orange, Riverside, San Bernardino, and Ventura counties in California. It offered parents basic strategies to attract reluctant readers, provided homework tips, stressed the importance of early vision screening, included lists of books appropriate for children of different ages, and much more—all with the aim of improving reading and parental involvement in education. Throughout the United States, local businesses are funding and community newspapers are distributing such guides written by child-education experts.[43]
- In the United Kingdom, schools support "Chaotic" (jargon for indifferent/uninformed parents) through parenting classes, while giving

teachers training right in their schools on practical disciplinary techniques for keeping order in class.[44]

These are but a few examples of numerous community programs, individual initiatives, and foundation, state, or federal efforts to mobilize parent involvement in children's education. In the past, parents were the primary providers of literacy for their children. In the 20th century, urbanization and industrialization shifted that obligation to public schools. However, many of the social building blocks of America are still dependent upon family self-help and the ability of parents to focus their children on the importance of educational attainment.[45]

Creating a Real Education Profession

A. What Makes a Good Teacher? Teaching at Risk: A Call to Action (2004) was the report of yet another blue-ribbon commission of experts on the growing national shortage of high-quality educators.[46] Why? The average public school teacher earned $44,499 in 2001–2002. California teachers received 121 percent of the national average while South Dakota teachers were paid only 70 percent. Average teacher pay resembles that of social workers or the clergy, not engineers and attorneys.

Between 1955 and 2000, the number of K–12 teachers in the United States almost tripled, but school enrollments grew by only 50 percent. Class size matters, especially in the early grades, for the teaching of reading. But smaller schools seem to matter even more. Perhaps somewhat larger classrooms after the primary grades could help us better reward excellent teachers.[47] Other possibilities offered by *Teaching at Risk* included performance-based pay, creating new career tracks, or providing premium pay in higher math, science, and special education areas. All these options will be difficult to implement unless the public can be motivated by a major overhaul of local schools that offers better results for more students.

Though teacher pay is not great, almost half of the new teachers who leave within the first five years do not cite pay as their biggest problem. What ultimately defeats them is lack of parental support, their own inadequate education, the breakdown of student discipline, the lack of mentoring or coaching, poor professional development, and little supervision or leadership. Otherwise, they say their jobs were wonderful![48]

All of these problems are compounded by a growing national teacher shortage (see Chapter 1). For instance, Illinois state officials estimate (2004) that schools will need almost 40,000 more regular teachers and 9,000 more special education teachers through 2007. The greatest demand in high schools will be for math and science teachers, where shortages already exist.

This serious shortage of degreed math teachers is exacerbated by a widespread lack of deep mathematical knowledge among many elementary school teachers. According to the American Association for the Advancement of Science (2001), the reason behind this is that too many U.S. students have been able to graduate from high school and college with little or no practical understanding of math and science principles.

David Goodstein, a professor of physics at the California Institute of Technology, observes that often the only way to graduate from college without taking a single science course is to major in elementary education. The result is that many teachers are not just ignorant of science, but are even hostile to it. The solution: Mandatory high school and college math and science for all students, regardless of career major.

These current conditions produce a broad, cascading effect by having functionally illiterate math and science teachers producing more science- and math-phobic students. This is ironic for a U.S. society so infatuated by technology![49]

Next to effective parenting, the quality of the teacher is the greatest factor in determining student learning. Many students testify that a dynamic teacher has motivated them to excel in school after years of poor academic performance.

At most high schools only the brightest students take advanced math. Yet at Lake View High School on Chicago's north side, any student can take Advanced Placement (AP) Calculus. "There's a history here that taking calculus is cool," states Steven Starr, a calculus teacher. To sign up a wide range of students, teachers appeal to student pride or how it will help later in college. Real-world lessons, like trying to calculate how many people will make the world too crowded, captivate many students.

"I can't believe it. I went from being a person who couldn't comprehend math to someone taking AP calculus," said Maribel Faulk, a 17-year-old with new-found math confidence that has encouraged her to pursue a career as a pediatrician. Teachers convinced her and many others that they are up to the challenge. They even promised to help them with tutoring after class. They changed the culture.

The Lake View AP program is paid for by the Golden Apple Foundation. Teacher interns are sent to Lake View to learn teaching and motivational techniques from the calculus teachers who pioneered the program. They can then use these teaching strategies in other city schools.

What can help veteran teachers keep on improving? It is clear that continuing professional development programs, like the one at Lake View, that focus on one topic and give teachers new knowledge and skills with a chance to practice them is a vital means of making sure that teachers keep learning and growing throughout their teaching careers.[50]

B. What Makes a Good Principal? School principals need to spearhead a culture of high academic standards and expectations that supports the development of an aptitude for abstract, logical thought in students. This requires the study of specific subjects at a very early age. There is a small window of opportunity for fostering this mental development, which closes even before puberty.

If all young Americans were required to master an academically more structured and demanding curriculum, the United States could possibly achieve universal math, science, and reading literacy at a higher level. Elementary and secondary school principals need to be leaders in articulating this message to parents.

It will also take far better preparation for principals and other school managers to be not just educational administrators, but people managers as well. The educational preparation of principals and other school managers seldom includes learning how to better motivate and lead people by taking graduate courses on the principles of leadership or basic supervisory management.

Granted, schools are not for-profit businesses, but they are staffed by men and women who need to be motivated and led as a team, not dictated to, in order to reach the goal of better overall student achievement. Parents, too, need the information and guidance that motivates them to be participants in the educational mission of a school.

Some urban school systems have established leadership development programs for their principals and other managers, but most school districts don't have them. This is a mistake. A number of academic disciplines offer preparation in how to become a successful leader. One example is a program developed by the California organizational researcher, Etienne Wenger, who uses a "communities of practice" framework. He focuses on the interactions and relationships between people. For those involved in various aspects of school management, this means seeing themselves as building and leading teams in which everyone's involvement is critical. Policy reform models can thus be turned into practical plans that can be implemented.[51]

By transforming education into a real profession, the United States can draw brighter and more academically prepared people to enter and stay in teaching. Higher education will be forced to treat more seriously the preparation of these professionals. The development of school administrators with solid leadership abilities and better-prepared teachers in all subject areas and all school levels will help begin raising the performance of more students so that they have the preparation to meet the challenges of the 21st century.

Developing a Greater Diversity of Local Schools

Now comes the hard part. What do we call and how do we start new, small, local, curriculum-diverse, parent- and /teacher-driven schools? Throughout the United States and in other countries as well, liberals and conservative ideologues have strewn landmines on the road to system change.

Some conservatives want to take a hatchet to public education and end its so-called monopoly. They believe that market forces will offer higher quality, more cost-effective or even cheaper educational choices to parents. They say that the money saved by pruning the current public school bureaucracy could then be redirected to pay teachers more, based on performance incentives. They see a conspiracy of the Left dumbing-down standards to make everyone equal rather than seeking to provide academic excellence.

On the other hand, some liberals accuse conservatives of wanting to dismantle a fundamental democratic institution—the public school. They see this institution (as it is currently structured) as the glue that holds our society together. In their view, any significant change in how local schools operate will further balkanize a racially divided society. They see a conservative conspiracy to concentrate resources on students with the most academic potential, or the back to basics movement as a plot to dumb-down public school education. The cultural reality of education in this watershed era lies somewhere in between these two conspiracy viewpoints.[52]

In 2003 Richard M. Daley, the mayor of Chicago, agreed to let about 60 community organizations open new schools in Chicago under a plan for sweeping change called Renaissance 2010. Interest in developing one of these new schools has come from Chicagoans and people from across America. Some would focus on a more traditional curriculum, while others would give parents many new options, such as a special-education charter school; an all-boy high school and an all-girl grammar school; a school of journalism; a white-collar, professional junior high school for minority students; an alternative school for dropouts; a fine arts and humanities academy; a farm school for at-risk students; and a Peace and Education school for gang members and dropouts.

By 2010 the mayor intends to re-create over 10 percent of the city's 600 schools—one-third as independently operated contract schools, one-third as charter schools, and the balance as new, small schools opened by the public school district. Two-thirds of these new schools will not be bound by certain state regulations or labor laws. Up to 20 current high schools will become 40 to 60 small schools.

Why did Daley do this? In 2003 the Civic Committee of the Commercial Club of Chicago, an organization that represents Chicago's top corporate leaders, criticized Daley's ongoing school reform efforts as doing too little to raise most student achievement levels, and not reducing a horrendous dropout rate. The slow rate of student improvement was going to be too little, too late in providing the entry-level, smart workforce that Chicago businesses increasingly can't find. Businesses are leaving Chicago behind as they need to find areas that have larger concentrations of well-educated, young knowledge technologists in other states or other countries.

After a great deal of shouting and behind-the-scenes negotiating, the Renaissance 2010 plan was born. The business community has formed a non-profit corporation, New Schools for Chicago, to assist in this initiative and to coordinate the effort to raise $50 million to cover start-up costs at these new schools. Half of these funds have already been committed by the Chicago Community Trust, the Gates Foundation, and others. This is a significant start for a large urban school system. Will its momentum ultimately sweep over all of the current 600 Chicago public schools?[53]

According to the Educational Commission of the States, a non-profit think tank funded by the 50 U.S. states, such new approaches to providing public education challenge earlier, 20th-century state school-finance regulations. They are shifting the focus from funding school districts to funding individual schools. This 21st-century education revolution now seems unavoidable because our society is beginning to see the real need to hold every local school to a much higher student performance standard.[54]

The question of how individual schools rather than school districts will be funded raises many new cultural and policy issues. These nuts-and-bolts issues will be worked out by each state as part of a new American education system. An essential element of this new system, say Brian C. Hassell and Lucy Steiner at the Education Commission of the States, is "designing a funding system that provides sufficient startup dollars and through which adequate resources follow children to their new schools."[55]

One point in this great school debate remains clear. If America is to provide a sound academic preparation for more of its children at the 2010 crossroad and beyond, we must develop more local school options. As we have seen in Chapter 6, this cultural change process has already begun and now needs to be adopted nationwide.

A Recipe for an Education Revolution

When I Turn 50

When I'm 50 I will be married and I will have two kids and I will make it a point not to be like other men I know. I will help my wife raise my kids and I will be a good Daddy. I will get myself a good job and buy my kids everything they need. I am going to work at a store and be the manager. I am going to be very nice to people and help people who need help. I am only going to be married once. I am going to have a nice life.

"Victor" R., Grade Four

Victor was enrolled at an elementary school where 99 percent of the students were from low-income families and only 22 percent were at grade level in reading. At his neighborhood high school only 10 percent of students read at grade level.

Less than 30 miles away, Valerie attended an elementary school with the same number of students. But 88 percent read a grade level, and 95 percent were at grade level in math. At Valerie's school 99 percent of the students were from middle- and upper-income families.

According the Illinois Board of Education, in 2002 about 500,000 children attended 920 schools where half of the students were from low-income families. Yet poverty does not always produce this achievement gap. For three years the Center for Governmental Studies at Northern Illinois University studied the remarkable local success stories of 59 high-poverty, high-performance schools scattered in 44 school districts across Illinois. What they found was eye-opening. These lessons aren't theoretical, " ...but about what people in local schools do each day to close the achievement gap," states Glenn McGee, the study's author.[56]

I have found this study's results to be a compelling short list of the essential ingredients for an American education revolution:

- Smaller schools
- Local schools near students' homes
- Different curricula that reflect diverse student aptitudes and interests
- Principals who are trained to be effective people managers, leaders, and administrators
- Teachers who receive continuous, quality professional development
- Teachers who like to work with young people and who love to teach
- Constant, two-way communication in plain English between teachers and parents about their child's current and future learning needs

- Accurate, up-to-date career information, beginning in elementary school and throughout high school
- Counselors who have the time to care and take a personal interest in a child[57]
- Tutoring after school in the classroom or the student's home
- A longer school day
- A longer school year with summer programming that helps students learn the increasing amount of knowledge needed for life in the 21st century

American education today is far too often a testament to enshrined mediocrity. This is not good enough. America's critical education mass, needed to sustain democracy and a high-tech economy, must grow rather than shrink. Schools must better prepare far more students than they do today for what lies ahead at the 2010 crossroad and beyond. America needs a revolutionary approach to community schooling.

Issue 3: Finding the People

'I'm not concerned about U.S. job losses so long as were feeding the front end of the pipeline with growth and innovation," states business thinker Stan Davis. The issue that concerns him is "Does the United States represent the front end of the pipeline?" In other words, do we have enough creative and innovative people throughout the culture and the economy? Smarter workers can lose, too, if they don't stay on the cutting edge of knowledge. This will require individual, business, community, and national effort. It won't just happen all by itself.[58]

How all this will happen concerns Elaine Chao, the U.S. Secretary of Labor in the George W. Bush administration. "I'm concerned about the flexibility of our workforce, the international competitiveness of our workforce," she says. "They've got to be better educated, trained, more skilled.... The way that America works has fundamentally changed, yet the way that Washington deals with workforce issues has not." She sees that federal job training efforts represent only the tip of a vast iceberg of under-lying education needs. Chao says that government programs are "venture capital for the 21st-century workforce ... offering hope to workers that the private sector hasn't reached out to yet."

Over 1,900 federally funded one-stop career centers are providing work-ers first-aid stations in changing careers. John Maynard became a dislocated worker when he lost his $10-an-hour coal mine job (2000) in Kentucky. The local Pike County Job-Sight Center steered him to an education program that provided two years of tuition and books at his local community college, plus financial support for food and gas. After finishing school, he took a night job doing electrical work in an industrial bakery. He also found a hospital day job. About a year later, he was offered a position teaching electronics at the technical college from which he graduated. For some people, like John, the system works.

But Chao makes one thing perfectly clear: "There is no way the federal government will have enough resources to train every single person in America who needs it. We need to partner with the private sector and the nonprofit sector to ensure that the training programs are providing the best training possible."[59] This has also been the policy of recent Democratic administrations.

Indeed, in recent years the federal government has set the performance goals for worker retraining provided by individual states at impossibly high levels. The states don't want to do this training because many of the people who need training enter the classroom at such a low level that they cannot meet the training targets in the mandated time period. States need to renegotiate with the federal government to get more training time for the lower-skilled workers.[60]

At an even more fundamental level, Chao is right about getting more employers involved given the evidence on the ineffectiveness of most generic public job-training programs. An alternative method is to allow federal money to be spent on economic development job training. This would allow federal funds to be given to employers for real, on-the-job training programs, particularly for minority or other disadvantaged workers.

For many smaller, anonymous businesses, finding the people is already a real issue. These businesses account for about half of America's 9.8 million manufacturing jobs. Without stockholders pushing them for maximum short-term results, such companies tend to be more flexible in facing the ups and downs of the marketplace. U.S. Tool & Die, Inc. is such a company. It spent 3,000 hours training workers because it feared it would be left without much-needed talent for future growth.[61]

Labor training expert Dow Scott, a professor in the School of Business at Loyola University–Chicago, sees this as an important part of any business performance improvement system.

Organizations today have flat structures with carefully defined jobs. A management system often is in place to carefully measure team and organizational results. A reward system can then be activated based on achieving these defined performance goals. But it is people development—training and education—that is increasingly necessary to move the whole performance improvement system forward. Smarter people now are needed across organizations who successfully cope with waves of new information and constant competitive change. The critical competencies of these knowledge workers often make the fundamental difference between profit and loss for most organizations.[62]

More educated workers are beginning to understand a basic fact of 21st-century employment. When they lose a job that has become redundant or obsolete because of flatter organizations or technology advances, many people are going back to school for technical education in fields that are hiring. At Alamance Community College in Graham, North Carolina, nearly 10 percent of the people enrolled in 2004 were individuals with Bachelor's degrees or higher. "We kind of jokingly call ourselves the new graduate school," says Dan Ensalaco, assistant vice president of community college development at Waubonsee Community College in Illinois. Twenty-six percent of those enrolled are college graduates.[63]

In 1995, when George David, the CEO at United Technologies Corporation (UTC), turned his employee tuition reimbursement program into one of the most generous in corporate America, some people thought he was nuts. The criticism from business people on the street was "People would take advantage of the corporation, be educated on our nickel, and then take off and go to work for somebody else," said Lee Dailey, back-to-school program director at UTC's Hartford, Connecticut headquarters.

About 4 percent did. UTC's regular employee attrition rate is between 8 and 10 percent a year. Sixteen percent of UTC employees now participate in these education programs (10 percent is the U.S. average). UTC pays all tuition and fees upfront for any college credit course, no matter what the subject!

Though UTC doesn't guarantee lifetime jobs, it offers skills and education that can help its workers evolve and grow in their careers. Half of the essential education revolution is needed in America's elementary and high schools. But according to George David, the other half is "a significant investment in education for the millions of Americans already in the workplace."[64] But what about the millions of workers who have been forced out of the workforce for various reasons? The 2010 crossroad will call many of them back.

As the demographic pool shrinks, where will America find workers to fill its ranks? They will be increasingly found among older workers, married women, the disabled, welfare-to-work participants, and members of the correctional population. Here's how.

Calling All Older Workers

A few years ago, a reader wrote the following letter in response to my article, "Help Wanted: Creating Tomorrow's Workforce," that appeared in the July, 2000 issue of *The Futurist*:

Dear Ed:

Being a fifty-something, junior executive that was displaced due to a RIF and concurrent reorganization, I have been looking for another position for over two years now. I would love for some company to give this old dog a chance to show them the new tricks he has learned over the last two years.

However, there is a problem—one that, by law, cannot exist—age discrimination. Yes, I can tell you from experience, that it is alive and well. Of course, it is cleverly disguised and classified using terms and phrases that are perfectly legal such as: "over qualified," "not the right fit for our organization" and "others had better qualifications." I found it interesting, however, that in almost all cases, the candidate selected was younger and usually female.

Yes, companies need to realize that there is a wealth of experience that is available from individuals that have exceptional skills, dedication, ethics and work habits. They need to realize that older individuals "want" to work, unlike many that are only putting time in as they "need" the money. They need to realize that old dogs can and do learn new tricks and can make contributions to their organizations. However, they need to look beyond the color of one's hair and the number of wrinkles in one's face to be able to tap that source of human potential.

Sincerely,
T.B.[65]

Most executives have not faced up to the problems of changing demographics. Companies must change their cultural bias and begin taking steps to retain and retrain baby boomers before they disappear with all their valuable skills. According the U.S. Bureau of Labor Statistics, by 2012 workers who are 55 and older will constitute about 19 percent of the labor force. This compares to 14 percent in 2002.[66] According to OECD calculations, just to maintain current employment-to-population ratios, from 2005 onward the U.S. labor force participation by those over 55 will have to increase by about 25 percent.[67] This population shift will provide a particular challenge to small businesses that, according to the U.S. Small Business Administration, represent more than 99 percent of all employers and provide about 75 percent of net new jobs.[68]

The attitude of many in the business world is that an increase in age correlates to a decrease of skills in newer technologies and the ability to learn them. An Institute of Electrical and Electronics Engineers survey reported that U.S. workers 45 years of age and older were better problem solvers and communicators than younger workers and were equivalent in technical knowledge and teamwork skills. Older workers were slower in adapting to new assignments and staying current on the latest tech developments. Older programmers seemed better in project management roles, while the younger workers were better at employing the technologies.[69]

In many cases, retirement is no longer a viable option. For personal or financial reasons, many people are postponing retirement or going back to work. Look at the numbers: In 2002, 20.7 million people aged 55 and above were in the workforce. According to the U.S. Bureau of Labor Statistics, in 2004 that number had risen to 22.7 million (a 9.6 percent increase). This increase in older workers seems to indicate that a major culture shift in business attitudes toward senior workers is beginning. Basically, it seems that companies want people who are reliable, and baby boomers often fit this job description.[70]

In 1997 Bonne Bell, a $100-million, family-owned cosmetics firm near Cleveland, launched a seniors-only production department. The company needed workers, and seniors were available. Jess Bell, 79, son of the founder, hired them.

By 2001, retirees made up about 20 percent of Bonne Bell's 500 workers. The retirees perform work that was once outsourced, saving the company over $1 million since the department's launch. Shipment goals are set and met. Employee turnover is near nil. Company skeptics have been silenced by a group of assembly-line workers whose average age is 70. The oldest person just turned 90.

These workers have many reasons for working into their seventh decade or beyond. Half need the money to help pay bills. For many, the job provides self-esteem and a sense of belonging. Says Juliana Carlton, 69, "Instead of sitting around, I wanted to do something with my life." She and others sent a Christmas card to the Bells. Their message: "Thanks for allowing us to do something useful."

Bob Wotsch, 56, who manages that department, attributes these workers' success to their generation's loyalty and work ethic. "They don't want or need anyone to tell them to get going," he says. This basic reliability is the main reason that Jess Bell's son, Jess Jr. (who is now the CEO) doesn't see the senior department as a temporary experiment. Nor do other companies with similar employment outreach efforts.[71]

Many firms now understand that making the workplace more appealing to aging workers may be a critical key to averting the demographic challenge at the 2010 crossroad and beyond. Organizations are introducing flexible work schedules, retraining, and health-and-wellness seminars, part-time positions, job-sharing, and other strategies in a bid to retain and recruit older workers. Companies that have embraced this approach include Deere & Company, the Principal Financial Group, Pitney Bowes, the Vanguard Group, and St. Mary's Medical Center in Huntington, West Virginia.[72]

International companies such as Quaker Oats now offer senior executives the choice of overseas office assignments. This can appeal to many senior executives nearing the end of their careers, and helps retain valuable knowledge and skills for important global expansion.

Microsoft, Productivity Point International, ExecuTrain, the National Education Training Group, and Alternative Resources Group are supporting Got/IT, a program of Green Thumb, Inc., a non-profit training and employment organization in Arlington, Virginia. Through alliances with these companies, Green Thumb has developed programs that prepare older workers to enter jobs at computer-related companies. These senior hires free up younger employees with more advanced IT skills to move up the career ladder to challenging new projects, thus increasing personal loyalty and motivation as well as reducing turnover of hard-to-find advanced technologists.[73]

In "Re-Visioning Retirement," a study published by the World Future Society (2005), about 80 percent of baby-boomer retirees expect to be working at least part-time in retirement. They intend to seek a balance between leisure and work.

The study's author Ken Dychtwald, a gerontologist and psychologist, believes, "In the decades ahead, the boomers will complete America's transformation into a gerontocracy, as they take control of the nation's social and economic power." He predicts the boomers will postpone old age by disposing of our current "linear life" culture in which people move lock-step through life, first through education, next a job, and then leisure and retirement. Instead, a new "cyclic life" baby-boomer culture is taking shape. Education, work, and leisure will be interspersed repeatedly throughout the life span. This parallels the increasingly rapid obsolescence of knowledge and the consequent growing importance of life-long learning.

For baby-boomers, it is becoming normal for 50-year-olds to go back to school and for 70-year-olds to reinvent themselves through new careers. "Phased retirement, part-time and flex-time work and `rehirements' will become common options for elder boomers who'll either need or want to continue working," believes Dychtwald

American business needs to rethink its attitudes about retirement. Our culture will better value the knowledge and skills of the baby boomers as it becomes more obvious that they will be needed in the workplace beyond the 2010 crossroad.

Another factor for employers to consider is that Generations X and Y are less focused on advancing in the workplace than were their predecessors. A 2004 study commissioned by the American Business Collaboration, a consortium of eight top U.S. companies, found that the next generation of workers is less interested in putting work above all else. The survey reported that both men and women who are university-educated are less focused on career advancement and increased work responsibilities than was found a decade earlier.

"These are highly motivated professionals who want to get the job done but also want to honor their obligations to their families," states Stan Smith, national director of Next-Generation Initiatives at Deloitte & Touche, a member of the business collaborative. "So it is important for businesses to offer informal work arrangements that permit reduced hours, compressed hours—you name it." The message is clear. The next generation of workers wants fewer hours. That will mean finding other people to make up the difference.[74]

The Mother Factor

Savvy companies know that impending skilled labor shortages make it important to reach out to the large, mostly untapped pool of so-called sequencing mothers who want to return to the labor market. Such women temporarily leave the workforce or scale back to raise their children. Later, when the children are older, these women return to their careers.

Erin Novak left her job six years ago to raise her two children. When she returned to the marketplace, it took her just over two months to land a human resources job. Sequencing mothers like Erin are discovering that businesses are now more interested in hiring them, despite career gaps. Why has this happened?

More companies are starting new programs to hire sequencing moms, or are seeking to retain them because of a seismic shift in women's cultural attitudes toward motherhood and work. "It's almost like our generation is trying to prove something," says Jennifer Juo, 33, of Oakland, California. She left her job as an international trade manager to raise her two-year-old son. "It's not just climbing to the top of the corporate ladder. Other things are important, such as family and a good marriage," Juo believes.

Many new mothers agree with her. Laborforce participation rates of new mothers aged 15 to 44 have shrunk from 59 percent in 1998 to 55 percent in 2002. Better-educated women with a Bachelor's degree or some graduate training are also working less, with 68 percent in 1990 declining to 63.5 percent in 2002.

For "The Motherhood Study" (2005), Enola G. Aird and Martha Farrell Erickson conducted a national survey of more than 2,000 working mothers. They found that only about 16 percent of those surveyed preferred full-time employment, while 33 percent would prefer part-time work and about 30 percent would like to work for pay from home. Most of these mothers wanted to spend more time with their children and families.

Now companies are reaching out to these women, giving them a year or longer for maternity leaves. A 2004 study by Chicago-based Corporate Project Resources reported that over 90 percent of Fortune 500 companies are trying to recruit sequencing moms on a contract or short-term basis. Many of these women are older, with more career experience and proven skills. Offering them flexible work schedules, part-time positions, telecommuting, or job-sharing helps employees move in and out of the workplace for personal reasons without being lost as human capital to an organization.

Deloitte & Touche and IBM have launched significant sequencing programs that allow such workers from three to five years off to focus on personal or family needs. "We've invested in them, trained them. We want to retain them," affirms Maria Ferris, IBM manager of work-life and women's initiatives.[75]

Making a Difference

According to the U.S. Census Bureau, about 20 percent of the U.S. workforce in 2004 were designated as disabled. Yet, a surprising additional 36 percent could also productively work if given the opportunity, according to Brewster Thackeray of the National Organization on Disability.

Ford, Hewlett-Packard, Procter & Gamble, Xerox, Motorola, Sears, Microsoft, and about 200 other companies helped to organize a consortium entitled Able to Work to hire disabled people. Managed by the National Business & Disability Council, which was established in 1952, the consortium offers a variety of services to businesses and disabled people across America. More businesses are becoming involved because of the shrinking pool of professional people in IT, engineering, and science.

Francene Tishman, the council's executive director, outlined the services it provides. The council offers companies staff training on the recruitment and interviewing of the disabled. It also maintains a National Resume Database that carries between 2,200 and 2,800 resumes of college-educated people. There is also a job posting service on the council's Web site where businesses can list positions they seek to fill.

The Americans with Disabilities Act (1990) guaranteed equal-opportunity employment for disabled people. Federal tax incentives include up to $5,000 a year to cover the costs of accommodating a disabled employee. Companies can also earn up to a $2,400 tax credit for each disabled employee working at least 400 hours annually.

About 5,000 non-profit organizations have been established to employ the disabled. One of the largest is Pride Industries, a California-based leader in providing outsourcing solutions using disabled workers for companies nationwide. Since 1966 Pride Industries has grown to nearly $100 million in annual revenue, delivering fee-based commercial services (custodial, recycling), government services (maintenance, food services), mail and fulfillment assistance (print, packaging, mail), and manufacturing and logistics support to organizations across America. Its full- and part-time workforce is composed of 4,500 workers in 14 states. Pride Industries has seven production facilities. Through U.S. Department of Labor funding, Pride partners with local non-profits, using their managerial expertise to garner more jobs for disabled people in large and small businesses as well as in government agencies.

"The disabled do need some support, but they do not need a lot of support," says Mike Ziegler, CEO of Pride Industries. "If companies want to make a difference, they can give them jobs." Employing disabled workers can also increase productivity, reduce costs, and improve customer satisfaction. It is a unique blending of meeting the employment needs of your business and contributing to the social welfare of the local community.[76]

The Brave New World of Welfare-to-Work

During the past decade, welfare-to-work reforms have opened up new opportunities for businesses to find workers. For such employees to succeed, however, carefully designed training and education are needed. There is now clear evidence that the most effective welfare-to-work programs are those that provide a balance between adult education and specific job training.

Carolyn Heinrich, a sociologist at the University of Wisconsin–Madison, evaluated a successful welfare-to-work program for the residents of Ford Heights, Chicago's most depressed suburban community. The program offered both education and job training at local businesses, and it also provided assistance to people who needed help with issues that hindered them from getting and holding a job. Five major problems that cause welfare-to-work adults to lose their new jobs were addressed:

1. Little knowledge of appropriate, daily, on-the-job employee behaviors
2. Poor basic education and unfamiliarity with the technical skills required for a job
3. Child-care problems
4. A personal view of work as a threatening experience
5. Transportation difficulties in getting to and from work

The Ford Heights program overcame these issues by taking a holistic service approach. It sequentially and concurrently provided all the necessary training, employment, and support services to keep people on the job. This program emphasized long-term education, intensive personal coaching, and job-specific, customized, employer-provided training. These are important components in enabling welfare-to-work participants reach the goal of long-term job retention.

The Ford Heights program's coaching activities helped each job trainee identify and work through any personal problems he or she experienced during the training period. To provide this assistance, company trainers also mentored the trainees by being very hands-on coaches. They made phone calls, even house calls after hours, to make sure the trainees attended classes and fulfilled job responsibilities.

Welfare-to-work job trainees often will need training featuring role-playing in mock interviews or meetings, as well as business vocabulary development, guidance on personal appearance, instruction in presentation skills, and motivational sessions. However, all of these support services will be of little use unless they are built around one major foundation—concurrent, good-quality, on-the-job training. In a study sponsored by the Center for Law and Social Policy, *Built to Last: Why Skills Matter for Long-Run Success in Welfare Reform* (2003), authors Karin Martinson and Julie Strawn also supported the holistic approach. They concluded, "There is clear evidence that providing a full range of employment, education, and training services is the most effective welfare-to-work strategy."[77]

A similar comprehensive program in Portland, Oregon provided some of the strongest evidence that a balanced program can produce dramatic results. Compared to previous efforts, the Portland program increased the number of adults who finished high school or passed the General Education Development (GED) test. Also, more of these individuals completed training for a skilled-trade license or a professional or occupational certificate. With this new, holistic approach, Portland's welfare-to-work participants saw a 21 percent increase in their employment and a 22 percent reduction in time spent on welfare. Those who earned a GED also had a 30 percent average increase in annual earnings.[78]

Another successful approach, a program called From the Streets to Geeks, was pioneered by N Power, a non-profit organization in New York City. The program assists low-income men and women between 18 and 25 in developing Internet design and networking skills. The trainees must have finished high school or earned a GED.

Most participants come from housing projects where drugs and crime are seen as "the only way to get money," says Ethan Richards, 22, who graduated from N Power. "The options there are death or jail, to be honest." These New York housing projects contain a huge underclass of minority youth who have mostly been excluded from new job growth.

In this program, job trainees learn not just IT skills, but trainers and coaches from companies also help them cross a culture gap. When the trainees visit the sleek Manhattan offices of the primary program sponsors, Accenture and J. P. Morgan Chase, they have eye-opening experiences. The contrast between the corporate work world and the trainees' neighborhoods is like being on two different planets. "I think we're demystifying work and the private sector for these kids," state Chris Wearing, managing partner of Accenture's New York office.

Trainees typically enter the program with low-skill jobs paying only about $10,000 a year. After graduation, the figure jumps to about $23,000. "I had [the] drive in me," said Marvin Mendez, 23, a recent graduate, "and just needed a little spark to get it going."[79]

Linking employment-focused training to finishing high school or obtaining a GED often results in more success for trainees and their employers, affirmed Barbara Van Horn, co-director at the Pennsylvania State University's Institute for the Study of Adult Literacy. "Adults supporting families cannot afford an up-front deferment of employment and earnings that may or may not have a longer-run payoff," she stated. Also, adults respond better to hands-on training that immediately applies what they are learning (even basic educational skills) to their day-to-day employment in the workplace.[80]

Businesses need to consider how to reach out to the gigantic underclass of Americans who can be profitably recruited for entry-level jobs through meaningful welfare-to-work programs. However, as is shown by the programs discussed here, cultural and educational issues must be addressed in addition to practical, good-quality job training.

From a Jailed Past to a Future Job?

A record 3.2 percent of the adult population of the United States is under the control of the criminal justice system (2004): Over two million are now inmates, and over four million Americans are on probation. Even though 2004 FBI data shows a drop in the overall crime rate, a 2001 study by the U.S. Justice Department's Bureau of Justice Statistics projects that in 2010, 3.4 percent of all adults (or about 7.7 million people) will be imprisoned. It seems we are on track to reach this projection. These shocking numbers ill-serve wider American society for many different reasons.

Using 2002 figures, "The cost of housing, feeding, and caring for a prison inmate is roughly $20,000 per year or about $20 billion nationwide," according to The Sentencing Project, a non-profit NGO. "That's a really upsetting number," states Jason Zeidenberg, director of policy and research at the Justice Policy Institute. Removing such a large population of people from the potential workforce at the 2010 crossroad will have significant demographic consequences for business.[81]

Approximately 70 percent of prison inmates have not completed high school. Two-thirds of all inmates arrive in prison unable to write a simple, coherent letter to explain their innocence or why they committed a crime, or to perform such simple calculations as an automobile's mileage per gallon based on the mileage printed on a highway map.

According to Allen J. Beck of the Bureau of Justice Statistics, about 614,000 people were released from prison in 2001. Based on his research, Beck projects that 62 percent of them will be rearrested and 41 percent will be sent back to prison. This overall recycling of inmates (recidivism) has deteriorated during the past 20 years, from 18 percent in 1980 to 36.4 percent in 1998.[82]

Attempts to rehabilitate prisoners were abandoned with the huge influx of inmates during the 1980s. Prison officials largely believed they had no responsibility for what happened after the release of offenders. "The objective became that prisons should be just for punishment and politicians competed to see who could make prisons more unpleasant," states Todd Clear, a professor at the John Jay College of Criminal Justice in New York City.[83]

In the 1990s this thinking began to change. The states were overwhelmed with a staggering population of new inmates and people who kept coming back. Prisons couldn't be built fast enough and people began to question whether states resources were being spent for the right reasons.

Cellblock or Classrooms? a 2002 report by the Justice Policy Institute, showed that between 1985 and 2000 state spending increases on corrections were nearly double those for higher education ($20 billion versus

$10.7 billion). Sadly, the report also estimated that in 2000 there were 791,600 African American men in prison versus 603,000 in college. Clearly, we are engaged in the wrong type of higher education.[84]

In 1994 Oregon voters passed a referendum mandating that prisoners work as long as the taxpayers who pay the bills—40 hours a week. Given this taxpayer mandate, prison managers asked Oregon business executives how to run prisons more productively. Out went low-pay/low-skill jobs such as making car license plates. In came comprehensive inmate career training for jobs that Oregon companies needed to have filled, such as telemarketing or using computers to map water and tax districts using aerial photographs.

For example, consider Todd Ragsdale's job. He enrolled in an advanced computer class while serving a 10-year sentence for assault. He now is building customized computers for state agencies. When he is released, he hopes to make over $50,000 a year as a computer service technician.

Prisoners like Ragsdale now leave prison with a professionally printed resume, a record of courses passed, and even letters of recommendation on their work record from prison job managers. "For guys whose lives have been way out of control," states Steven J. Ickes, as assistant director of the Oregon Department of Corrections, "a resume puts them back in control of their lives."

Since this prison jobs program began, fewer former inmates are coming back. Recidivism among Oregon inmates was 47 percent in 1995; in 2000 it was only 25 percent. Oregon businesses are collaborating to expand the jobs program. Prison violence has also lessened. Bad behavior can lead to automatic expulsion from the more coveted career assignments such as the computer program. Since 1995 there has been a 60-percent decline in major discipline problems such as fighting or attempted escape.

Admission to the better job training and career programs requires a high school diploma or passing the GED. This has motivated more of Oregon's inmates to enroll and pass the GED. In fact, Oregon prisoners' overall success rate in passing the GED exceeds that of the state's 17 community colleges! Can this be a sign that career training and the hope it provides for a better future are boosting inmates' motivation regarding education? Many people think the answer is yes. The movement for career and job training in prisons has spread to Missouri, Pennsylvania, Ohio, and Washington state.

Texas, with the second-largest state prison system (150,000 inmates), now requires mandatory schooling for prisoners with less than a seventh-grade education.[85] There is evidence, however, that education alone may not be enough. A study (2003) by John Tyler, a professor at Brown University, and Jeffrey Kling, a professor at Princeton, found that just passing the GED alone does not reduce recidivism or enable released prisoners to find meaningful work in the labor market.[86] Correctional institutions must link basic education with meaningful job training to achieve these objectives.

The Walt Disney Company, Hometown Buffet, Irvine Suites, United Parcel Service, several telemarketing firms, auto repair shops, and other large and small businesses came to a job fair held in 2004 at an Orange County, California minimum security prison. Prisoners who had completed comprehensive prison-to-work program were interviewed for entry-level jobs. In Chicago, the non-profit Safer Foundation has offered the same approach to inmate job training for more than three decades. They provided successful career training to Annette Stevens, who once stole credit cards and forged checks to support her drug habit. Today, she works as a nursing assistant at assisted living facility in suburban Chicago. "The public needs to learn that this approach can work and for many businesses to partner with us by offering more jobs for qualified individuals," says Cornell Hudson, program director of the PACE Institute at the Cook County Correctional Facility in Chicago.[87]

As the demographic belt tightens, many American businesses may need to find ways to broaden the job applicant pool. Many of the projected seven million people in prisons could be both punished for their crimes and successfully redeveloped into valuable workers though local business collaboration. They could become another important component of the answer to the 2010 crossroad issue of Finding the People.

TOWARD A NEW AMERICA

At the beginning of the 21st century, the United States is torn by two visions of itself. One is an Old America of mass-production, the Cold War, and plentiful low-skill/high-wage jobs. The second is a New America of technology, globalization, and the demand for highly skilled people to fill high-wage jobs. There is little consensus on how to bridge the growing skills gap between these two worlds. We lack the optimistic "New World Order," as forecast by President George H. Bush in 1991. Instead, America has slid into a stressful watershed era, trapped between these two worlds.

These mighty social and economic forces and an aging population in many parts of the world have helped to create a 21st-century American workforce divided (as I described in Chapter 2) into three parts: The smart people, those who are well educated and affluent; the walking dead who were educated for jobs that are disappearing and who, unless they opt for further education or training, are now often forced to accept lower paying jobs; and the techno-peasants whose poor general education and lack of special skills condemn them to a life of low-skill/low-pay jobs. This new face of the American workforce is leading to the erosion of the American middle class.

A 2004 study funded by the Annie E. Casey, Ford, and Rockefeller foundations disturbingly showed that one in four working families in the United States earns so little in wages that they are considered to be in the low-income category. U.S. labor market trends clearly demonstrate the further hollowing out of moderately skilled, good-paying jobs that have supported much of the traditional American middle class.[88]

This growing economic disparity is also beginning to hinder America's capacity to produce the high-tech products and services needed to compete in a global marketplace. As the U.S. trade deficit soars, middle-class families increasingly struggle to make ends meet; personal debt increases and market demand falls. This, in turn, produces many of the social problems inherent in our society (See Figure 7.1).

In my consulting and research on how these cultural forces are shaping the skill wars and propelling the world to the 2010 crossroad, one of my main conclusions is that, worldwide, people in local communities can change the culture and reconstruct a 21st-century world to make their lives better. The principal problem today is that people must overcome their personal feelings of anxiety and helplessness. Many believe that these issues are too complex to solve except by larger-than-life political leaders or so-called experts. Yet, massive change has rattled the world before. How did the American people respond?

In the 1890s, with the closing of the U.S. western frontier, Frederick Jackson Turner attempted to explain what he called the American phenomenon—the national personality that had settled the country. "With each advance of settlement westward from the Atlantic coast," Turner wrote, "as pioneers

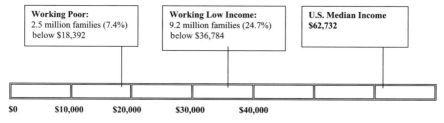

Figure 7.1—Types of U.S. Working Families (Based on annual household income for a family of four)
Source: Annie E. Casey Foundation, 2004.

confronted the primitive conditions of the frontier, a growing nation had been compelled to adapt, build and reinvent its institutions."[89]

Much now depends on how many other communities respond to these labor and economic challenges in the run-up to 2010. If levels of community activism don't begin to rise across America, we can expect more of the same inertia. Yet the question remains: If the U.S. economic situation worsens through a combination of declining education and the loss of high-paying jobs to global competitors, will enough Americans call for fundamental changes? They will, only if they begin to understand the strong connections between workforce development, on one hand, and its linkage to economic opportunity and quality of life issues, on the other.

This calls for ordinary people, through community activism, to muster around these dynamic solutions for a New America. We have done this before, during the so-called Progressive Era, through coalitions of Democrats and Republicans, liberals and conservatives, business, labor, educators, and other activists who helped establish many of the civic institutions that are now fraying at the edges. We need to again forge these community coalitions for change in every state across the nation.

Many people in the past have predicted the demise of America's greatness: in the Viet Nam era of the 1960s, during the 1970s Watergate affair, the severe inflation of the 1980s, or because of the corporate greed and corruption scandals of the late 1990s.

But now America is faced with a more subtle worldwide shift of social and economic forces that is eroding its industrial and economic power base. Though these forces have been building over the past 20 years, only now are more jobless, middle-class Americans becoming truly desperate, and many others fear for the future.

There is a time window of about five years, from 2005 to 2010, during which the working-age population will be at an historic high. But once we reach the 2010 crossroad, the baby boomers will start to retire in large numbers. They will begin to empty out our public and private workplaces. Once that change begins, there will be plenty of high-skill jobs for those who want them, if qualified people can be found.

We need to move quickly to expand the knowledge base of those future replacement workers. The longer American communities postpone the steps to make our knowledge economy sustainable, the more abrupt, damaging, and painful this process will become.[90]

In the cult Paul Newman movie *Cool Hand Luke*, the Southern sheriff that runs the chain gang tells Luke, after he has been recaptured, "What we've got here is a failure to communicate, a failure to communicate!" America is now beginning to suffer the consequences of the major long-term failure to communicate that we are losing the skill wars.

Every nation must sustain a critical education mass if it is to prosper, advance, and survive politically and economically. The facts, problems, and solutions presented in *The 2010 Meltdown* try to delineate these economic challenges and offer solutions for local communities to revive their critical education mass.

Education can be oversold. Without more positive developments in American capitalism and inventiveness, a college or technical education isn't a guarantee against losing a job. But I still agree with David Wessel's statement in *The Wall Street Journal* that "Education remains ... the best insurance policy for succeeding in the existing and future economy. That means streamlining the creaky system for getting vulnerable workers the skills still in demand in the U.S. and doing better at fixing schools so the next generation of Americans can compete with what surely will be better-educated workers elsewhere in the world."

Business leaders understand what is happening. In 2004 Dan Gillmor was a reporter at the *San Jose Mercury News* in California's Silicon Valley. Early that year, Craig Barrett, then chief executive at Intel, stopped by for a chat. Barrett warned that global shifts in the labor pool had brought changes that Silicon Valley and America, in general, were not even beginning to address.

Gillmor asked him if this meant "a generation of lowered expectations for Americans." His reply was that he "didn't see any way around it." Barrett then stated that "America's political leaders are disturbingly oblivious to the shift. They would rather increase the nation's unsustainable twin deficits, budgetary and trade, than boost a serious national commitment to the things that might make a difference in the long term, such as investments in education."[91]

What is the basic social factor that is the foundation of wealth for most individual Americans? In my opinion, it is the "C" (culture) factor, as was described in Chapter 3 and Figure 3.5. This factor drives the new policies that will improve the quality of life for the next generation. Economists Frank Levy and Richard J. Murnane agree that improved education is the most important part of the labor market equation. "The job market is changing fast, and improving education is a slow and difficult process. Nonetheless, over the long run, better education is the best tool we have to prepare the population for a rapidly changing job market," they said.[92]

There are very few cultural icons that have a greater long-term reach than education. American society values personal success. How many skills we attain defines who we are and what life career choices are open to us. That is why the United States has always been the nirvana of the world's immigrants. That is how the son of a carpenter whose Scottish ancestors came to America over 140 years ago can be writing this book.

On a much bigger scale, these same forces are at work defining the quality of life for American cities and regions. After a meeting of the Chicago Workforce Board, Paul O'Connor, executive director of World Business Chicago, the regional agency for new business development, turned to me and said, "It's all about education, isn't it?"

The quality level of a region's labor pool, particularly for entry-level and mid-level workers, is linked to our perceptions about the quality of education. What comes out of a city's schools and colleges goes into its hospitals, manufacturing facilities, offices, and government. Residents, business owners, and corporate boards often make their decisions on where they will work, live, or relocate based on their perceptions of the quality of a community's schools and its cultural attitudes toward education.

But is educating its people a core cultural value for most American businesses? How important do the majority of parents think quality education is for increasing the life potential of their children? Make no mistake: These community cultural attitudes feed one upon another. But people must also invest money and effort to back up their words.

Faith is the realization of what is hoped for and evidence of things not yet seen. I have faith that American communities will master the challenges of the 2010 meltdown. As more people begin to understand what is at stake, their enlightened self-interest will respond to this challenge, replacing despair with hope and ignorance with action. And they will begin an honest self-examination that will demand cultural change. As Brian Ross wrote to the editor of *The Santa Fe New Mexican* about the future:

The fault with the public school lies not in the schools, the children, or even the teachers, but within ourselves.

The politicians don't want to talk about it. They worry about a backlash.

The school board has tried blaming the tests and the teachers.

Be honest: Too many parents in Santa Fe do not put a premium on their child's education or the need to study at home.

Why should they?

Other than the government and the labs, [Los Alamos] there aren't businesses with high-skills jobs that require a great education.

Gov. Richardson needs to bring in businesses that will stimulate the tax base and give the students and their parents some reason to improve the quality of education at school and at home.

We can't expect the schools to make learning better if we don't do anything at home with our own kids—or at the ballot box for the community.[93]

America is entering a new era of reconstruction that will create a better-educated and smarter nation. This era has already begun with Santa Ana's Bridge to Careers program, with the Philadelphia Academies, in community efforts like those in Fargo, North Dakota and in Mansfield, Ohio, through innovative welfare-to-work, prison-to-work programs, and the host of other efforts we have seen starting across the United States. Linked to the continuance of free trade and the introduction of new U.S. technologies that increase productivity, America will remain a world-class economic power throughout the entire 21st century.

We need to get the message out to all Americans that if the number of well-educated, smart people remains static or is drained away in desperate attempts to cut social costs, America's overall standard of living will begin a long, downward slide as the economy stagnates. The stakes are high for all of us. Soon, America will arrive at the 2010 crossroad.

During this era of reconstruction, we need to focus not just on fulfilling life promises to our families. We also need to embrace the future as citizens of our communities, regions, and nation. The future depends on our individual and collective will to make these necessary culture changes now, for a New America and a new world.

Notes

INTRODUCTION

1. Seymour N. Lotsoff, "The Luddites and Static Versus Dynamic Analysis," The *LCM* (Lotsoff Capital Management) *Perspective*, October 9, 2003, 4.
2. David McCullough, *Brave Companions* (New York: Prentice Hall, 1992), 223.
3. Ibid., 210–216.
4. Simon London, "Computers Hollow out the Job Market," *Financial Times,* June 17, 2004, 11.
5. Richard Tomkins, "A Progressive Society Is One That Postpones Its Pleasures," *Financial Times,* March 1, 2005, 10.
6. Donald L. Miller, *City of the Century* (New York: Simon & Schuster, 1997), 196–197.
7. "Building a World-Class Workforce," *Chicago Tribune,* November 28, 1993, sec. 4, 2.
8. Daniel Henninger, "Time to Wring Out Our Waterlogged Civic Institutions," *The Wall Street Journal,* October 19, 2001, A18.

1. THE 2010 CROSSROAD

1. Erla Zwingle, "Goods Move. People Move. Ideas Move. And Cultures Change," *National Geographic,* August 1999, 12.
2. "School Brief—One World?" *The Economist,* October 18, 1997, 79–80; "Globalization and Its Critics," *The Economist,* September 29, 2001, 3, 9; William R. Cline, "Trade and Income Distribution: The Debate and New Evidence," Washington, D.C.: Institute for International Economics, International Economic Policy Brief no.99-7, September 1999, 5.
3. Timothy Aeppel, "Workers Not Included," *The Wall Street Journal,* November 19, 2002, B1, B11.

4. "A Survey of the New Economy," *The Economist,* September 23, 2000, 7; It has also been alleged that Bill Gates once predicted that "185K is enough for any person." Diane Stafford, "Majority of U.S. Workers Use PCs," *Chicago Tribune,* October 28, 2002, sec. 1, 3.

5. Jim Krane, "Biggest Gains Lie Ahead as PCs Shrink, Grow Smarter," *Chicago Tribune,* August 13, 2001, sec. 1, 6; "A Survey of the New Economy," 6.

6. D. Ian Hopper, "Transistors Taken Down to Size: A Single Molecule," *USA Today,* November 12, 2001, 90; "Fastest Computer Is No Longer from U.S.," *Chicago Tribune,* April 22, 2002, sec. 1, 6; "Domino Effect in Computer Circuits," *Financial Times,* October 31, 2002, 9; Barbara Rose, "Motorola Reveals Wireless Advances," *Chicago Tribune,* October 23, 2003, sec. 3.3; Tom Foremski, "Intel Steps Ahead in Microchip Contest," *Financial Times,* November 5, 2003, 21.

7. "A Survey of the New Economy," 6–8.

8. Bob Greene, "You Must Remember This (Unless You Don't)," *Chicago Tribune,* April 9, 2000, sec. 1, 2.

9. Edmund S. Phelps, "Crash, Bang, Wallop," *The Wall Street Journal,* January 5, 2004, A14.

10. Charles P. Kindleberger, *Manias, Panics and Crashes,* 4th ed. (New York: John Wiley & Sons, 2000), 2, 15, 16.

11. "History Lesson: Bubbles of the Past," *The Wall Street Journal,* January 18, 2000, C14; Christopher Silvester, "Echoes for Bursting Bubble." Review of *A Very English Deceit: The Secret History of the South Sea Bubble and the First Great Financial Scandal* by Malcolm Balen, *Financial Times,* August 11, 2002, Weekend, IV; Jon Swartz, "Dot-Com Decline Sees No End Soon," *USA Today,* June 7, 2001, B1. This article states Webmergers.com reported that 493 dot-coms failed between January 2000 and May 2001.

12. "History Lesson: Bubbles of the Past," *The Wall Street Journal,* January 18, 2000, C14; Edward E. Gordon, *Skill Wars, Winning the Battle for Productivity and Profit* (Boston: Butterworth-Heinemann, 2000), 287–288.

13. Jeremy Siegel, "Good Things Come to Those Who Wait," *Financial Times,* July 15, 2002, 18; Greg Burns, "Quick Work Made of 11,000 Mark," *Chicago Tribune,* May 4, 1999, sec. 5, 1; E. S. Browning and Lanthe Jeanne Dugan, "Aftermath of a Market Mania," *The Wall Street Journal,* December 16, 2003, C1; Paul Abrahams, "Rationalisation Looms as 'Liquidity Events' Run Dry," *Financial Times,* October 16, 2002, 7; Steven Lipin, "Done That? Flashback to '60s Echoes 'New Paradigm' Talk," *The Wall Street Journal,* January 18, 2000, C1; Andrew Sum, Irwin Kirsch, and Robert Taggert, *The Twin Challenges of Mediocrity and Inequality: Literacy in the U.S. from an International Perspective* (Princeton, New Jersey: Educational Testing Service, 2002), 29.

14. "A Survey of the New Economy," 7; Kindleberger, *Manias,* 7; Thomas Frank, *One Market under God* (New York: Doubleday, 2000), 15; R. C. Longworth, "CEO Pay 531 Times that of Workers," *Chicago Tribune,* August 28, 2001, sec. 3, 4; Jack Beatty, *The World According to Peter Drucker* (New York: The Free Press, 1998), 23.

15. Theodore Roosevelt, as quoted in Daniel Broder, "Bush Could Learn Some Things from Roosevelt," *Chicago Tribune*, January 29, 2002, sec. 1, 7;

16. R. C. Longworth, "Suddenly Our Manuals Are Out of Date," *Chicago Tribune*, April 9, 2000, sec. 2, 1, 7; Yochi J. Dreazen, Greg Ip, and Nicholas Kulish, "Why the Sudden Rise in the Urge to Merge and Form Oligopolies?" *The Wall Street Journal*, February 25, 2002, A2, A10; Michael Skapinker, "Only the Strong Survive," *Financial Times*, June 11–12, 2005, W1, W3.

17. Jesse Eisinger, "Out of Options," *The Wall Street Journal*, July 9, 2003, C1; John Plender, "How to Take a Little Air from Those Bubbles," *Financial Times*, July 28, 2003, 19; David Wessel, "For Well-Paid CEOs, No Passing the Buck," *The Wall Street Journal*, February 28, 2002, A1.

18. John Kay, "Profits Without Honor," *Financial Times*, June 29–30, 2002, 9; Sinclair Stewart, "Options Value Payments Keep Soaring," *Financial Post*, May 20, 2002, FP 2; Andrew Hill, "S&P Lines Up Corporate Performance Reforms Despite Business Opposition," *Financial Times*, May 13, 2002, 1; Andrew Parker and Andrew Hill, "Standard-Setters Are Targeting Stock Options Again. After Enron, Reform Will Be Harder to Resist," *Financial Times*, November 11, 2002, 11; Richard Waters and Scott Morrison, "Microsoft Ends Employee Stock Options, *Financial Times*, July 9, 2003, 1.

19. Mark Hulbert, "A 16-Year Slump, If So, Blame It on the Boomers," *The New York Times*, December 1, 2002, BU7; "Getting On," *The Wall Street Journal*, July 3, 2001, A1; Harold Hodgkinson, "The Future of Jobs and Workers: A Demographic View," Institute for Educational Leadership, Washington, D.C. Keynote Address, Sixth Annual Workplace Learning Conference, December 2, 2001, Chicago, Illinois; Aaron Bernstein, "Too Many Workers? Not for Long," *Business Week*, May 20, 2002, 128. Robert Stowe England, *The Fiscal Challenge of an Aging Industrial World* (Washington, D.C.: Center for Strategic and International Studies, 2002), 6.

20. Julie Edgar, "Wake-Up Call," *Chicago Tribune*, February 4, 2001, C1; "A Survey of America—U.S. Versus Us," *The Economist*, November 8, 2003, 7; Kristen B. Donahue, "Time to Get Serious about Talent Management," *Harvard Management Update*, July 2001, 6.

21. Larry Wheeler, "Report on Social Security Spurs Capitol Hill Debate," *The Desert Sun*, March 27, 2002, A13; Hodgkinson, "The Future of Jobs"; "U.S. Birthrate Hits New Low," *Chicago Tribune*, June 26, 2003, sec. 1, 14; Gary Marx, "10 Trends for Tomorrow's Kids," *The Futurist*, May 2001, 4–5.

22. Bernstein, "Too Many Workers?", 129.

23. "The Next Society: A Survey of the Near Future," *The Economist*, November 3, 2001, 5; "Aging," *OECD in Washington*, January 2000, 1; "Demography: Population Growth Slows," *The Futurist*, July–August 2003, 12; "Japanese Elderly Hit Record High," *Financial Times*, September 16, 2002, 4; Fen Montaigne, "Russia Rising," *National Geographic*, November 2001, 24; England, *The Fiscal Challenge*, 6; Roger Herman, "Herman Trend Alert: Global Demographics," *The Herman Group*, December 2, 2003, 1.

24.   Quentin Peel, "No Room for the Intolerant," *Financial Times*, May 13, 2002, 13; "The Next Society: A Survey of the Near Future," *The Economist*, November 3, 2001, 6; Francesco Guerrera, "How Much Will It Take to Defuse the Time Bomb?" *Financial Times*, May 21, 2003, 11; Paul Betts, "Aging Europe Faces Up to Need for Pension Reform," *Financial Times*, August 28, 2003, 14; "Half a Billion Americans?" *The Economist*, August 24, 2002, 22; Mark Landler, "Empty Maternity Wards Imperil a Dwindling Germany," *The New York Times*, November 18, 2004, A3.

25.   Robert Samuelson, "Retirement is Now More than a Notion," *Chicago Tribune*, August 2, 2002, sec. 1, 25; Joanne Cleaver, "For Many, Work is Never Done," *Chicago Tribune*, August 11, 2002, sec. 5, 5; Kelly Greene, "Many Older Workers to Delay Retirement until after Age 70," *The Wall Street Journal*, September 23, 2003, D2; Norma Cohen and Clive Cookson, "The Planet is Ever Greyer," *Financial Times*, January 19, 2004, 11; Richard Jackson, "The Challenge of Global Aging: The Threat to World Stability and What To Do About It," Washington, D.C.:U.S. Center for Strategic and International Studies, 2002, 4–5.

26.   Melissa Allison, "Computer Bug Silences NYSE," *Chicago Tribune*, June 9, 2001, sec. 2, 1–2; "Nasdaq Extends Trading after Computer Glitch," *Chicago Tribune*, June 30, 2001, sec. 2, 1–2; Kate Kelly, "Nasdaq Logjam Halts Platforms for Two Hours," *The Wall Street Journal*, July 2, 2001, C1; "2,000 Idled ATMs Back in Operation," *Chicago Tribune*, September 6, 2001, sec. 3, 2; James P. Miller and Leon Lazaroff, "Computer Glitch Nearly Stops Tribune Presses, *Chicago Tribune*, July 20, 2004, sec. 3, 1; Jathon Sapsford and Paul Beckett, "Crash Dodging: Financial Firms Work to Revive Old Technology," *The Wall Street Journal*, September 7, 2001, C1; Tom Rybarczyk and John McCormick, "Computer Glitch Grounds Flights," *Chicago Tribune*, August 2, 2004, sec. 2, 1, 5; "Bush Delayed by Helicopter Breakdown," *Akron Beacon Journal*, April 18, 2002, A3.

27.   "Needed: Experienced Workers," *Harvard Business Review*, July–August, 2001, 20; Cheryl Hall, "Shortage of 'Human Capital' Envisioned," *Chicago Tribune*, November 18, 2002, sec. 4, 2; John A. Challenger, "The Coming Labor Shortage," *The Futurist*, September–October 2003, 24–28.

28.   Carlos Tejada, "Why Some Jobs Go Begging Despite Weak Labor Market," *The Wall Street Journal*, September 2, 2003, B1; Saul Carliner, "The Economy–Training Op Connection," *TD*, August 2003, 66.

29.   Cynthia G. Wagner, "Economics—The Impending Jobs Crisis," *The Futurist*, March–April, 2003, 6; Roger E. Herman, Tom G. Olivo, and Joyce L. Gioia, *Impending Crisis: Too Many Jobs, Too Few People* (Winchester, Virginia: Oakhill Press, 2003), 96–99.

30.   Mark Henricks, "Evaporating Labor Pool," *American Way*, June 15, 2003, 69–70; Kristine Ellis, "Mind the Gap," *Training*, January 2002, 30–35.

31.   Jon E. Hilsenrath, "Slump in Job Market is Longest in Decades," *The Wall Street Journal*, January 13, 2003, A2; Peter G. Gosselin, "Productivity Surge Backfiring, Some Say," *Chicago Tribune*, sec. 5, 1; James Mackintosh, "Robots Lose Out to the Human Touch," *Financial Times*, May 1, 2003, 7.

32.   Ellis, "Mind the Gap," 31.

33. Kelly O'Connor, "A Call to Care," *Desert Sun*, November 14, 2003, D1; "Shortage of Skilled Health-Care Workers Requires New Recruitment Solutions," *The Wall Street Journal*, November 12, 2002, B9; Carol Kleiman, "Amid Shortage, Nurses Lobby for Better Jobs, Lives," *Chicago Tribune*, January 28, 2003, sec. 3, 1; Sarah Laitner, "Shortage of Nurses Prove Headache for U.S. Hospitals," *Financial Times*, February 7, 2003, 4; Maura Kelly, "Nursing Supply in Critical Condition," *Chicago Tribune*, December 26, 2001, sec. 8, 1, 8; Barbara Varro, "Colleges Leading Charge in Battle to Recruit Nurses," *Chicago Tribune*, July 14, 2002, Special Education Section, 1; Francesca Donlan, "No End in Sight to Valley's Nursing Shortage," *Desert Sun*, October 22, 2000, A11; Francesca Donlan, "Hospitals Working Overtime to Recruit and Retain Nursing Staff," *Desert Sun*, October 22, 2000, A18; Kris Maher, "Enrollment in Nursing Rises, but Crisis in Field May Linger," *The Wall Street Journal*, May 27, 2003, B12.

34. Robert Pear, "Health Spending Hits Record Level: 15% of Economy," *Desert Sun*, January 9, 2004, A3. This article states that a 2001 OECD study gave the following international comparisons with other countries: Switzerland, 10.9 percent, Germany, 9.7 percent, Canada, 9.7 percent, and France, 9.5 percent; Kelly, "Nursing Supply in Critical Condition," 1; Laitner, "Shortage of Nurses," 4.

35. Mitchel Benson, "California Moves to Designate Levels for Nurse Staffing," *The Wall Street Journal*, January 23, 2002, B1; Steven Hymon, Jia-Rui Chong, and Lisa Richardson, "Some Hospitals Giving Up Hope," *Los Angeles Times*, January 16, 2004, B6; "Eisenhower Medical Center, ICU/ED/Telemetry Nurses," *Desert Sun*, Career Builder, January 7, 2004, E2; Rachel Osterman, "Filipinos Carry On Legacy of Nursing," *Chicago Tribune*, October 24, 2004, sec. 2, 2; Bob Davis, and Jon E. Hilsenrath, "Conflicting Data," *The Wall Street Journal*, October, 24, 2004, A1. In a December, 2003 cross-country drive, the author saw nursing recruitment roadside billboards along interstates in Missouri and New Mexico. Other hospitals offered new cars, gift certificates, and other perks.

36. Greg Wright, "Study: More Entering Nursing Field, but Shortage Looms," *Desert Sun*, November 13, 2003, A11; Hugh Dellios, "U.S. Takes Care in Recruiting Mexico Nurses," *Chicago Tribune*, August 17, 2003, sec. 1, 9.

37. M. William Salganik, "Breast-Test Centers Decline as Need for Them Increases," *The Baltimore Sun*, October 28, 2001, C1; David Crary, "Small Towns across America Facing Dentist Shortage," *Chicago Tribune*, September 21, 2003, sec. 5, 5.

38. Jon Hilkevitch, "Air Traffic Shortage on Radar," *Chicago Tribune*, August 13, 2001, sec. 1, 1, 10; Frank James, "Government Faces Wave of Retirements," *Chicago Tribune*, April 28, 2001, sec. 1, 1; Scott McCartney, "Crowded Chicago Skies Raise Safety Concerns," *The Wall Street Journal*, January 14, 2004, D1; Jon Hilkevitch, "Air Controllers Want 1,000 Hires," *Chicago Tribune*, July 8, 2004. sec. 2, 3.

39. Susan Carey, "Airlines Find Good Mechanics in Short Supply," *The Wall Street Journal*, May 10, 2001, B1; Gerard J. Arpey, "Maintaining Our Commitment," *American Way*, September 1, 2003, 6; Andy Pasztor, "Study Cites Maintenance Risks," *The Wall Street Journal*, April 21, 2004, D1.

40. Timothy Aeppel, "Plants Face Challenge as Boomers Retire," *The Wall Street Journal,* July 12, 1999, A1; "Industry Report Shows Need for More Skilled Workers," *School-To-Career Report,* February 2002, 15–16; Michell Higgins, "Latest Car-Repair Problem: Finding a Mechanic," *The Wall Street Journal,* September 23, 2004, D6; Greg Bluestein, "Program Puts Minorities into Technician Jobs," *Chicago Tribune,* November 28, 2004, sec. 12, 5; Virginia Groark, "Mechanic Gap Puts Mowers in Lawn Line," *Chicago Tribune,* August 5, 2000, sec.1, 8.

41. Nancy Dunne, "Securing Jobs While Keeping the Nation Safe," *Financial Times,* January 16, 2004, 9; Edward E. Gordon, "FutureWork : The Revolution Reshaping American Business," Keynote presentation, California Apprenticeship Council, San Diego, California, October 24, 1996; Tanya Mohn, "Construction Site Sees Technology Adapt," *Chicago Tribune,* April 28, 2002, sec. 10, 1, 3.

42. "Bring Your Teaching Degree to California," display ad in the *Chicago Tribune,* August 10, 2001, sec. 1, 10; Crystal Yednak, "Schools Fight for Teachers," *Chicago Tribune,* January 20, 2003, sec, 2, 1; Evan Osnos, "Schools Left Dry by Wave of Teacher Retirements," *Chicago Tribune,* July 29, 2001, sec. 1, 1.

43. Kris Maher, "Many Jobless Turn to Teaching, but Not Enough to Fill the Need," *The Wall Street Journal,* July 29, 2003, B8; Richard M. Ingersoll, "Teacher Turnover and Teacher Shortages: An Organizational Analysis," *American Education Research Journal 38* (Fall, 2001): 499–534; Sheryl Silver, "Accelerated Certification Programs Target Teacher Shortage," *Chicago Tribune,* October 14, 2001, sec. 6, 3.

44. Greg Toppo, "Teacher Wages Beat Inflation by a Hair," *Chicago Tribune,* April 8, 2002, 8; Diana Jean Schemo, "For Oklahoma's Teachers Big D is Dollars (and Dallas)," *New York Times,* July 6, 2002, A7.

45. David B. Caruso, "Hey, What Ever Happened to the Teacher Shortage?" *Chicago Tribune,* August 17, 2003, sec. 5, 5.

46. Stephanie Overby, "U.S. Stays on Top," *CIO,* January 20, 2004, 44; Carol Jonas-Morrison, "The IT Career Model at TVI Community College," Presentation Paper at National Council for Workforce Education National Conference, October 26, 2003, Westminster, Colorado; Hodgkinson, "The Future of Jobs"; Alex Pham, "Tech Sales, Not Jobs, Surging," *The Los Angeles Times,* January 26, 2004, C4.

47. Sharon Begley, "As We Lose Engineers, Who Will Take Us into the Future?" *The Wall Street Journal,* June 6, 2002, B1; Kemba J. Dunham and Kris Maher, "Fewer Engineering Graduates, Budget Cuts and Loss of 'Cool' Make Hiring Tougher for Agency," *The Wall Street Journal,* February 4, 2003, B1.

48. "A Moment of Insight that Helped Secure the Future," Boeing employment advertisement in *Los Angeles Times,* January 12, 2004, A6; Advertisement, *The Wall Street Journal,* January 27, 2004, B11; Rick Stephens, "Success in Education through Collaboration," Presentation at the National Tech Prep Conference, October 17, 2001, Dallas, Texas.

49. "Final Report of the Commission on the Future of the United States Aerospace Industry," Washington, D.C., 2002.

50. Martin Crutsinger, "Greenspan: Lost Jobs Replaceable," *Desert Sun,* January 27, 2004, E1.

51. Jon E. Hilsenrath, "Why for Many This Recovery Feels More Like a Recession," *The Wall Street Journal*, May 29, 2003, A14.

52. Adam Geller, "Workers Struggle to Stay Upbeat as Factories Leave," *Chicago Tribune*, August 11, 2003, sec. 4, 6.

53. Clare Ansberry, "Outsourcing Abroad Draws Debate at Home," *The Wall Street Journal*, July 14, 2003, A2; Charles Pretzlik, "Finance Companies 'Plan Shift to Low-Cost Countries,'" *Financial Times*, April 9, 2003, 7; Eric Auchard, "One in 10 Technology Jobs May Move Overseas," *Chicago Tribune*, August 3, 2003, sec. 5, 5; Julie Bennett, "Scientific Hiring Strategies Are Raising Productivity While Reducing Turnover," *The Wall Street Journal*, February 10, 2004, B7.

54. Eric Hazard, "Study: Labor Is Not In for Shortfall," August 28, 2003; *Planspower.com*, 2; Richard Waters and Tom Foremski, "Intel Insider Looks to Asia," *Financial Times*, September 22, 2003, 8; Jon Healey, "Intel Founder Looks to the Future," *Chicago Tribune*, January 22, 2001, sec. 4, 7.

55. Peter Marsh, "Dresden Fulfills California Dreams of Growth," *Financial Times*, July 8, 2002, 8.

56. Jon Van, "Foreign Plants Not Always Key to Profit," *Chicago Tribune*, August 30, 2003, sec. 2, 3; Michael Skapinker, "A Cost Effective Way to Lose Control of Your Business," *Financial Times*, October 15, 2003, 8.

57. Gordon, *Skill Wars*, 21–25; James Kynge, "Phoney Police Add to China's Fake List," *Financial Times*, June 21, 2002, 6; Skapinker, "A Cost Effective Way"; Edward Luce and Khozem Merchant, "Dell Cuts Back Indian Customer Service Venture," *Financial Times*, November 26, 2003, 8; Ray Marcelo, "Extending the Net Gain," *Financial Times*, January 23, 2004, 28.

58. Letter from Douglas Swanson to Edward E. Gordon, April 23, 2002. An interview had preceded this correspondence. James Mackintosh and Peter Marsh, "Toyota Executive Backs French Workers over U.S. Counterparts," *Financial Times*, March 3, 2003, 1; "(Still) Made in Japan," *Financial Times*, April 10, 2004, 57–59.

59. Khozem Merchant, "India on Hunt for IT Staff," *Financial Times*, October 18, 2004, 20; "China Help Wanted," *The Economist*, October 9, 2004, 39; Alexandra Harvey, "Going Home: Chinese Migrant Workers Shun Long Factory Hours and Low Pay," *Financial Times*, November 3, 2004, 15.

60. Rebecca Theim, "Coming Soon: Plenty of Jobs," *Chicago Tribune*, April 13, 2003, sec. 5, 5; Edward Alden, "Companies to Pay High Price for U.S. Visa Expansion," *Financial Times*, November 24, 2004, 3.

61. "Greenspan Warns U.S. Lawmakers about Protectionism," *Los Angeles Times*, January 27, 2004, C5.

62. Hodgkinson, "The Future of Jobs."

63. Warren Veith, "He'll Take Your Job and Ship It," *Los Angeles Times*, April 27, 2001, 1.

64. ———, "Fed Chief Warns of Barriers to Growth," *Los Angeles Times*, February 12, 2004, C1; Gordon Lafer, "Bush's Call for Job Training: Cruel Joke on Unemployed," *Los Angeles Times*, January 25, 2004, M5; Gordon, *Skill Wars*, 294–296.

65. Simon London, "How to Free the Boffins from the Lab," review of *Open Innovation* by Henry Chesbrough, *Financial Times,* May 15, 2003, 10.

66. Christopher Caldwell, "A Chill Wind from Offshore," *Financial Times,* February 7, 2004. 7.

2.   THE RISE OF THE TECHNO-PEASANTS

1. Melita Marie Garza, "Jobs in Manufacturing No Longer Build Futures," *Chicago Tribune,* April 22, 2001, sec. 1, 1, 14.

2. Kris Maher, "The Outlook, Labor Pains: Closing the 'Skills Gap'," *The Wall Street Journal,* November 22, 2004, A2.

3. Beatriz Pont and Patrick Werquin, "Literacy in a Thousand Words," *OECD Observer,* November 2, 2000, 1, 2; Horst Kohler and James Wofensohn, "We Can Trade Up to a Better World," *Financial Times,* December 12, 2003, 12; Susan Ohanian, "Capitalism, Calculus and Conscience," *Phi Delta Kappan* 84 (June, 2003): 737.

4. Richard Waters, "The Enigma within the Knowledge Economy," *Financial Times,* February 2, 2004, 5; "Choose to Compete," *Computer Systems Policy Project,* Washington, D.C., 2004, 4, 6, 7, 9, 10; Scott Donnelly, "GE Taps a World of Local Skills," *Financial Times,* February 18, 2004, 8.

5. Tom Foremski, "Samsung to Overtake Intel as Biggest Buyer," *Financial Times,* January 9, 2004, 18; John O'Dell, "Toyota Cuts in Front of Ford as No. 2," *Los Angeles Times,* January 24, 2004, A1, A14; "Efficient Japanese Top U.S. Big 3," *Chicago Tribune,* June 15, 2001, 3; Ricky Popely and Jim Mateja, "UAW Seen Focusing on Benefits vs. Jobs—U.S. Big 3s Market Share Has Declined," *Chicago Tribune,* September 13, 2003, sec. 1, 1, 19; George A. Clowes, "Getting Our Priorities Right," *School Reform News,* July 2000, 20; Robert L. Simison and Joseph B. White, "Reputation for Poor Quality Still Plagues Detroit," *The Wall Street Journal,* May 4, 2000, B1; Earle Eldridge and Stephanie Armour, "Ford Employees to Get Computers," *USA Today,* February 4, 2000, B1; "Group: High School Diploma a Broken Promise," *Desert Sun,* February 10, 2004, A4.

6. "The Misery of Manufacturing," *The Economist,* September 27, 2003, 61; "Manufacturing Shows Healthy Growth," *Chicago Tribune,* September 3, 2003, sec. 3, 3; Jon E. Hilsenrath, and Rebecca Buckman, "Factory Employment is Falling World-Wide," *The Wall Street Journal,* October 20, 2003, A2; Rick Popely and Jim Meteja, "Toyota Pulls Ahead in Productivity," *Chicago Tribune,* June 3, 20054, sec. 3, 1; "The Car Company in Front," *The Economist,* January 29, 2005, 65–67.

7. Melissa Allison, "Manufacturing's Woes Drain Its Pool of Workers," *Chicago Tribune,* February 24, 2003, sec. 4, 1; Clare Ansberry, "Why U.S. Manufacturing Won't Die," *The Wall Street Journal,* July 3, 2003, B1; Pont and Werquin, "Literacy in a Thousand Words," 3; *Higher Skills, Bottom Line Results* (Washington, D.C.: Center for Workforce Preparation, U.S. Chamber of Commerce, 2002), 2.

8.   Bettina Lankard-Brown, "The 'New Economy:' Real or High-Tech Bubble?" No. 27 (Columbus, Ohio: ERIC Clearinghouse on Adult, Career, and Vocational Education, 2003).

9.   Dannah Baynton, "America's $60 Billion Problem," *Training,* May 2001, 51; *Literacy in the Information Age: Final Report of the International Adult Literacy Survey* (Paris: Organization for Economic Cooperation and Development, 2000), 14, 17; *Workplace Testing, Basic Skills, Job Skills, Psychological Measurement* (New York: American Management Association, 2000); *Workforce Academy Model Project* (Washington, D.C.: Center for Workforce Preparation, U.S. Chamber of Commerce, 2002); *The Language of Opportunity: Expanding Employment for Adults with Limited English Skills* (Washington, D.C.: Center for Law and Social Policy, 2003); Patrick O'Driscoll, "Mayors: Lack of Skilled Workers Hurting Cities," *USA Today,* September 23, 1999, 4A; "Half of Adults in Los Angeles Lack Literacy Skills, Action Plan Sought," *Report on Literacy Programs,* September 16, 2004, 137–138; "Study: 90 Million Americans Have Low 'Health Literacy'," *Desert Sun,* April 9, 2003, A23.

10.   Gordon, *Skill Wars,* 13, 25–29; Adrienne Fox, "Leaders Offer Insights on the Workforce of the 21st Century," *HR News,* May 1999, 3.

11.   Edward E. Gordon and Elaine H. Gordon, *Literacy in America, Historic Journey and Contemporary Solutions* (Westport, Connecticut: Praeger, 2003), 274, 285–288, 295–296.

12.   "First 'State of Literacy'" Report Predicts Upswing in Illiteracy," *Report on Literacy Programs,* November 27, 2003, 179.

13.   "States Make Progress on Standards for Adult Education Achievement," *Report on Literacy Programs,* August 21, 2003, 121, 125.

14.   Andrew Sum, Irwin Kirsch, and Robert Taggert, *The Twin Challenges of Mediocrity and Inequality: Literacy in the U.S. from an International Perspective* (Princeton: Policy Information Center, Educational Testing Service, 2002), 29; Organization for Economic Co-operation and Development, Document 28, December 6, 2004.

15.   "If U Can Read This … ," *The Wall Street Journal,* October 27, 2000, W17.

3.   WHERE HAS THE SCHOOLHOUSE GONE?

1.   V. Dion Haynes, "Nation Tries to Prepare for Problems Tied to Surge in Youth Population," *Chicago Tribune,* December 14, 2000, sec. 1, 35; "Census: Schools Fuller, Much More Diverse," *Desert Sun,* March 23, 1001, A11; Roger Herman, "The Future of Training," *Herman Trend Alert,* February 11, 2004, 1.

2.   "Computers in Schools, Pass the Chalk," *The Economist,* October 26, 2002, 74; Jean-Paul Renaud, "Putting Knowledge in Their Grasp," *Los Angeles Times,* February 9, 2004, B4; "Reading: Sure, But Why Bother?" *National Institute for Literacy Workplace,* May 17, 2001, 1; Mary Beth Marklein, "E-Textbooks Let Collegians Take Byte Out of Bookstore," *USA Today,* August 2, 2000, 9D.

3. "Anyone Read a Good Book Lately?" *Chicago Tribune*, May 17, 2001, sec. 1, 26; Richard Tomkins, "The Mysterious Tales of the Disappearing Book Readers," *Financial Times*, July 16, 2004, 8; Mary Schmich and Eric Zorn, "A Sorrowful Tale, or Just Another Cultural Trend," *Chicago Tribune*, September 12, 2004, sec. 4, 1.

4. *Reading at Risk* (Washington, D.C.: National Endowment for the Arts, 2004); David Henninger, "Love of Reading's a Labor Lost for Many Now," *The Wall Street Journal*, July 16, 2004, A12; Ronald R. Morgan, *Learning to Love Reading*, Loyola University–Chicago research report, January 2004, 3.

5. "Digital Divide: Web Sites Tough for Limited-Literacy Users to Navigate," *Report on Literacy Programs*, November 13, 2003, 175; Renaud, "Putting Knowledge in Their Grasp," B4; "Pass the Chalk," *The Economist*, October 26, 2002, 74–75; "Screen It Out," *The Economist*, October 26, 2002, 13; Andrew Trotter, "International Study Questions Computers' Aid in Learning," *Education Week*, December 8, 2004, 13. This is a report on the OECD study, "Computers and Student Learning: Bivariate and Multivariate Evidence on the Availability and Use of Computers at Home and at School"; Lisa Black, "New Algebra: Batteries Required," *Chicago Tribune*, sec. 1, 1, 28; David J. Hoff, "Tapped Lessons Offer Insights into Teaching," *Education Week*, April 2, 2003, 1, 24.

6. Tracy Dell'Angela, "A Look at Life in High School," *Chicago Tribune*, October 12, 2003, sec. 1, 1, 4; Debra Viadero, "Homework Not on Rise, Studies Found," *Education Week*, October 1, 2003, 1, 16; George A. Clowes, "Homework Burden Not So Crushing after All," *School Reform News*, December 2003, 12–13.

7. Roger Alford, "No Library and Kentucky County Likes It that Way," *Chicago Tribune*, November 24, 2000, sec. 1, 20; Kimberly Hefling, "Scrimping Schools Try a 4-Day Week," *Los Angeles Times*, November 9, 2003, A19; "Colorado Mulls Cutting 12th Grade," *Chicago Tribune*, November 19, 2003, sec. 1, 16. "Public Agenda Releases Decade's Worth of Findings on View of Education," *Reading Today*, August/September 2003, 29; Joel L. Swerdlow, "Changing America," *National Geographic*, September 2001, 50–51; Rob Stein, "Pediatrician Discovers 'Hogwart's Headaches,'" *Chicago Tribune*, October 30, 2003, sec. 1, 11; Dennis L. Evans, "Technological Progress: An Oxymoron?" *Education Week*, November 6, 2002, 37; "Screen Time Outweighs Reading Time for Nation's Youngest Children," *Report on Literacy Programs*, October 30, 2003, 164; Siobhan McDonough, "Too Much TV May Impede Reading Skills," *Chicago Tribune*, October 29, 2003, sec. 1, 20; "Many Parents Doubt Ability to Raise Kids," *Chicago Tribune*, October 31, 2002, sec. 1, 11.

8. Sharon Darling and Jon Lee, "Linking Parents to Reading Instruction," *The Reading Teacher* 57 (December 2003/January 2004): 382–384; Miranda Green, "OECD Warns on the Future of Education," *Financial Times*, September 17, 2003, 8.

9. Daniel W. Kirkpatrick, "A Nation Still at Risk," *School Reform News*, April, 2003, 1; Judith Graham, "Try Swallowing a Byte of This," *Chicago Tribune*, sec. 1, 18; "12th Graders Score Low on Science Test," *Chicago Tribune*, sec. 1, 20.

10. Tony Wagner, "Leadership for Learning: An Action Theory of School Change," *Phi Delta Kappan* 82 (January 2001): 378–383.

11. James S. Braswell et al., *The Nation's Report Card Mathematics 2000*, Washington, D.C.: U.S. Department of Education, 2001, xiii, 17–19, 24, 31–33; Kathleen Kennedy Manzo and Michelle Galley, "Math Climbs, Reading Flat on '03 NAEP," *Education Week,* November 19, 2003, 1, 16; Diana Jean Schemo, "U.S. School Tests Show Steady Gain in Mathematics," *Desert Sun,* November 14, 2003, A3; "Reading Study Highlights Student Progress, Pitfalls," *Report on Literacy Programs,* June 26, 2003, 93.

12. "Good News, Bad News," *Reading Today,* August/September 2003, 1, 4; Kathleen Kennedy Manzo, "Math NAEP Delivers Some Good News," *Education Week,* August 8, 2001, 24; June Kronholz, "Math Scores Don't Add Up to Progress," *The Wall Street Journal,* August 3, 2001, A2; David J. Hoff, "Progress Lacking on U.S. Student's Grasp of Science," *Education Week,* November 28, 2001, 1, 14.

13. Gary Hoachlander, Ann Dykman, and Steven Godowsky, "Attending to Attendance," *Education Week,* May 16, 2001, 40.

14. Robert Holland, "High School Crisis: 3 in 10 Drop Out," *School Reform News,* January 2003, 1, 4; Andrew Sum, Paul Harrington, et al., "The Hidden Crisis in the High School Dropout Problems of Young Adults in the U.S.: Recent Trends in Overall School Dropout Rates and Gender Differences in Dropout Behavior," Boston: Center for Labor Market Studies, Northeastern University, 2003.

15. Mary Ann Zehr, "Reports Spotlight Latino Dropout Rates, College Attendance," *Education Week,* June 18, 2003, 12.

16. Tracy Dell'Angela, "Study: Graduate Rate is Inflated," *Chicago Tribune,* February 26, 2004, sec. 2, 1, 8.

17. Sum et al., "Hidden Crisis," 13. This study cites the 1992 National Adult Literacy Survey and a 1991 survey by the U.S. Bureau of Justice Statistics.

18. David J. Hoff, "U.S. Graduation Rates Starting to Fall Behind," *Education Week,* November 25, 1998, 1, 11.

19. Sum et al., "Hidden Crisis," 40–42.

20. Mike Schmoker, "The Crayola Curriculum," *Education Week,* October 24, 2001, 42, 44; Donna Harrington-Lueker, "Crayola Curriculum Takes Over," *USA Today,* September 16, 2002, A13.

21. Kathleen Kennedy Manzo, "Panel Calls for Writing Revolution in Schools," *Education Week,* April 30, 2003, 10; Diane Rado, "Report Hits Students' Writing Skills, *Chicago Tribune,* April 26, 2003, sec. 1, 10; "Panel Calls for Focus on Student Writing," *Report on Literacy Programs,* June 26, 2003, 90.

22. Erika Hayasaki, "Term Papers Becoming a Relic," *Chicago Tribune,* May 28, 2003, sec. 1, 8; Kathleen Kennedy Manzo, "Relegating Student Research to the Past," *Education Week,* November 20, 2002, 1.

23. Stephanie Banchero, "Students 'Abysmal' U.S. History Scores Alarm Educators," *Chicago Tribune,* May 10, 2002, sec. 1, 8; Tamara Haney, "Kids Get 'Abysmal' Grade in History," *USA Today,* May 10–12, 2002, A1.

24. E. D. Hirsch, *Cultural Literacy: What Every American Needs to Know* (Boston: Vintage Books, 1987), 11, 13, 31; Sam Wineburg, "Crazy for History," *The Journal of American History* 90 (March 2004), 1410.

25.   Bess Keller, "Afghanistan? Young Americans Can't Find It on Maps, Survey Finds," *Education Week,* November 27, 2002, 1; Michael Kilian, "Poll Finds World Is a Mystery to Many," *Chicago Tribune,* November 21, 2002, sec. 1, 13; "Young Americans Flunk Geography," *School Reform News,* March 2003, 5.

26.   Anne Marie Chaker, "Schools Say 'Adieu' to Foreign Languages," *The Wall Street Journal,* October 30, 2003, D1; Ted Sanders and Vivien Stewart, "International Knowledge: Let's Close the Gap," *Education Week,* May 28, 2003, 31, 44.

27.   Mary Beth Marklein, "Math SAT Scores Rise, but Virtual Scores Fall, *USA Today,* August 29, 2002, 8D.

28.   "Group: High School Diploma a Broken Promise," *Desert Sun,* February 10, 2004, A4; Lynn Olson, "States Must Beef Up Diploma Demands, Study Maintains," *Education Week,* February 11, 2004, 1, 9.

29.   Debra Viadero, "Review of Transcripts Says College Concerns May Be Unwarranted," *Education Week,* February 18, 2004, 14; Michael Kirst and Andrea Venezia, "Bridging the Great Divide between Secondary Schools and Postsecondary Education," *Phi Delta Kappan* 83 (September 2001), 94.

30.   *Remedial Education at Degree-Granting Postsecondary Institutions in Fall 2000,* (Washington, D.C.: U.S. Department of Education, Institute of Education Sciences, 2004), iii–vi.

31.   Sara Hebel, "Cal State Sees Reduced Need for Remediation, but Finds English Skills Lacking," *Chronicle of Higher Education,* January 29, 2003; George A. Clowes, "Most Children Left Behind in Urban Public Schools," *School Reform News,* February 2004, 5.

32.   Karen Arenson, "Enrollment and Standards Rise at CUNY," *The New York Times,* September 10, 2001, B1, B3.

33.   "A Survey of the New Economy, Untangling E-Conomics," *The Economist,* September 23, 2000, 39–40; Jim Sulski, "Science Shortage," *Chicago Tribune,* November 12, 2000, sec. 18, 18; David Wessel, "Professor Romer Goes to Washington," *The Wall Street Journal,* January 25, 2001, A1.

34.   *Choose to Compete* (Washington, D.C.: Computer Systems Policy Project, 2004), 10.

35.   David Wessel, "Hidden Costs of a Brain Gain," *The Wall Street Journal,* March 1, 2001, A1; Robert Becker, "U.S. Grad Schools Lose Foreign Applicants," *Chicago Tribune,* February 26, 2004, sec. 1, 20.

36.   Candace Stuart, "Nano Tries Hurdling the Education Gap," *Small Times,* December 1, 2003, 16; Evelyn Iritani, "U.S. Firms Lament Cutback in Visas for Foreign Talent," *Los Angeles Times,* February 16, 2004, C1, C6.

37.   Steve Lohr, "Microsoft, Amid Dwindling Interest, Talks Up Computing as a Career," *The New York Times,* March 1, 2004, C1.

38.   David J. Hoff, "A World-Class Education Eludes Many in the U.S.," *Education Week,* April 11, 2001, 1, 14–15; June Kronholz, "Some U.S. Suburban Students Score High, Urban Pupils Trail on Math, Science Test," *The Wall Street Journal,* April 5, 2001, A13.

39. David J. Hoff, "U.S. Students Rank among World's Best and Worst Readers," *Education Week,* December 12, 2001, 7; *Reading for Change,* PISA, Paris: OECD, 2001; Mary Ann Zehr, "U.S. Lagging in Graduation Rate, Report Says," *Education Week,* November 6, 2002, 5; "U.S. System Helps Educate World, Yet Fails at Home," *USA Today,* November 8, 2001, 15A; "Public Schools Get Decent Grade," *USA Today,* November 14, 2001, 16A.

40. "U.S. System Helps Educate World," *USA Today,* November 8, 2001, 15A.

41. Bonnie Miller Rubin, "Reading, Writing, Retailing: Field Trips Flock to Stores," *Chicago Tribune,* February 22, 2004, sec. 1, 1, 18; Hugh Dellios, "New Train of Thought in Mexico," *Chicago Tribune,* February 22, 2004, sec. 1, 3.

42. Carly Fiorina, "Be Creative Not Protectionist," *The Wall Street Journal,* February 13, 2004, A12.

43. Paul A. Gigot, "Beltway 101: Teddy Takes George to School," *The Wall Street Journal,* May 4, 2001, A14.

44. Olson, "Beef Up Diploma Demands," 1, 9; John Gehring, "Report Examines Motivation among Students," *Education Week,* December 10, 2003, 5; Stephanie Banchero, "'Broken' High-School System Targeted," *Chicago Tribune,* February 28, 2005, sec. 1, 12.

4. HELP WANTED IN AMERICA AND THE WORLD

1. Sean Cavanagh, "Congress Notes Shifting Trends in Higher Education," *Education Week,* March 17, 2004, 49.

2. Tom Vander Ark, "America's High School Crisis: Policy Reforms that Will Make a Difference," *Education Week,* April 2, 2003, 52.

3. "Nation's Jobless Youth Face Training Obstacles," *School-to-Work Report,* September, 2000, 70.

4. "Private Companies Losing Interest in Partnership, Advocate Says," *School-to-Work Report,* July 1999, 52.

5. W. J. Reeves, "College Isn't for Everyone," *USA Today* (Magazine), May 2002, 12; Michael E. Wonacott, "Everyone Goes to College," No. 25 (Columbus, Ohio: ERIC Clearinghouse on Adult, Career, and Vocational Education, 2003), 1; Gordon, *Skill Wars,* 215–218; Cavanagh, "Shifting Trends," 49. *Preparing Youth for the 21st Century: The Transition from Education to the Labour Market,* Proceedings of the Washington, D.C. Conference, 23–24, February 1999, OECD, 159.

6. Gordon, *Skill Wars,* 228–229; Gordon and Gordon, *Literacy in America,* 275.

7. Howard R. D. Gordon, *The History and Growth of Vocational Education in America* (Prospect Heights, Illinois: Waveland Press, Inc., 2003), 83–86, 88–89, 98; Gordon, *Skill Wars,* 228.

8. Chuck Devarics, "Lack of Interest among Students, Not Employees, Hurts Program," *School-to-Work Report,* March 1999, 19; Chuck Devarics, "Data Problems Hinder Efforts to Track Effects of Transition," *School-to-Work Report,* October 2000, 74; Chuck Devarics, "Slants & Trends," *School-to-Work Report,* July 2001, 49;

Kim Kiser, "Tapped-Out," *Training,* July 1999, 48; Chuck Devarics, "Tech-Prep Helps Schools but Students Efforts Mixed," *School-to-Work Report,* March 1999, 22; Mike Perrault, "'Real World' School Falls by Wayside," *Desert Sun,* February 9, 2004, B1.

9.   Lynn Olson, "The Career Game," *Education Week,* October 2, 1996, 31–32.

10.   Chuck Devarics, "Students Confident, but Often Lack Knowledge of Careers," *School-to-Work Report,* November 2000, 82; Peter Y. Hong, "Money Trap Goal of College Freshmen," *Los Angeles Times,* January 26, 2004, 83.

11.   Chuck Devarics, "Career Guidance Falls Short in Most Schools: Report," *School-to-Work Report,* May 2002, 38; Sean Cavanagh, "Advocates Call for Breakdown of Gender Barriers in Voc. Ed.," *Education Week,* June 12, 2002, 9; Gordon, *Skill Wars,* 220; *Decisions without Direction,* Ferris State University, Grand Rapids, Michigan, 2002.

12.   Barbara Schneider and David Stevenson, "The Ambitious Generation," *Education Week,* April 14, 1999, 41, 60. See also their book, *The Ambitious Generation: America's Teenagers, Motivated but Directionless,* Yale University Press, New Haven, Connecticut, 1999.

13.   Gordon, *Skill Wars,* 220–221; George L. Wimberly and Richard J. Noeth, "College Readiness Begins in Middle School," ACT Policy Report, Iowa City, IA: ACT, 2005; Author interview on May 27, 2005 with Richard J. Noeth, Director, ACT Office of Policy Research.

14.   "Economic Focus, The Education Shibboleth," review of *Myths about Education and Economic Growth* by Alison Wolf, *The Economist,* June 8, 2002, 7; Paul Blaum, "College Degree No Substitute for Realistic Goals," *Penn State Newswire,* September 28, 2001.

15.   Justine Law and Richard McGregor, "The ABCs of Taking English to the Chinese," *Financial Times,* March 20, 2004, 8; Peter Marsh, "World's Manufacturers March into China," *Financial Times,* June 21, 2004, 8; Leslie Chang, "China's Grads Find Jobs Scarce," *The Wall Street Journal,* June 22, 2004, A17; "Golden Boys and Girls," *The Economist,* February 14, 2004, 37; "Chronic Overinvestment, Excess Supply and Economic Corruption: Can China Keep Its Booming Economy on Track?" *Financial Times,* September 23, 2003, 15; "Rich Man, Poor Man," *The Economist,* September 27, 2003. 39; *Encyclopedia Britannica Almanac 2003,* 434; James Kynge, "Cancer of Corruption Spread Throughout Country," *Financial Times,* November 1, 2002, 6; Patrick Barta, "Asia's Rebound Faces Squeeze," *The Wall Street Journal,* August 4, 2004, A4; Mei Fong, "A Chinese Puzzle," *The Wall Street Journal,* August 16, 2004, B4; Alexandra Harvey, "Chinese Growth Shrinks Labor Supply," *Financial Times,* August 16, 2004, 4; Peter Marsh, "Fear of High-Tech Piracy Makes Some Microchip Companies Cool about China," *Financial Times,* July 15, 2004, 8; Alexandria Harney, "Laying a False Trail: How Chinese Factories Dupe Western Buyers and Cheat Their Staff," *Financial Times,* April 22, 2005, 13; Ching-Ching Ni, "5 Girls' Deaths Highlight Child-Labor Woes in China," *Chicago Tribune,* May 22, 2005. sec. 1, 8; "A Brother for Her," *The Economist,* December 18, 2004, 51.

16. "The Tiger in Front–A Survey of India and China," *The Economist*, March 5, 2005, 6; Ray Marcelo, "Colleges Set to Take on Rivals," *Financial Times*, March 22, 2005; Uli Schmetzer, "Literacy Unchains Indian Women in Radical Change," *Chicago Tribune*, February 13, 2000, sec. 1, 6; *Encyclopedia Britannica Almanac 2003*, 506; Edward Luce, "Can India Shake up Its Bureaucracy and Spur Change in a Two-Speed Economy?" *Financial Times*, July 13, 2004, 11; *The World in Figures* (London: The Economist, 2003), 1151; Khozem Merchant, "Shrines to Knowledge and Wealth," *Financial Times*, September 7, 2004, 10; "The Bangalore Paradox," *The Economist*, April 23, 2005, 69; Rebecca Buckman, "U.S. Bank Plays 'Concierge' to Tech Start-Ups in India, *The Wall Street Journal*, March 30, 2005, B1.

17. "Immigration in Japan, the Door Opens, a Crack," *The Economist*, September 2, 2000, 37; Randall Morck and Masao Nakamura, "Japan Inc. Feels Crushing Weight of History," *Financial Times*, July 3, 2003, 9; "Higher Education in Japan, Scandal on the Campus," *The Economist*, March 1, 2003, 42.

18. Sarah Laitner and George Parker, "Brussels Looks at 'Green Cards' for Migrants," *Financial Times*, December 14, 2004, 2; George Parker, "Brussels Points the Finger at Lax EU States," *Financial Times*, January 22, 2004, 5; "Room for Improvement," *The Economist*, March 16, 2002, 70; *Going for Growth, The Economy of the EU*, (Brussels: European Communities, 2003), 21–22.

19. Tom Hundley, "Cultural Attitudes Blamed for Italy's Labor Crisis," *Chicago Tribune*, February 23, 2001, sec. 1, 4.

20. "Economic Indicators, Finland," *The Economist*, August 19, 2000, 88.

21. "Survey Portugal," *The Economist*, December 2, 2000, 16.

22. Tony Major and Bertrand Benoit, "Euro Erodes Germany's Role as an International Powerhouse," *Financial Times*, January 13, 2004, 14.

23. Gordon, *Skill Wars*, 180, 182; David Wessel, "American Economy Offers a Model Others Both Envy and Fear," *The Wall Street Journal*, January 18, 2001, A12.

24. "Dummkopf," *The Economist*, December 15 2001, 43.

25. Hugh Williams, "Germany Goes Back to Basics over Education," *Financial Times*, August 23–24, 2003, 2.

26. Gordon, *Skill Wars*, 186–188.

27. "Europe's Immigrants, a Continent on the Move," *The Economist*, May 6, 2000, 25–27; "Brains Not Welcome Here," *The Economist*, May 11, 2004, 50.

28. "A Schooling Nightmare," *The Sunday Times*, October 13, 2002, 18; Gordon, *Skills Wars*, 190.

29. "Hard Numbers," *The Economist*, April 19, 2003, 47–48; James E. Green, *Education in the United Kingdom and Ireland* (Bloomington, Indiana: Phi Delta Kappa Educational Foundation, 2001), 30.

30. Major, "Euro Erodes Germany's Role," 14; Dan Roberts, "Innovation and Diversity Shine through Gloom," *Financial Times*, April 22, 2003, 10; Chris Giles, "Industrial Jobs Are Not Always Beneficial," *Financial Times*, April 13, 2005, 11.

31. "British Panel Calls for Changes in Adult Ed Service Delivery," *Report on Literacy Programs*, April 1, 1999, 5; "Blame the Bosses," *The Economist*, October 12, 2002, 52.

32. "Canada's Census, Please Come, We Need You," *The Economist*, April 13, 2002, 38–39; Ken Warn, "Canada Bucks the Trend by Looking for Immigrants," *Financial Times*, July 11, 2002, 2; "Slants & Trends," *Report on Literacy Programs*, June 24, 1999, 97; Peter Calamai, "Odds Are Good You're Bad at Math," *Literacy at Work*, ABC Canada, September 2002, 6–7; "Chief Economist Drives Literacy Roadshow," *Literacy at Work*, ABC Canada, September 2002, 9.

33. "Education in Latin America, Cramming Them In," *The Economist*, May 11, 2002, 34.

34. Paul Keller, "Peru Faces a Battle to Keep Children in Schools and Out of Hard Labor," *Financial Times*, January 29, 2002, 4; *Encyclopedia Britannica Almanac 2003*, 601.

35. "Education in Chile, Back to School," *The Economist*, June 16, 2001, 38; "Poor Education Leaves Latin Income Gap Wide," *The Wall Street Journal*, April 24, 2000, A1.

36. "A Survey of Brazil, Starting at the Beginning," *The Economist*, February 22, 2003, 13–14; "Education in Latin America," 34–35; Robert Miller, *Literacy Instruction in Mexico* (Bloomington, Indiana: Phi Delta Kappa Educational Foundation, 2003), 14, 114; *Encyclopedia Britannica Almanac 2003*, 565.

37. Aaron Schaney, "Education without Opportunity Will Not Stimulate Development," *Financial Times* (letter to the Editor), June 20, 2002, 12; "Dreaming with BRICS: The Path to 2050," *Global Economics Paper No. 99*, Goldman Sachs, 1–2; Michael E. Porter, *The Competitive Advantage of Nations* (New York: The Free Press, 1990), 628.

38. "Education in Poor Countries: Down with School Fees," *The Economist*, December 13, 2003, 44; Leyla Boulton, "Reform Becomes Political Battlefield," *Financial Times*, April 1, 2003, World Report: Turkey, III; *Encyclopedia Britannica Almanac 2003*, 650.

39. "Primary School Attendance," *The Economist*, December 14, 2002, 94; "Report Roundup, World's Children," *Education Week*, January 7, 2004, 15; Jim Kelly, "More Than 70 Countries Seen as Likely to Miss Education Targets," *Financial Times*, November 14, 2002, 5.

40. "Education," *The Economist*, December 13, 2003, 102; "Girls Continue to Face Sharp Discrimination in Access to School," *Education Report*, UNESCO, November 5, 2003, 1, 2; Alan Beattle, "Rich Nations Tackled over Education Initiative Fund," *Financial Times*, March 25, 2003, 7; Ashleigh Collins, "Not Enough Girls in World's Classrooms," *Los Angeles Times*, April 21, 2004, C6.

5. SIGNPOSTS AT THE WORKFORCE CROSSROAD

1. Edward E. Gordon, "Retool and Revitalize," *Employee Benefit News*, June 15, 2003, 25; Author interview with Dale Ward, executive vice president, Santa Ana Chamber of Commerce, July 7, 2004.

2. Daniel Altman, "Experts Urge Strong Education Rather Than Big Tariffs," *New York Times*, July 28, 2003; Edward E. Gordon, "How Fargo, N.D. Restarted

the American Dream Machine" *Employee Benefit News,* March 1, 2004, 50; Author interviews with Carissa Richter, July 12, 2004 and Justin Andrist, Fargo–Cass County Economic Development Commission, July 14, 2004; Nancy Dunne, "State Hopes to Reap Innovative Harvest," *Financial Times,* August 26, 2004.

3. *The Shawshank Redemption* is an acclaimed 1994 motion picture in which a straight-arrow banker, Andy DeFrame (Tim Robbins) is wrongly convicted for the murder of his wife and her lover and sent to the Shawshank Prison on a life sentence. There his fellow inmate (played by Morgan Freeman) as well as other prisoners come to admire Robbins' moral code of helping others in spite of a corrupt warden and brutal prison guards. Robbins sets up a prison library, helps inmates learn to read, and gives many of them hope for the future and their own personal redemption.

4. Edward E. Gordon, "Worker Training Portends Another Shawshank Redemption," *Employee Benefit News,* September 15, 2001, 57; Author interview with Robert Zettler, vice president, Workforce and Community Development, North Central College, July 19, 2004.

5. Edward E. Gordon, "You Get What You Ask For," *Training,* November 2004, 32; Author interviews with Homer M. Hayes, president, College of the Mainland, Texas City, Texas, July 20, 2004 and Denis Link, manager of learning and development, British Petroleum (BP), August 30, 2004; "Student Success Stories in Process Technology," Texas City, Texas: Center for the Advancement of Process Technology, 2003, 5, 8.

6. David Wessel, "Socks Are Odd: Made in America." *The Wall Street Journal,* May 3, 2001, A1; Angelou Economics, "Yadkin County Economic Development Strategy," December 2003, 1–3; 11–22; Author interviews with Anita Bullin, Surry Community College, June 30, 2004 and Tom Carter, Employment Security Commission, Yadkin County, North Carolina, July 5, 2004.

7. *Preparing Youth for the 21st Century,* Proceedings of the OECD Conference, Washington, D.C., February 23–24, 1999, 168; Constance Majka, Presentation at the 2002 Connecting Conference, Beaver Creek, CO, July 2, 2002; Author interview with Constance Majka, director of public relations and national partnerships, Philadelphia Academies, Inc., June 29, 2004.

8. Timothy Aeppel, "Better Off Blue Collar," *The Wall Street Journal,* July 1, 2003, B1.

9. Mary Ann Roe, "Cultivating the Gold-Collar Worker," *Harvard Business Review,* May 2001, 32–33.

10. Gordon, *Skill Wars,* 24; Author interview with Dr. Jean Calahan, Tulsa Technology Center, Tulsa, Oklahoma, July 16, 2004.

11. Dennis Littky, et al., "Moment to Moment at the Met," *Educational Leadership* 61 (May 2004): 39–43; Author interview with Phil Price, Met Building principal, September 7, 2004.

12. Joel Rubin, "Auto Tech Academy Helps Put Teens Back on Track," *Los Angeles Times,* March 24, 2004, B2; Jonathan Fahey, "Bumper-to-Bumper Education," *Forbes,* September 6, 2004, 77, 80; Author interview with Robert

McCarroll, academy director, San Clemente High School, San Clemente, CA, July 15, 2004.

13. Rhea R. Borja, "Brave New Science," *Education Week,* September 17, 2003, 27–30; Author interview with Thomas Markham III, director of community relations and development, Minuteman High School, Lexington, Massachusetts, July 15, 2004.

14. Carlos Tejada, "These Students Wear Hardhats and Learn How to Cut Tiles," *The Wall Street Journal,* May 20, 2002, B1, B2; Interview with Lanette Meyer, principal, Construction Career Center, St. Louis, Missouri, July 15, 2004.

15. Ana Beatriz Cholo, "Hard Work Paying Off for Students and School," *Chicago Tribune,* May 21, 2003, sec. 2, 1, 7; Ann Therese Palmer, "Cristo Rey Crafts a School Model that Works," *Chicago Tribune,* December 26, 2003, sec. 3, 1, 3; Author interview with Joshua Hales, director of development and public relations, Cristo Rey High School, Chicago, Illinois, August 6, 2004.

16. V. Dion Hayes, "In California, Experimental School Bids to Turn Out High-Tech Workers," *Chicago Tribune,* December 26, 2000, sec. 1, 20.

17. Rhea R. Borja, "New Tech Haven," *Education Week,* May 29, 2002, 27–31; Author interviews with Mark Morison, principal, New Technology High School, August 30, 2004, and Susan Schilling, president and CEO, New Tech Foundation, September 13, 2004.

18. James J. Kemple and Judith Scott-Clayton, "Career Academies Impacts on Labor Market Outcomes and Educational Attainment," New York, Manpower Demonstration Research Corporation (MDRC), March 2004, 1–10.

19. Joel Rubin, "Career Academies Benefit High School Grades, Student Says," *Los Angeles Times,* March 16, 2004, B5; David Stern, Neal Finkelstein, James R. Stone III, John Letting, and Carolyn Dornsife, *School to Work Research on Programs in the United States,* (Washington, D.C.: Falmer Press, 1995), 125–126.

20. John Gehring, "School-to-Work Results," *Education Week,* February 21, 2001, 5.

21. Paul M. Barrett, "A Baltimore Academy Focuses on Careers—and Staying in School," *The Wall Street Journal,* May 31, 2001, A1; "National Organizations Get Ready to Announce Standards of Practice for Career Academies," *Connections* (National Career Academy Coalition), May 2004, 1, 3; "Connecting the Dots: Linking School and Work to Accelerate Student Results," *Workforce Economics,* February 1999, 3; OECD, "Preparing Youth," February 23–24, 1999, 168–172; Stern, *School to Work Research,* 127–129; Kevin Hollenbeck, *Classrooms in the Workplace* (Kalamazoo, Michigan: W. E. Upjohn Institute, 1993).

22. Edward E. Gordon, "Work-Based Learning In America: Solutions for a New Century," *Corporate University Review,* November/December 1997, 36; "Tech Prep," *Boeing Education Relations,* July 14, 2004; Author interview with Mark Turner, The Boeing Company, Educational Partnerships/Tech Prep, August 2, 2003; Rick Stephens, "Success in Education through Collaboration," Presentation delivered at the National Tech Prep Conference, Dallas, Texas, October 11, 2001.

23. Jeff Barbian, "Get 'Em While They're Young," *Training,* January 2004, 44, David Wessel, "Workers Get Dessert: Bigger Slice of Pie," *The Wall Street Journal,* April 19, 1999, A1.

24. Michael A. Fletcher, "Caltech Gets $600 Million Donation," *Washington Post,* October 28, 2001, A2; David Wessel, "Intel Cost-Cutting Spares a College Tour," *The Wall Street Journal,* June 14, 2001, A1.

25. Barbian, "Get 'Em," 44–46.

26. "Young, Cheap and American," *The Economist,* November 1, 2003, 70.

27. Roe, "Gold Collar," 33.

28. Tal Barak, "Competition Inspires Students to be Inventive," *Education Week,* June 23, 2004, 12.

29. "Maryland Uses Recent Grads to Boost School/Work Links," *School-to-Work Report,* September 2000, 71; *2003 Annual Report,* Maryland Business Roundtable for Education, 10–16; Author interview with June E. Streckfus, executive director, Maryland Business Roundtable for Education, July 7, 2004.

30. Jon Van, "Robots Rally School Spirit," *Chicago Tribune,* April 5, 2003, sec. 2, 3; Rhea R. Borja, "Robotics Students See Real-World Lessons," *Education Week,* October 31, 2001, 8; Author interview with Marian Murphy, communications manager, FIRST, Manchester, New Hampshire, September 1, 2004.

31. Lynn Olson, *The School-to-Work Revolution* (Reading, Massachusetts: Addison-Wesley, 1997), 67–71, 258.

32. Andrew Trotter, "S. Korea Tops U.S. in Key Education Ratings," *Education Week,* September 24, 2003, 3.

33. "Banking on Education to Propel a New Spirit of Growth," *The Economist,* December 3, 2003, 37–38.

34. *A Community of Fifteen: Key Figures Edition 2000,* (Luxembourg: Office for Official Publications of the European Communities, 2000), 34.

35. Gordon, *Skill Wars,* 171–209.

36. Stefan Wagstyl, "An Endangered Species: Fewer Births Make Old Europe Fear for Its Future," *Financial Times,* June 11, 2004, 11; "Bridging Europe's Skills Gap," *The Economist,* March 31, 2001, 55–56; *How Europeans See Themselves,* (Luxembourg: Office for Official Publications of the European Communities, 2001), 43.

37. *Towards a Knowledge-Based Europe,* (Luxembourg: Office for Official Publications of the European Communities, 2003), 12.

38. *European Employment and Social Policy: A Policy for People,* (Luxembourg: Office for Official Publications of the European Communities, 2000), 16; *Passport to Mobility,* (Luxembourg: Office for Official Publications of the European Communities, 2001), 5.

39. Davi Woodruff, "In New Europe, Mobile Workers Find Jobs in Nations Offering the Best Opportunities," *The Wall Street Journal,* August 5, 1999, A14.

40. Hugh Williamson, "Skills that Keep Silicon Saxony in the Picture," *Financial Times,* May 21, 2004, 8.

41. T. Diessinger, "Vocational Training in Small Firms in Germany: The Contribution of the Craft Sector," *Education & Training,* 43 (2001), 17–37; Author

interview with Peggy Luce, vice president for education and training, Chicagoland Chamber of Commerce, on the findings regarding workforce education of a nine-person delegation study trip to Germany, Holland, and Denmark, July 20, 2004.

42. Jabeen Bhatti, "Germans Rethink Immigration," *The Wall Street Journal,* July 2, 1004, A9.

43. Hugh Williamson, "Immigration Law Hailed as a Vital Turning Point in Germany's Attitude to a Multiracial Society," *Financial Times,* July 9, 2004, 5.

44. Tom McCann, "Irish Immigrants Learning Chicago for New Prosperity in Old Country," *Chicago Tribune,* April 4, 2000, sec. 1, 1; James O'Shea, "'Celtic Tiger' Tames Ireland," *Chicago Tribune,* June 25, 2000, sec. 2, 1; Robert Kuttner, "Ireland's Miracle: The Market Didn't Do It Alone," *Business Week,* July 10, 2000, 23; Christopher Rhoads, "U.S. Slowdown Muffles the Volume of Ireland's Boom," *The Wall Street Journal,* March 6, 2001, A18; John Murray Brown, "Ireland Proves to be a Shining Example of Membership," *Financial Times,* April 22, 2004, 3.

45. "Britain Scores," *The Economist,* December 8, 2001, 52.

46. "Sliding into Recession," *The Economist,* July 28, 2001, 55; "Hunting the Snark," *The Economist,* June 23, 2001, 51; "The Politics of Literacy Policy," *Literacy Across the Curriculumedia Focus,* Montreal: The Centre for Literacy, Volume 15, No. 2, 2001, 1–2; Fiona Frank, "Workplace—United Kingdom Developments," *Workplace Basic Skills Network* (Lancaster, UK: Lancaster University, March 1, 2001), 1–2; "Improving Adult Basic Skills, Addressing a Generation of Neglect," *The National Needs and Impact Survey of Literacy, Numeracy and ICT Skills* (Norwich, UK: The Stationery Office, November 3, 2003). "Britain Celebrates Achievement in Adult Literacy: 750,000 Learners," *Report on Literacy Programs,* December 23, 2004, 199.

47. Charlotte O'Brien, "Bridging the Skills Gap," *Manchester Guardian,* (Guardian Unlimited Web site), August 27, 2003; Debbie Andalo, "Clarke Announces Apprenticeship Shake-Up," *Manchester Guardian,* (Guardian Unlimited Web site), May 10, 2004; Lucy Ward, "Job Training Plan for 14–16s Unveiled," *Manchester Guardian,* (Guardian Unlimited Web site), May 11, 2004.

48. Angela Jameson, "British Gas to Plug Skills Shortage with 2,000 Jobs," *The Times,* October 9, 2002, 27; Amanda Kelly, "Education: It's Back to the Grindstone," *The Times,* October 10, 2002, 20.

49. Frederick Studemann, "Blair Announces School Reform Plan," *Financial Times,* July 9, 2004, 5.

50. Jim Kelly and Parminder Bahra, "Bridging the Great Education Divide," *Financial Times, A Comprehensive Guide to the UK's Leading Schools,* October 6–7, 2001, 1; Christopher Swann, "Selective System in the Eye of a Political Storm," *Financial Times,* July 9, 2003, 5.

51. Alvise Cassagrande, "Long-Time Employee Remembers Days at Central Shops," *Cape Breton Post,* May 21, 2002, B3; Heather Scoffield, "Rock Solicits Federal Funding to Close Shipyards," *The Globe and Mail,* May 21, 2002, A1; Wade Kearley, "Riding the Tides," *Atlantic Business,* November 2, 2002, 12–13; Sandra Phinney, "Nova Scotia Brink of Prosperity," *Atlantic Business,* November 2, 2002;

Natural Resources in Atlantic Canada, NR6-NR5; Author interview with Joseph Brown, July 28, 2004.

52.   Terry K. Peterson, Alan L. Ginsburg, Lenore Y. Garcia, and Mariann Lemke, "Educational Diplomacy," *Education Week,* November 22, 2000, 48.

53.   Author interview with Hilary Pennington, CEO of Jobs for the Future. Also see Richard Kazis, Joel Vargens, and Nancy Hoffman, editors, *Double the Numbers: Increasing Postsecondary Credential for Underrepresented Youth,* (Cambridge, Massachusetts: Harvard University Press, 2004). A collection of provocative essays about strategies to strengthen career preparation.

54.   *2001 Report,* Career and Technical Education Challenge Task Force, Illinois Community College Board, Illinois State Board of Education, 7–9; Author interview with Leonard R. Wass, chief executive officer, Wass Consulting Group, member of the Illinois Career and Technical Education Challenge Task Force, member of the Education Workforce Quality Committee, Chicagoland Chamber of Commerce, August 2, 2004.

6.   THE "SIXTH DISCIPLINE"

1.   Edward E. Gordon, "Are We Writing the Obituary for the Learning Organization?" *Employee Benefit News,* April 2001, 68; S. Gary Snodgrass, "Insider Column, Learning Never Steps for Successful People," *Chicago Tribune,* Working Section, January 21, 2001, 1; Peter Senge, *The Fifth Discipline: The Art and Practice of the Learning Organization* (New York: Currency Doubleday, 1990).

2.   "Annual Training Industry Reports," *Training 1990–2004*; "Labor Force Statistics 1994–2004," Washington, D.C.: U.S. Department of Labor, Bureau of Labor Statistics.

3.   Richard Donkin, "Keeping Qualifications in Tip-Top Condition," Special Report, Continuing Professional Development, *Financial Times,* November 25, 2002, 1; David Pringle, "Learning Gurus Adapt to Escape Corporate Axes," *The Wall Street Journal,* January 7, 2003, B1; Jonathan Hunt, "Adapting to the Needs of the Market," *Financial Times,* November 24, 2003, 3; Barbara B. Buckholz, "Short Circuit, In a Down Cycle Companies Disconnect Employees from Training," *Chicago Tribune,* October 2, 2001, 5.

4.   Michael J. Trimble, "Service Suffers as Companies Lose Incentive to Train Staff," *Financial Times* (letter to the Editor), August 29, 2001, 12; Carlos Tejada, "Work Week—A Special Report—and Trends Taking Shape There," *The Wall Street Journal,* August 28, 2001, A1; Ed Michaels, Helen Handfield-Jones, and Beth Axelrod, *The War For Talent* (Cambridge, Massachusetts: Harvard University Press, 2001), 86.

5.   "Low Jobless Rate Backfires," *Desert Sun,* December 31, 2000, D4.

6.   Florence M. Stone, "Will We Win the Skill War?" *Training Zone,* American Management Association, 2003; Gill Plimmer, "Emphasis Should Be on More Skills Investment," *Financial Times,* October 11, 2004, Professional Development Section, 1.

7. Linda Anderson, "The Downturn, A Steely Nerve Becomes a School's Essential Weapon," *Financial Times*, May 17, 2004, 5; Andrew Sum, Irwin Kirsch, and Robert Taggert, *The Twin Challenge of Mediocrity and Inequality: Literacy in the U.S. from an International Perspective* (Princeton, New Jersey: Educational Testing Service, 2002), 31.

8. "Life-Time Training Expectancy," *Education Policy Analysis*, Paris: OECD, 1999.

9. World Future Society Seminar, October 14, 2003, Chicago, Illinois.

10. "Understanding E-Learning," *Financial Times*, Spring 2002, 1–15; Linda Anderson, "Fresh Ways of Learning at the Touch of a Finger," *Financial Times*, March 24, 2003, Special Report Business Education, 10; Sumathi Baba, "Time to Break Out from Campus," *Financial Times*, July 26, 2004, 8; Donna Goldwassor, "Beyond ROI," *Training*, January 2001, 82; Jack Hupple, "The Future of Corporate Innovation Centers." Presentation at Annual Meeting of the World Future Society, Minneapolis, Minnesota, July 30, 2001.

11. Edward E. Gordon, "Can America Keep Pace?" *Employee Benefit News*, June 2000, 39–40; John Seely Brown and Paul Duguid, *The Social Life of Information* (New York: McGraw-Hill, 2000); Nicole Lee, "Learning How to Make the Best of Workplace Education," *Financial Times*, August 19, 2002, 8.

12. Peter J. Smith, "Workplace Learning and Flexible Delivery," *Review of Educational Research* 73 (Spring 2003), 53–88.

13. Two *Information Week* studies cited in "Why Classroom Training Is So Effective," *Training* Zone, American Management Association, 2004.

14. Lee, "Best of Workplace Education," 8.

15. Linda Anderson, "Flexible Courses Prove Popular If Unfulfilling," *Financial Times*, May 12, 2003, 7.

16. Eunice N. Askov, Jerome Johnston, Leslie I. Petty, and Shannon J. Young, *Expanding Access to Adult Literacy with Online Distance Learning* (Cambridge, Massachusetts: National Center for the Study of Adult Learning and Literacy, Harvard Graduate School of Education, 2003), 15–27.

17. Robert M. Bernard et al., "How Does Distance Education Compare with Classroom Instruction?" *Review of Educational Research* 74 (Fall 2004), 379–429.

18. Christine Mahr, Adults Continue Their Educations from the Comfort of Their Homes," *Desert Sun*, February 9, 2004, B6.

19. Della Bradshaw, "E-Learning Alliance Bears Fruit," *Financial Times*, June 24, 2002, 7; Robert McGarvey, "Training 24/7," *American Way*, September 15, 2003, 62.

20. Maria Atanasov, "Savings, Convenience, a Draw for E-Learners," *Chicago Tribune*, December 17, 2001, sec. 4, 1; Kevin Oakes and David Green, "The Answer is Blended Learning, Now What Was the Question Again?" *T&D*, October 2003, 17–19.

21. Edward E. Gordon, "Bridging the Gap," *Training*, September 2003, 31–32; Morgen Witzel, "Birth of the Living Company," *Financial Times*, August 21, 2003, 7; Buckholtz, "Short Circuit," 5.

22.   William Rothwell, *Beyond Training and Development* (New York: Amacon, 2001).

23.   William J. Rothwell, *What CEOs Expect from Corporate Training* (New York, Amacon, 2003).

24.   Edward Gordon, *Skill Wars*, 3–4; Author interview with Tom Monaghan, executive vice present, Human Resources, Wabash National, August 19, 2004.

25.   Kathryn Tyler, "Brushing Up on the Three R's," *HR Magazine*, October 1999, 82–88; Edward E. Gordon, Ronald R. Morgan, and Judith A. Ponticell, *FutureWork The Revolution Reshaping American Business* (Westport, Connecticut: Praeger, 1994), XV; Michael R. Bloom and Brenda Lafleur, *Turning Skills Into Profit: Economic Benefits of Workplace Education Programs* (New York: The Conference Board, 1999), 44, 53, 58, 130.

26.   Sandra Chereb, "Beyond Words: Businessman's Feat Awarded," *USA Today*, June 9, 1999, 5A.

27.   Mary T. Moore, David Myers, and Tim Silva, *Addressing Literacy Needs at Work: Implementation and Impact of Workplace Literacy Programs* (Washington, D.C.: Mathematica Policy Research, Inc., 1997), xiii, xvi, xviii, 1; Mary T. Moore, David E. Myers, and Tim Silva, *Addressing Literacy Needs at Work: A Profile of Institutions, Courses, and Workers in the National Workplace Literacy Partnerships* (Washington, D.C.: Mathematica Policy Research, Inc., 1997), 1, 24, 27.

28.   Gordon, *Skill Wars*, 151–157; Edward E. Gordon, Ronald R. Moran, and Judith A. Ponticell, "Adult Basic Education: Riding Hi-Tech Rails to the Future," in *Transferring Learning to the Workplace*, ed. Mary L. Broad. (Alexandria, Virginia: American Society for Training and Development, 1997), 37–56; Author interview with John Wagner, manager of training and development, METRA, September 13, 2004.

29.   Gordon, *Skill Wars*, 163–167; Suzanne Knell, *Learning That Works: Basic Skills Programs in Illinois Corporations* (Champaign, Illinois: Illinois Literacy Resource Development Center, 1993); Hank O'Roark, "Basic Skills Get a Boost," *Technical Training*, July/August 1998, 10–13; "Canadian Firms Pick up Awards for Fostering Workplace Literacy," *Report on Literacy Programs*, June 24, 2004, 102; Conference Board of Canada, "Awards for Excellence in Workplace Literacy," 2004. Retrieved from www.conferenceboard.ca/education/awards/literacy; Author interview with Linda Scott, program manager, education and learning, The Conference Board of Canada, July 8, 2004; *Canadian CEO*, ABC Canada, September 2004, 6–17; Information on Verizon Foundation programs is available at www.verizon.com/foundation.

30.   Julia Kirby, "Reinvention with Respect," *Harvard Business Review*, November 2001, 117–123.

31.   Tammy Galvin, "The 2003 Training Top 100," *Training*, March, 2003; "The 2004 Training Top 100," *Training*, April, 2004.

32.   Michael Oneal, "Win Cycle for a Maytag Town," *Chicago Tribune*, June 20, 2004, sec. 5, 1, 10.

33.   Suzy Wetlaufer, "The Business Case against Revolution: An Interview with Nestlé's Peter Brabeck," *Harvard Business Review* February 2001, 113–119.

34.   Alan Greenspan, "The Evolving Demand for Skills." Remarks made at the U.S. Department of Labor National Skills Summit, Washington, D.C., April 11, 2000.

35.   Laurie J. Bassi and Mark E. Van Buren, *The 1999 ASTD State of the Industry Report* (Alexandria, Virginia: American Society for Training and Development, 1999), 2; Edward E. Gordon, "Training Investments: The Global Perspective," *Technical and Skills Training,* July 1996, 14.

36.   Sarah Murray, "Bigger Profits Are the Prize for Education," *Financial Times,* October 13, 2003, 7.

37.   Edward E. Gordon, "Human Capital" in *Business the Ultimate Resource* (Cambridge, Massachusetts: Perseus, 2002), 115; Gordon, *Skill Wars,* 82–83.

38.   Edward E. Gordon and Boyd Owens, "Measuring the Impact of Basic Skills Training" in *Measuring Return on Investment,* ed. Jack J. Phillips (Alexandria, Virginia: American Society for Training and Development, 1997), 267–282.

39.   Gordon, *Skill Wars,* 75–63.

40.   *Human Capital Investment,* Paris: OECD, 1998, 35, 63.

41.   Laurie Bassi, "Counterpoint Interview with Daniel Goleman," *Training & Development,* April 1999, 30.

42.   Michael Moskow, "Invest in Skills to Safeguard Growth in Wages," *Financial Times,* September 10, 2004, 13; John S. McClenahen, "The Worrisome Weight of Wall Street," *Industry Week,* November 2004, 46–50.

43.   "What's Left" *The Economist,* May 12, 2001, 80.

44.   OECD, *Human Capital Investment,* 92; Ian Cunningham, "Learning in Organizations" in *Global Management* (American Management Association International, 1999), 66–68; Tom Davenport, *Human Capital: What It Is and Why People Invest It* (San Francisco: Jossey-Bass, 1999); Sherri Caudron, "The Myth of Job Happiness," *Workforce,* April 2001, 36.

45.   "Innovation in Industry Survey," *The Economist,* February 20, 1999, 5–28.

46.   Richard E. Dauch, "Productivity Starts on Plant Floor," *Chicago Sun-Times,* February 9, 2002, 17; Simon London, "A Highly Calculated Recovery Act," *Financial Times,* October 26, 2004, 10.

47.   Michiyo Nakamoto, "How to Turn the Tables on Outsourcing," *Financial Times,* January 6, 2005, 6.

48.   Anna Fifield, "S. Korean Businesses Learn that Less Work Can Still Pay," *Financial Times,* January 7, 2005, 12.

49.   Clare Ansberry, "What's My Line?" *The Wall Street Journal,* March 22, 2002, A1.

50.   Elizabeth Craig, John Kimberly, and Hanid Bonchikhi, "Can Loyalty Be Leased?" *Harvard Business Review,* September 2002, 24.

51.   Peter F. Drucker, "Looking Ahead: Implications of the Present," *Harvard Business Review,* September/October 1997, 22.

52.   Peter Drucker, "Meeting of the Minds," *Across the Board,* November/December 2000, 16–21.

53. Michael Gelb, "Lessons from Leonardo," *Training*, June 1999, 38.

54. Nancy Dunne, "Goodwill Hunting in the Name of Efficiency," *Financial Times*, June 3, 2004, 10.

55. Michael H. Jordan, "Tired of Playing Quarters," *The Wall Street Journal*, September 14, 2004, B2.

56. Thomas Petzinger, Jr., "A New Model for the Nature of Business: It's Alive!" *The Wall Street Journal*, February 26, 1999, B1, B4.

57. Gail Johnson, "Good to Great," *Training*, July/August 2003, 38–42.

7. BEYOND THE 2010 CROSSROAD

1. "Labor's Future of 'No Guarantees,'" *Chicago Tribune*, September 4, 1995, sec. 1, 10.

2. Remarks by Alan Greenspan, "The Evolving Demands for Skills," U.S. Department of Labor National Skills Summit, Washington, D.C., April 11, 2000.

3. John Colville, *The Fringes of Power* (Guilford, Connecticut: Lyons Press, 1985), 651.

4. Richard Florida, "America's Best and Brightest Are Leaving and Taking the Creative Economy with Them," *Across the Board*, September–October 2000, 37.

5. Kohzem Merchant, "Shrines to Knowledge and Wealth," *Financial Times*, September 7, 2004, 10.

6. *Learning Partnerships: Strengthening American Jobs in the Global Economy* (Washington, D.C.: New Economy Information Service, 2004).

7. Edward E. Gordon, Ronald R. Morgan, and Judith A. Ponticell, *FutureWork, the Revolution Reshaping American Business* (Westport, Connecticut: Praeger, 1994), 207; Edward E. Gordon, *Skill Wars: Winning the Battle for Productivity and Profit* (Boston: Butterworth Heinemann, 2000), 281; Marvin J. Cetron, and Owen Davies, *50 Trends Shaping the Future* (Bethesda, Maryland: World Future Society, 2003), 22.

8. Stephen Franklin, "The Future of Success," *Chicago Tribune*, January 28, 2001, sec. 14, 3.

9. Kathleen W. Fitzgerald, "Those Who Refuse to Reflect Die Off," *Chicago Tribune*, July 18, 2004, sec. 2, 1.

10. Michael Skapinker, "The More America Changes, the More It Stays the Same," *Financial Times*, August 4, 2004, 6.

11. Robert D. Putnam, *Bowling Alone: The Collapse and Revival of American Community* (New York: Simon & Schuster, 2000), 287; "Human and Social Capital, What Money Can't Buy," *The Economist*, May 12, 2001, 73; Kathleen Burke, "American Life Is No Longer Like That," *Financial Times*, April 3–4, 2004, W4.

12. Putnam, *Bowling Alone*, 380, 382–384, 389, 393, 397.

13. S.D. Cameron, "Community Development Starts at Grass Roots," *The Sunday Herald, Atlantic Canada*, May 26, 2002, C3.

14. Nancy Dunne, "Self-Help Drive Boosts Nation's Skill Base," *Financial Times*, September 9, 2004, 12.

15. Gregg Edwards and David Pearce Snyder, "High Tech, Free Trade and a Century of Progress." Paper given at Australian Institute of Company Directors Annual Conference Hobart, Tasmania, May 10, 2002, 18–19; Lisa Aldisert, "Global Visions," *Professional Speaker*, December 2001, 14.

16. Harry Levinson, "Why the Behemoths Fell," *American Psychologist*, May 1994, 428–429.

17. Jessica T. Mathews, "Power Shift," *Foreign Affairs*, January/February 1997, 63.

18. Sarah Murray, "Partnerships on the Rise, Special Report, Business & Development," *Financial Times*, June 24, 2004, 5; "Major Gates Foundation Grants to Support High Schools," *Education Week*, June 16, 2004, 28–29.

19. Peter Willets, "What Is a Non-Governmental Organization?" *Encyclopedia of Life Support Systems*, 2002, http://www.eolss.net; Olena P. Maslyukivska, "The Role of Non-Governmental Organization in Development Cooperation," Research paper, UNDP/Yale Collaboration Program, 1999 Research Clinic, New Haven, 1999; International Center for Non-Profit Law, *The Handbook on Good Practices for Laws Relating to Non-Governmental Organizations* (Washington, D.C.: World Bank, 1997).

20. Dunne, "Self-Help Drive."

21. Marcelo Suarez-Orozco and Howard Gardner, "Educating Billy Wang for the World of Tomorrow," *Education Week*, October 22, 2003, 44.

22. David Broder, "Making Educators and Pols Accountable," *Chicago Tribune*, May 8, 2001, sec. 1, 17; Lynn Olson, "User-Friendly Reports on Student Test Scores Help Guide Instruction," *Education Week*, May 26, 2004, 9; David A. Goslin, "Student Engagement," *Education Week*, October 22, 2003, 34.

23. Ted Hershberg, Ian Rosenblum, and Virginia Adams Simon, "Adequacy, Equity, and Accountability," *Education Week*, February 19, 2003, 33; Diane Rado and Geoff Dougherty, "Test Success Can Come Cheap," *Chicago Tribune*, November 25, 2001, sec. 2, 1; Stephanie Simon, "Schools: A $2 Billion Study in Failure," *Chicago Tribune*, May 30, 2001, sec. 1, 8; "Fate of Ailing School System in Arkansas Justice's Hands," *Los Angeles Times*, January 23, 2004, A13.

24. Robert J. Taggart, "The Reform of Reform: How Business-Led Reformers Have Changed Their Tune," *American Educational History Journal* 28 (2001): 225–226.

25. Henry M. Levin, "Educating for a Commonwealth," *Educational Researcher* 30 (August/September 2001): 33.

26. James S. Coleman and Thomas Hoffer, *Public and Private High Schools: The Impact of Communities* (New York: Basic Books, 1987), 94, 133–135, 229, 231. For contrary evidence, see Stephen L. Morgan and B. Spresson, "A Test of Coleman's Social Capital Explanation of School Effects," *American Sociological Review* 64 (1999): 661–681.

27. Anne T. Henderson and Nancy Berla, *A New Generation of Evidence: The Family Is Critical to Student Achievement* (Washington, D.C.: National Committee for Citizens in Education, 1994), 1.

28.   Frank Levy and Richard J. Murname, "Preparing Students for Work in a Computer-Filled Economy," *Education Week*, September 1, 2004, 44, 56.

29.   Kathleen Parker, "Today's Scatological Behavior a Broken Window of Our Civilization," *Chicago Tribune*, December 1 2004, sec. 1, 27.

30.   Jean Johnson, "Why Is School Discipline Considered a Trivial Issue?" *Education Week*, June 23, 2004, 39; "Stressed Teachers Showing Strain of Added Responsibilities—Study," *Edmonton Journal*, July 14, 2001, A11; Ana Beatriz Cholo, "Teachers Give Reasons for Leaving," *Chicago Tribune*, July 1, 2003, sec. 2, 3.

31.   Hayes Mizell, "Not for the Timid," *Education Week*, January 22, 2003, 48; Putnam, *Bowling Alone*, 302; "The High Cost of Lax Parenting," *Chicago Tribune*, August 22, 2004, sec. 2, 8.

32.   Paul R. Lehman, "Ten Steps to School Reform at Bargain Prices," *Education Week*, November 26, 2003, 36.

33.   "The Cosby Show," *The Economist*, July 10, 2004, 30.

34.   Larry E. Suter, "Is Student Achievement Immutable? Evidence from International Studies on Schooling and Student Achievement," *Review of Educational Research* 70 (Winter 2000): 529–545; Linda Teran Strommen and Barbara Fowles Mates, "Learning To Love Reading: Interviews with Older Children and Teens," *Journal of Adolescent and Adult Literacy* 48 (November 2004): 188–200.

35.   John Merrow, "Making the Achievement Gap Disappear: Meeting Superman," *Phi Delta Kappan* 85 (February 2004): 455–460.

36.   Michael Ryan, "An American Success Story," *Parade*, June 30, 2002, 4–5.

37.   David J. Armor, "Environmental Effects on IQ, from the Family or from Schools?" *Education Week*, November 19, 2002, 32–33.

38.   Jeff Donaldson, "Teachers Now Make House Calls," *The Desert Sun*, March 17, 2002, A8.

39.   Deborah Davis, "Parenting 101," *The Santa Fe New Mexican*, May 9, 2004, A!, A5.

40.   Practical Parenting Partnerships, Jefferson City, Missouri. See Web site: www.pppctr.org.

41.   Linda Jacobson, "Parent Power," *Education Week*, October 22, 2003, 29.

42.   "Dolly Parton's Home State Adopts Imagination Library Program Statewide," *Reading Today*, August/September 2004, 36.

43.   "Parent Reading Guide 2004, Reading by 9," A Literacy Initiative for Southern California, *Los Angeles Times*, 2004. See Web site: www.latimes.com.

44.   "Behave, or Else," *The Economist*, December 4, 2004, 55.

45.   Gordon and Gordon, *Literacy in America*, 300–301.

46.   Michael D. Usdan, "Teaching Commissions, Then and Now," *Education Week*, March 31, 2004, 36.

47.   Suzanne Loeb, "Public Policy and Teacher Labor Markets: What We Know and Why It Matters." Paper given at Michigan State University Education Policy Center Conference, 2004; Julian R. Betts, Andrew C. Zau, and Larren A. Rice,

"Determinants of Student Achievement: New Evidence from San Diego," Public Policy Institute of California, 2003.

48. Vivian Troen and Katherine C. Boles, "The 'Trilemma' Dysfunction," *Education Week*, May 14, 2003, 32, 34.

49. Stephanie Banchero, "More Teachers Stay in Schools," *Chicago Tribune*, August 19, 2004, sec. 1. 1. 6; Robert E. Reys, "Curricular Controversy in the Math Wars: A Battle with No Winners," *Phi Delta Kappan* 83 (November 2001), 256; National Council on Teacher Quality, *The Teacher Quality Bulletin*, August 31, 2001, 7.

50. Tracy Dell'Angela, "School Counting Up Successes," *Chicago Tribune*, August 3, 2004, sec. 2, 1, 4. Great ideas for teachers and parents on increasing math comprehension and overcoming the math phobia that pervades American education can be found in: Robert Moses and Charles Cobb, Jr., *Radical Equations: Math Literacy and Civil Rights* (Boston: Beacon Press, 2001). Robert Moses is the founder of the Algebra Project.

51. Diana Nelson, "Middle Mismanagement," *Education Week*, November 24, 2004, 38–48.

52. Robert Lowe and Joan Whipp, "Examining the Milwaukee Parent Choice Program: Options or Opportunities?" *Educational Researcher* 32 (January/ February 2002), 34.

53. Ana Beatriz Cholo and Tracy Dell'Angela, "100 New Schools to be Created," *Chicago Tribune*, June 23, 2004, sec. 2, 1, 7; Ana Beatriz Cholo, "City School Ideas Delve into Unusual," *Chicago Tribune*, September 22, 2004, sec. 2, 2.

54. Janet S. Hansen, "21st Century School Finance: How is the Context Changing?" Education Commission of the States Issue Paper, Denver, Colorado, 2001.

55. Brian C. Hassell and Lucy Steiner, "Stimulating the Supply of New Choices for Families in the Light of NCLB: The Rose of the States," Issue Brief, Education Commission of the States, Denver, Colorado, 2004.

56. Glenn W. McGee, "Closing the Achievement Gap: Lessons from Illinois' 'Golden Spike' High-Poverty High-Performing Schools," *Journal of Education for Students Placed at Risk* 9 (2004): 2, 9, 97–125. Author interview with Glenn W. McGee, October 29, 2004.

57. Richard Kazis, Kristin D. Conklin, and Hilary Pennington, "Shoring up the Academic Pipeline," *Education Week*, March 24, 2004, 39.

58. Matthew Budman, "Will We All Be Unemployed?" *Across the Board*, January/February 2004, 16–17.

59. T. Shawn Taylor, "I've Got an Open Mind," *Chicago Tribune*, September 2, 2001, sec. 6, 1, 7; "Feds Propose More Aid for Workforce Boards, *School-to-Work Report*, July 2001, 53; David Wessel, "Clues to the Cure for Unemployment Begin to Emerge," *The Wall Street Journal*, October 13, 2003, A1.

60. *Workforce Investment Act Improvements Need in Performance Measures to Provide a More Accurate Picture of WIA's Effectiveness* (Washington, D.C.: United States General Accounting Office, February 2002), 27–28.

61. Clare Ansberry, "By Resisting Layoffs Small Manufacturers Help Protect Economy," *The Wall Street Journal*, July 6, 2001, A1.

62.   Author interview with Dow Scott, professor, School of Business, Loyola University–Chicago, June 25, 2004.

63.   Jon E. Hilsenrath, "More Americans Are Leaving the Work Force," *The Wall Street Journal,* February 17, 2004, B10.

64.   David Wessel, "Capital—How Loyalty Comes by Degrees," *The Wall Street Journal,* February 17, 2004, B10.

65.   Author interview and letter from an insurance company executive, August 4, 2000.

66.   Kathy Chu, "Older Employees Gain New Favor," *The Wall Street Journal,* September 1, 2004, D3.

67.   "Needed Experienced Workers," *Harvard Business Review* 79 (July/August 2001): 20–21.

68.   "Futurist Update," June 2001; "News and Previews from the World Future Society," June 2001, 1.

69.   Lisa B. Song, "Washed up at 40?" *Chicago Tribune,* April 15, 2001, sec. 6, 1.

70.   Brad Foss, "Older Workers, Employers Comfort Each Other in Maturity," *Chicago Tribune,* June 28, 2004, sec. 4, 5.

71.   Clare Ansberry, "The Gray Team, Averaging Age 70, Staff in This Cosmetics Plant Retires Old Stereotypes, *The Wall Street Journal,* February 5, 2001, A1, A15.

72.   Chu, "Older Employees."

73.   Susan J. Wells, "Novices Fill Technology Gaps," *HR Magazine,* November 1999, 77.

74.   Ken Dychtwald, "Ageless Aging: the Next Era of Retirement," *The Futurist,* July–August 2005, 16–21; "Forget the Overtime: Family Comes First," *International Harold Tribune,* October 9–10, 2004, 19.

75.   Stephanie Armour, "Moms Find It Easier to Pop Back into Workforce," *USA Today,* September 23, 2004, B1-B2; Michelle Quinn, "More Moms Take Work Force Hiatus," *The Santa Fe New Mexican,* May 9, 2004, D5. Enola G. Aird and Martha Farrell Erickson, "Their Saving Graces," *Chicago Tribune,* May 8, 2005, 1. The full text of "The Motherhood Study" can be obtained at http://www.motherhoodproject,org. Support groups for sequencing mothers include: International Moms Club, www.momsclub.org; Mothers and More, www.mothersandmore.org; and Mocha Moms, www.mochamoms.org.

76.   Nancy Dunne, "Getting a Toehold in America's Job Market," *Financial Times,* September 12, 2003, FT Careers USA, 1; Author interview with Francene Tishman, October 22, 2004. For more information on the National Business & Disability Council, contact them at www.businessdisability.com or (516) 485-1519. For information on their Serving Customers with Disabilities, call (516) 465-1520; Author interview with Rochele Burton, executive affairs manager, Pride Industries, November 1, 2004. For more information, contact Pride Industries at www.prideindustries,com or (800) 550-6005.

77.   Eunice N. Askov and Edward E. Gordon, "The Brave New World of Workforce Education," in *The Welfare-to-Work Challenge for Adult Literacy Educators,* ed. Larry G. Martin and James C. Fisher (San Francisco: Jossey-Bass, 1999), 59–67;

Carolyn J. Heinrich, "The 'True Grit' Demonstration Program Evaluation Findings: One-Year Follow-up Report." Paper presented to the program funders: the John D. and Catherine T. MacArthur Foundation, Cook County President's Office of Employment Training, and the Private Industry Council of Suburban Cook County, January 1996.

78.   "Adult Ed, Job Training Provide Skill Base for Welfare Recipients," *Report on Literacy Programs,* May 15, 2003, 68.

79.   Kris Maher, "The Jungle, Focus on Recruitment, Pay and Getting Ahead," *The Wall Street Journal,* August 10, 2004, B4.

80.   Barbara Van Horn, "Functional Context Education for Welfare-to-Work Programs," *National Institute for Literacy Research Notes,* November 18, 2001, 1.

81.   Fox Butterfield, "U.S. 'Correctional Population' Hits Record 6.9 Million," *Chicago Tribune,* July 26, 2004, sec. 1, 14; "Prison Ranks Grow Despite Crime Drop," *Chicago Tribune,* July 28, 2003, sec. 1, 8; Curt Anderson, "Study: 2.7% of Adults Do Prison Time," *Chicago Tribune,* August 18, 2003, sec. 1, 8; Meg McSherry Breslin and J. Linn Allen, "Course Cuts Slam Door on Future, Inmates Say," *Chicago Tribune,* December 16, 2001, sec. 4, 1–2.

82.   Fox Butterfield, "Inmate Rehabilitation Returns as Prison Goal," *New York Times,* May 20, 2001, 1, 36.

83.   Ibid.

84.   *Cellblock or Classrooms?* (Washington, D.C.: Justice Policy Institute, 2002).

85.   Butterfield, "Inmate Rehabilitation."

86.   John H. Tyler and Jeffrey R. Kling, "What is the Value of a 'Prison GED'?" National Center for the Study of Adult Learning and Literacy, February 2003, 1–32.

87.   Stanley Allison, "O. C. Inmates Take First Steps from Jail to Jobs," *Los Angeles Times,* March 11, 2004, B7; Rick Jervis, "Ex-Cons Get Hand to Help Find Jobs," *Chicago Tribune,* October 26, 2003, sec. 2, 1, 20; Author interview with Cornell Hudson, October 21, 2004.

88.   Barbara Rose, "1 in 4 Working Families Is Low Income, Study Finds," *Chicago Tribune,* October 12, 2004, 1.

89.   Dayton Ducan, *Miles from Nowhere, in Search of the American Frontier* (New York: Penguin Books, 1993), 3–4.

90.   "Forever Young," *The Economist,* March 27, 2004, 4, 16.

91.   David Wessel, "Better Answers to Tough Questions on Jobs," *The Wall Street Journal,* October 21, 2004, A2; Dan Gillmor, "Not the Very Worst Thing To Have Happened," *Financial Times,* April 6, 2005, 6.

92.   Frank Levy and Richard J. Murnane, *The New Divisions of Labor* (New York: Russell Sage Foundation, 2004), 155.

93.   Brian Ross, "Fault Line," *The Santa Fe New Mexican* (letter to the Editor), May 11, 2004, A5.

Index

About the Author

EDWARD E. GORDON is president of Imperial Consulting Corporation in Chicago and Palm Desert, California. He is an internationally recognized expert on the future of labor market development and many education reform issues, applying a broad multidisciplinary approach to today's complex business and socioeconomic problems. During his over thirty years of consulting experience, he has assisted a wide variety of clients—from Fortune 500 corporations to universities, school systems, and trade/professional organizations—and has taught at DePaul, Loyola, and Northwestern Universities in the Chicago area. He is the author of sixteen books, including *FutureWork* (Praeger, 1994), *Skill Wars* (Butterworth-Heinemann, 2000), and *Literacy in America* (Praeger, 2002), and has been quoted in or written over 200 articles in newspapers, popular magazines, business publications, and education journals.